# THE OUTPUT-ORIENTED ORGANIZATION

*OTHER BOOKS BY W. J. REDDIN*

Campus Countdown
Situational Management
The Best of Bill Reddin
Managerial Effectiveness
Effective Management by Objectives
Problems in Economic and Business Statistics
How to Make Your Management Style More Effective
Handbook of Management by Objectives
The Manager's Book of Lists
Effective Management
Money Management
The Money Book

# The Output-Oriented Organization

Bill Reddin, PhD

Gower

Published by
Gower Publishing Company Limited,
Gower House,
Croft Road,
Aldershot,
Hants GU11 3HR,
England

Reprinted 1990

**British Library Cataloguing in Publication Data**
Reddin, Bill
    The output oriented organization.
    1. Organizations. Productivity. Measurement.
    Improvement
    I. Title
    658.3'14'0287

ISBN 0 566 02710 0

Printed in Great Britain by
Dotesios Printers Ltd, Trowbridge, Wiltshire

*This book is dedicated to Bob White of Westpac Banking Corporation, who together with his 1,700 most senior managers, implemented most of the ideas found here and who contributed in many ways to making this book more practical for those who want to change organizations.*

# Contents

# Preface

Bookshops and libraries are now full of books describing organizational effectiveness. So how, then, is this book different? The aim
of the book is to show how to change organizations, or parts of
organizations, in order to make them more effective. The units in
the organization might be the individual manager, a work team, a
production or administrative system or the organization as a whole.
This book demonstrates a method of identifying units in the organization which need change and then specifying the objectives for
each. Objectives might range from moving decision levels downwards to reorganization, or to increasing organizational flexibility.
The book provides readers with tested methods on how each of
these objectives may be achieved.

This book is the natural outgrowth of the Outputs Planning
Meeting, which has now been conducted in many organizations in
many countries. The essence of the meeting is to show how
managers can get better control of their organization, so that they
may change it.

Embedded in the book are some rather interesting assumptions
about people. One is that, in the majority of organizations, the
resources to solve most matters that arise lie within the group; the
trick is to get the solution out. Here of importance is Chapter 8 on
'putting theory into practice'. It is about novel types of meeting
that are definitely not of the normal kind. These meetings harness
human resources; while not generally recognized, this is an assumption of the Harvard Business School. In my two years there,
studying for my MBA, we were given a total of one book to read.
That happened to be Carl Rogers's *Counselling and Psychotherapy*
– of all things! Beyond that we received no advice, no lectures and
three cases to talk about each day! There the case study was taken
to its absolute limits, for they believed – as do I in this book – that
'wisdom cannot be told'. Wisdom must rather be found within the
people of the organization.

Another assumption running through this book is that people
need two kinds of help to use what they already know. One is

simple frames, often called lists, in order to look at their situation in a clearer way. Such clarity will lower defensiveness and encourage people to read situations for what they really contain. This lowers resistance. The other kind of help needed is discussion with others, to increase objectivity, leading to a public commitment to do something.

The book also has a theme that commitment is preferable to elegance when it comes to being effective; in matters involving change, commitment to an effective solution is preferable to the elegant solutions proposed by outsiders. This book may well strive for elegance in thought, and in proposed actions, but not at the expense of obtaining commitment. The position is that managers themselves can best decide the objectives and methods for planned change, hence a preoccupation which underlies the book is how to lower resistance to change. Here, my approach has been to show situations where managers can become more objective, while lowering their natural resistances, in order to lead to an action plan.

By studying this book readers will obtain many ideas by which they can improve the effectiveness of their organization, or the part of the organization in which they work, and I have presented many proposals for self-development, for team improvement and for organization-wide planned change. Readers should obtain a sound basis for creating productive planned change for themselves, their team and their organization.

However, some readers may be surprised at the lack of prescriptive advice in this book. You will search hard to find statements along the lines of 'all organizations should be thus' or 'all managers should be this'. In fact there is no ideal style of managing; and there is no one way to make an organization more effective. Moreover, no list exists in the world showing characteristics of effective managers, or of effective organizations, which apply generally. What this book substitutes for prescriptions is advice on how to diagnose what is the true situation and what are the true needs. This is intended to enable managers to make a sound decision on how best to arrive at their planned change objectives.

Many managers will be surprised at the prominence given to clarity of thinking – even to theory. Some may wonder if this is another long-haired theoretical textbook, or whether it is in fact a guide to action. However, the book and the theory itself are meant to be both theoretical and practical, for there is nothing more practical than a good theory properly applied – or so costly as one applied inappropriately. The effectiveness potential of sound

behavioural theory for managers is only now beginning to be realized. It has been seen by some as the opposite of action, yet we
could not design a bridge, a radio or even an egg-timer without it.
A poor theory leads to idle speculation, inaction or impractical
proposals; while a sound theory shows us how things are related,
and how and when that relationship changes.

Sound management theories are intended to clarify, not to
mystify; they are designed to make sense out of what may appear
to be a confusing situation; they show relationships not previously
identified and hence lead to actions that would not otherwise be
considered; and they provide positive, direct guides to action.
Useful theory is a reality in the physical sciences. It will become
so in the social sciences, of which management is an applied branch.

The point here is that we can build bridges, but we are not sure
about building organizations. We can predict what will happen to
a beam under stress, but not what happens to a manager under
stress. However, our knowledge will continually improve; and
universities of the future will teach courses in 'management styles'
or 'situational management' with the same precision, and with the
same guides to immediate, proven application, as we now teach
courses in concrete structures. The professional manager as a social
engineer will emerge as a reality, as the professional engineer has
similarly emerged. It is true that, at this point in development,
much of management skill is an art; the manager who has learned
from errors may still be ahead of the one who has learned from
books. At one time, this statement was also true of medicine, but
today the thought of a self-trained doctor is not attractive. So too
it will be with managers – intuition will never cease to be useful,
but the scientific approach will continue to assume more and more
importance.

Perhaps the best way to utilize this book is to distribute a copy
to every member of your team. Ask them to read it and to come
together to discuss it. In particular, they might discuss what sections
of the book they would like to start to apply to the team of which
they are a part. The team might be (as it has been in the past) the
top team of an organization of 35,000 people, the top team of one
of the *Fortune 500* companies or the top team of a firm with less
than 100 employees, or again, it might be a team of a subunit such
as a warehouse function, a marketing function or whatever.

Chapter 8 describes the Team Meeting. It consists of a full team
of the top member and all immediate team members. It should
always be residential, away from the work base, and deal with
making the team a more effective unit. The Outputs Planning

Meeting is described in Chapter 9. Normally it is a three-day non-residential, with the ideas in this book used as prework. Sometimes it is conducted in-company for the top team of a unit or the company as a whole, and it is sometimes conducted on a public seminar basis. As it is a workshop and managers are coming to solve their own problems, there is really no problem over how many might attend. Some of these meetings have been attended by 80 people from fifteen different companies spending the three days at the workshops solving their own problems. As in the Team Meeting, there is little in the way of formal talks. A workshop is a workshop.

Avid readers of my prefaces over the years will perhaps like to know how my writing in Canada is progressing, together with my particular writing situation. When I first wrote, it was in an unheated cabin overlooking a large lake with an outdoor toilet. As the royalties came in, I was able to afford a larger cabin with my own lake with an indoor toilet! As I have decided to start writing even more, I had the lodge winterized, so that now I can use it when the weather outside is 20 degrees below zero. There is a deer yard down two miles in the woods, where the deer hole up for the winter, and there are about 70 of them there, and there are also several moose around this year. I have two squirrels that have gotten into the roof of my lodge and they keep running over the place where I write. They were beginning to keep me awake at night. I heard that camphor was a good thing to use and I decided to encourage them to go and live in a tree somewhere. I could not get any camphor flakes, so I decided to put up mothballs instead. This was an error. Right now the two squirrels are playing something like ping-pong with them! I do find that living in settings like this and writing here helps me think more clearly about what my true work really is.

Technically, I see myself as an occupational sociologist, that is I am concerned with people and their work effectiveness. I do not find that reading *Business Week* or thinking about profits or the stockmarket reports helps me to write a book like this. This book is about people and organization. It is natural.

Some readers will be familiar with one or more of my other books. *Effective Management by Objectives* (McGraw-Hill, 1971) dealt primarily with the concept of outputs and the concept of team implementation of management by objectives. It was the first book to link management by objectives and organization development; it was the second-generation management by objectives. Another book, *Managerial Effectiveness* (McGraw-Hill, 1970), dealt with the individual manager and situations. It emphasized managerial style and managerial situation and had the basic argument that style must match situation needs in order for effectiveness to be created. Alternatively, the situation must be changed; this is known as situational management. So one of these books has dealt primarily with the team, and the other with the individual. The present book concentrates on collectivities of teams, that is the organization as a whole, or units of it composed of more than one team. Two more recent books include *The Best of Bill Reddin* (IPM, 1985), which is a collection of articles and forms a summary of my writings over more than twenty years, and *How to Make Your Management Style More Effective* (McGraw-Hill, 1987), which is a practical handbook dealing exclusively with style, which forms but one part of the present book.

I hope that *The Output-Oriented Organization* will be seen as making several contributions to management literature. First, it takes the field of organization development out of the hands of professors, psychologists and human relations types and puts it squarely into the hands of the manager; and the main part in accomplishing this is to render social science jargon into everyday terms. True, there is some jargon in this book; for instance, what organization development specialists call 'interventions' I call meetings, and what they refer to as 'interpersonal authenticity' I refer to as being candid about effectiveness. Finally, when people say, as has been proposed to me more than once, that 'Only those highly trained with PhDs should conduct some of the meetings described in this book, I say: 'Please go away and let the managers do it.'

Broadly, this book has been designed around the idea of Kurt Lewin that change in social systems may be looked at in the same way as change in physical systems. If you want to change a block of ice, you first unfreeze it, then you change it and, finally, stabilizing the new shape. So it is with organizations; some kind of unfreezing is necessary. This may simply consist of questioning the past; some kind of change is needed and this is best accomplished by talking about the right things, with a shared interest in effectiveness. Something must be done to stabilize change and this may range all the way from improved corporate strategy to reorganization to new systems, or on to new policies and operating methods in general.

As far as I can see, nothing in this book is in serious conflict with what might be called 'traditional organization development'. The primary difference is that mystique is removed and commonsense given more emphasis, and the central value is in improving organization effectiveness. For some the central value in organization development is interpersonal authenticity and openness and candour, and while these are critical (in fact essential) elements, they have to be seen as inputs to the broader objective of improving organization effectiveness.

This book has not been 'armchaired'. It is grounded in practice: I know with certainty that the ideas here are easily understood by managers, are widely accepted by them and may be easily implemented to increase effectiveness. The book is a direct outgrowth of my experience as an organization change agent. I have worked in this role for over thirty years with organizations both large and small. Here is contained all that I believe managers need to know, in addition to their commonsense about creating planned change in their own organization. I have planned the book to represent absolutely the best organization development method; and again, I know these ideas work routinely and well in making units and organizations more effective. Unlike some others, I have never felt the need to appeal to authority ('So-and-so said it') or to appeal to organization behaviour experiments and the specialists who conduct them, whose lives seem to be spent in the pedantic pursuit of the decimal point!

I have found it useful to transmit the ideas on which this book is based through three rather different kinds of method. These are all diagnostic and action planning workshops, but having somewhat different focuses. The most important and longest running is the Managerial Effectiveness Seminar described in Chapter 7; the second is the Team Meeting and other meetings, Chapter 8; and the third is the Outputs Planning Meeting, Chapter 9. Certainly, if you want to create a more output-oriented organization, then you will make plans to arrange to conduct some of the seminars on an in-company basis; and a detailed design is given, so that you can proceed.

The seminars and meetings mentioned in this book have been conducted in many countries for up to twenty-five years, and this does seem to give some credence to the view that the ideas are reasonably widely applicable. These countries include: Argentina, Australia, Austria, Belgium, Brazil, Canada, Ethiopia, Finland, Guyana, Hong Kong, Ireland, Jamaica, Kenya, Mexico, the Netherlands, New Zealand, Norway, Singapore, South Africa, Spain, Sweden, Trinidad, the UK, the USA, Venezuela and West Germany. Several of the case studies in this book, and some of the examples, have appeared in other books written by me over the last twenty-five years. If a case study or example makes the point well there seems little need to change it.

I would like to acknowledge the help of many people. John Fry and Valerie Richardson were very helpful, as usual, in producing the right kind of documentation in the right form at the right time, all the way to sending this book to the publisher. Malcolm Stern, of Gower, made many suggestions to make this book more helpful.

Angela Wood used the magic of the word processor, and Joan Wilson helped a great deal with earlier drafts and Val Barrett with the later ones. Claudia Maconick was very helpful in the editing process.

In particular, I wish to acknowledge the co-operation and support of those companies who used this approach to organization change, and especially to record my thanks to these companies for advancing these ideas, making them even more practical and being willing to share their information and experiences. I am deeply indebted to them.

One company has undoubtedly contributed to making this book highly practical in having tested and used its ideas over several years. This company is the Westpac Banking Corporation, and this book is dedicated to their CEO.

I am indebted to many writers, colleagues and friends who have helped develop the ideas on which this book is based. These include: Warren Bennis, Peter Drucker, Henri Fayol, Kurt Lewin and Douglas McGregor.

I am also indebted to many CEOs who have asked me to help them with organization change. Working with them has helped me develop the practice in organization change that is represented by this book. These include: Reg Tweeddale, New Brunswick Electric Power Commission; Les Kirkpatrick, Nova Scotia Power Commission; Cecil McNeil, Westinghouse Switchgear Division; Geoff Iden, John Player & Sons; Bill Morrow, National Sea Products; Colin Ward, Atlas Air Australia Pty Ltd; Bob White, Westpac Banking Corporation; and Gordon Slade, Falconbridge Nickel Mines.

W. J. Reddin
Station Road
Motspur Park
New Malden
Surrey KT3 6JH
UK

# Acknowledgements

We gratefully acknowledge the following sources:

AMACOM
> Change in an accounting firm – Marksbury, Henry, 'Managerial team building: Casting light on what makes us tick' (Part 1) and 'Exercises in team building' (Part 2): 'A Manager's trip through the hall of mirrors of the psyche', *Management Review*, September 1979, pp. 8–14, and October 1979, pp. 53–7; reprinted by permission of the publisher, from *Management Review*, (issue: September–October) 1979 © 1979 AMACOM, a division of American Management Associations, New York. All rights reserved.

Falconbridge Nickel Mines Ltd
> Change in a nickel mine – Buckland, G. R. 'Organisation development at Sudbury operations', *Update '79*, May 1978, pp. 11–15, 'Update interview with Jack Boyd', pp. 16–17.

Financial Times
> Change in a cigarette manufacturing firm – Dodsworth, Terry, 'How Player's changed management style', *Financial Times*, 22 September 1972; reprinted by permission of Financial Times.

International Institute for Applied Systems Analysis (IIASA)
> Paper presented by Dr D. Hempel at IIASA Task Force Meeting, 'Human Factors in Innovation Management', Helsinki, Finland, October 1983.

International Management
> Change in a computing firm – Clutterbuck, David, 'Computer managers learn to be more effective', *International Management*, vol. 31, no. 12, December 1976, pp. 51–3; reprinted with special permission from International Management. Copyright © McGraw-Hill Publications Company. All rights reserved.

## McGraw-Hill Book Company (UK)

Extracts from Reddin, W. J., *How To Make Your Management Style More Effective*, McGraw-Hill Book Co. (UK), 1987; reprinted with permission.

## Southam Publishing

Tweeddale, R. E., 'Change in a power commission', *3-D Executive*, vol. 9, 30 January 1967, pp. 26–8.

## Geoff Thompson, WESTPAC

Change in a bank – 'Organisation change and the Westpac Merger'; reprinted by permission of Geoff Thompson, Westpac Banking Corporation, Australia.

## Colin Ward

Ward, Colin, 'Change in an air conditioning installation firm. (What happens when you remove your desk and take your team away for the weekend)', Managing Director, Atlas Air Australia Pty Ltd, 133 Victoria Road, Rozelle, New South Wales, Australia 2039.

## Bob White, WESTPAC

Extract from CEO's talk given to a meeting of the International Monetary Conference in Boston, USA; reprinted by permission of Bob White, CEO Westpac Banking Corporation.

# PART I

# Creating the Output-Oriented Organization

# 1 What is the output-oriented organization?

> The manager has the task of creating a true whole that is larger than the sum of its parts, a productive entity that turns out more than the sum of the resources put into it.
>
> Peter F. Drucker
>
> The great end of life is not knowledge but action.
>
> Thomas Huxley

The objective of this chapter is to clarify the nature of the output-oriented organization by explaining the nature of its seven major characteristics.

The essence of the output-oriented organization is a tight integration of all the organization systems around specific output statements concerning the organization, specific output statements concerning units composing the organization and specific output statements concerning every individual manager in it.

There are many reasons for senior and middle managers wanting to get better control of their organizations. These include greater competition, lower margins, problems in running multinationals, the increasing number of mergers and acquisitions, new developments in technology, growth and, for some, the belief that 'small is beautiful'.

Clearly, the reasons for this interest do not all relate to profit. It is also obvious that poorly designed organizations have serious negative effects on those who inhabit them. These are well recognized as stress, heart-attacks, alcoholism, psychosomatic illnesses, low trust levels, alienation and (certainly) death.

## YOUR LEVEL DECIDES YOUR ARENA OF CONCERN

Some readers of this book will be chief executive officers (CEOs) of large or small organizations, some will be heads of a division or other type of major unit, some will be heads of a particular smaller unit and some will be managers who feel somewhat cast adrift and are concerned that something must be done. But what? The principles in this book apply to all. Certainly, output orientation, and all that it involves, applies just as well to the system as a whole as to the individuals within it.

The book does comment on what to do about corporate strategy. For some readers this will be critical, while for others it will be out of reach. Also the book comments on your personal managerial style and personal managerial effectiveness – and how one should measure one's managerial effectiveness. This, then, applies to all readers. Naturally as you read through the book, you will fit what is said to your particular level in the organization.

This book is designed to help you change your part of the organization. It does this by showing you how to create a special mind set in all of those who report to you and those who report to them. This mind set concerns outputs rather than inputs. The ideas in this book have been used by the CEO and top teams of large organizations. It has also been widely used by the CEO and top teams of small organizations and by the managers of many production and administrative units such as bank branches and life insurance offices. These ideas should apply to you; the aim of the book is to help you make yourself and your part of the organization more effective.

You may find that this book will simply organize your existing knowledge. You may well say, 'I knew all of this, really, but it was not organized in quite this fashion and now I know what I knew'. This comment has often been made when the ideas in this book are given in seminars. There is surely nothing wrong with this kind of comment. It is all too easy to make things in management difficult; it is hard to make them simple and still right. The only problem with commonsense in management is that it is not very common! What this book may do for you is to clarify what you knew already. It will make your knowledge more coherent, so that you can do a better job at acting on what you know.

The book contains many ideas on how to improve managerial effectiveness. However its main thrust is how to improve organizational effectiveness. Obviously this is based in part upon the effectiveness of individual managers, but it does take a broader view. Therefore, the book does not offer notions on 'how to delegate', but it does provide ideas on how to approach the issue of 'moving decision levels downward'. The book is concerned with organization development rather than management development.

## THE CHARACTERISTICS OF THE OUTPUT-ORIENTED ORGANIZATION

In this chapter there are seven characteristics of the output-oriented organization which we consider:

- An organization output statement.
- An organization design which will achieve the organization output statement.
- A clear understanding by all managers of the meaning of outputs and effectiveness.
- Integration of key systems with the concept of outputs.
- Linking of organization, unit and manager outputs.
- A flexible response to achieve outputs.
- Creation of one's own approach to outputs, not copying those of others.

## THE ORGANIZATION OUTPUT STATEMENT

Output-oriented organizations need clear output statements. Properly derived and used, they drive the firm in many ways; and organization output statements have been referred to as a 'driving force', a 'company strategy', a 'company goal', and so on.

Here are some examples of effective output statements:

- To be a research-based company by spending at least 60 per cent more on research and development than the nearest competitor and at least 1.6 per cent of sales.
- To be a quality order company by accepting no contracts under 400,000.
- To be a flexible company by owning no single fixed asset valued above 500,000, and by having no leases of a term longer than four years.

Key elements of corporate strategy statements include the proportion of sales spent on specific functions or services. For example, should research and development (R & D) expense be 0.5 or 3.5 per cent? Should the company match its competitors brand for brand, and tactic for tactic, or should it not? Until these strategy decisions are known, the R & D manager or a brand manager cannot really do a satisfactory job in setting objectives. Fortunately, strategy decisions like these tend to change infrequently, and when they do change, all those concerned know about it quickly.

An output statement can be regarded as a statement of an organization's basic purpose. This is apart from the fact that a large business organization serves the interests of many groups, including its owners, its employees, its customers, the government and the community as a whole.

Some strategy statements are simply window dressing for external consumption. Such strategy statements as these are not a guide to action, and they are no aid in planning:

- To build public confidence and continuing friendly feeling for products and services bearing the company's name and brands through sound, competitive advertising, promotion, selling, service and personal contacts.
- To provide good jobs, wages and working conditions, work satisfaction, and opportunities for advancement conducive to the most productive performance and also the stablest possible employment, in exchange for loyalty, initiative, skill, care, effort, attendance and teamwork on the part of employees – i.e. the contributions of individual employees that result in 'value to the company' and for which the employee is being paid.
- To co-operate both with suppliers and with distributors, contractors and others facilitating distribution, installation and servicing of company products, so that company efforts are constructively integrated with theirs for mutually effective public service and competitive, profitable progress.
- To adapt company policies, products, services, facilities, plans and schedules to meet continuously, progressively, foresightedly, imaginatively and voluntarily the social, civic and economic responsibilities commensurate with the opportunities afforded by the size, success and nature of the business, and with the public's confidence in it as a corporate enterprise.

When we have achieved all these, we will ask the Lord to 'move over'!

It is vital that the output statement is published, and is shared by all members of the organization. In her study of entrepreneurship in larger organizations, *The Change Masters*, Rosabeth Moss Kanter found that those organizations which shared a common philosophy between all the departments and sections were much quicker to change and respond to their environment. Likewise, those organizations which were strongly 'segmentalist' and had different departmental philosophies were less able to solve problems which arose as the world around them changed.

The output statement is a summary of the direction in which an organization wishes to head. It highlights the area of an organization's operations that is considered the most important when strategic decisions are made.

All large business organizations involve many different operations. One way of classifying operational areas is by use of the following list:

- Products offered;
- Market needs;
- Technology;
- Production capability;
- Selling method;
- Distribution method;
- Natural resources;
- Size/growth;
- Profit.

All these areas of operation are important and strategies should be developed for each one. However, one area of operation, at any time, will be considered more important than the others in making strategic decisions. This area is highlighted by the output statement.

In all organizations the operational area that is most strategically important may change as circumstances alter, particularly those in the organization's environment. If such change occurs, then the organization's output statement should change correspondingly.

In any organization different teams have unique circumstances and objectives. Therefore, many individual teams should adopt their own output statement in addition to, but consistent with, the organization's output statement. A team's future direction, including the need for a unique summary output statement, should be regularly discussed by the team.

**The organization outputs statement of a bank**

A large bank has made the following summary of its organization outputs statement:

- The bank's output statement is: 'The competitive servicing of customers' needs.'
- The output statement highlights our customers' needs as the

most important factor in our corporate life. It recognizes the fact that we could not exist without our customers.

- Our output statement also recognizes that we must focus on being better than our competitors at servicing customer needs.
- Our output statement means that we must change from a bank driven by our own concerns to one driven by our customers' needs. For example, we must learn to be more influenced by our customers' requirements than by the requirements of our trading bank computer system or the fact that we have a branch network.
- Our output statement gives direction to the many changes occurring in the bank. It guides our product and market strategies and should also help in many day-to-day management decisions.
- The importance of our output statement is reflected in the fact that every submission to the bank executive committee must include a Customer Impact Statement.
- The bank has four medium-term output statement goals:
  - being better at understanding the financial needs of our customers so as to produce the right products for each customer segment;
  - being better at providing a total financial management service to our customers;
  - being better in the customer service orientation of all our people, particularly their friendliness and helpfulness;
  - being an organization which encourages excellent performance by its managers.
- The achievement of these goals is critical to the future success of the bank.
- The achievement of these goals requires the contribution of all bank managers. Managers are expected to explain the goals to their team members and to set them an example by their efforts towards achievement of the goals.

## Deriving the organization output statement

It is true that some organization output statements have been decided and then announced by a CEO. A more common method is for the top team to derive it collectively. This derivation is not best done by a short meeting leading up to the announcement of a short statement. The words must have meaning, and they will only acquire meaning to the degree that they are reflected in the organization's plans and practices. The best method of derivation is probably the corporate strategy meeting, described at pp. 138–42. This puts the outputs statement into a wider context of corporate strategy and encourages – in fact virtually forces – the top team to take a close look at all factors which impinge on the outputs statement, on corporate strategy in general and methods of achieving higher organization, unit and managerial effectiveness.

## THE ORGANIZATION DESIGN FOR ACHIEVEMENT OF THE ORGANIZATION OUTPUT STATEMENT

The organization design, particularly at the top, must reflect the organization output statement. There is one type of organization which has more than a hundred to one span of control. The top person is seen by some as an autocrat; the effectiveness areas for every job are tightly defined. The organization works well; and it produces an array of beautiful outputs and job satisfaction is extremely high. Some of the reasons for its effectiveness are said to be that everyone is well trained, everyone knows what effectiveness means and how to measure it and the firm as a system was designed over the years by experts. There is an immediate feedback system, so that everyone knows very quickly how they are doing – and a reward system operates. This organization is the symphony orchestra: why not design other organizations this way? Clearly, satisfaction can occur in a well-designed organization like this. People, then, can obtain satisfaction from work itself if the structure and system are well designed.

What about the orchestra and output orientation? Every orchestra is fully output oriented; if it were not, it could not operate. Think of it: there is an organization, with all roles clearly defined; there is an insistence on tight teamwork, together with high performance visibility, and there is a tight linking of outputs both vertically and horizontally, and in addition, a reward system operates. Naturally, all this leads to a high motivation and performance. But to what else could it lead?

Well-designed organizations are quiet places in which to work. Poorly designed organizations are death-traps since role conflict can, and does, kill. All of us can draw on our knowledge in our own companies, of the clumsy change followed by a heart attack or the hard-working person in a non-job getting an ulcer or a lifetime of organization stress leading to a breakdown. If we believe that we have some humanity, let us also be honest and helpful. If two people are responsible for the same function, then one of them is not needed; and out of respect to both, the issue needs to be resolved.

There is no distinction between well-designed work and play. The hockey or football team and the orchestra are highly bureaucratic. They have elaborate rules, a punishment system that works and rewards for only the best; they need a tough results-oriented manager and an arch-bureaucrat to act as referee. Everyone enjoys playing, and people do it for fun. Why not design all organizations on this principle? There is simply no reason why we shouldn't!

We have all heard of the 'matrix organization', where individuals belong to overlapping teams: is this the organization of the future? The answer is: no, it is only one of them, to be used when appropriate. One firm had a superb matrix organization of 200 people, designing and making aerospace products. The management decided to change from what was essentially an R & D shop in order to exploit fully the technology that had been created. It decided to move from a creative organization to a production one, and this included a planned growth from 200 to 2,000 employees over a short space of time. The management met for three days to design the new organization, changing to the conventional status pyramid. Although change was not welcomed, the management recognized that the status pyramid is right for long production runs of routine products, while being wrong for short production runs of products requiring high creativity from different people.

## One organization's thoughts on design of organization structure

One highly sucessful organization re-designs its top three levels at least once a year and sometimes more often. They have been in a turbulent environment, are large and are – without doubt – the best-managed organization in their line of work. This is their point of view on structure:

- The structure we choose for ourselves tells us 'who does what' in our organization.
- There is no single ideal structure for a large organization like ours. There are always alternative ways of organizing such that our organization's goals are achieved in an efficient manner.
- Our structure is regularly reviewed to ensure it adapts to new ideas, to changes in our customers' needs and to changes in the aspirations of our people.
- When we review our structure, we start by asking ourselves: 'what do we want to be?'

• We consider our organization output statement, and ask how we can structure ourselves to service our customers' needs most competitively.

**Deriving the appropriate organization design**

There are many well-known ways to reorganize. One way is for the chief executive officer (CEO) to do it over a weekend, another is for the top team to decide and yet another is to call in consultants. All these methods have worked and failed at times; here the method proposed is the large group meeting design, shown on pp. 142–4. Often this has been used for total company reorganization around outputs, and it has not been known to fail. In addition to producing a far more effective organization design, the method of reaching that design leads naturally to a sharp lowering of resistance and an equally sharp increase in commitment to the new design.

**A CLEAR UNDERSTANDING BY ALL MANAGERS OF THE MEANING OF OUTPUTS AND EFFECTIVENESS**

An essential characteristic of an output-oriented organization is that all managers know it, live and breathe it, and implement it. They need to take the concept to heart and express it in all of their work. The concept of outputs is the subject both of this chapter and the next. Here it is in brief.

The definition of managerial effectiveness is 'the extent to which managers achieve the output requirements of their positions'. This must lead on to a precise definition of what 'output' means. The difference between inputs and outputs is illustrated by the following examples:

| | Input | | Output |
|---|---|---|---|
| *Not* | machine maintenance | *but* | machine availability |
| *Not* | changing attitudes | *but* | changing behaviour |
| *Not* | calls made | *but* | sales made |
| *Not* | speed reading | *but* | speed learning |

It is common for managers to think in terms of inputs rather than outputs and a dramatic reorientation is needed if a true output orientation is to be created.

**An organization's statement on outputs and effectiveness areas**

The following list comes from an organization which is output-oriented. It used many, or even most, of the ideas in this book to achieve that condition. This is how they view the importance of effectiveness areas and outputs for managers.

Effectiveness areas (EAs) are descriptions of the output requirements of a managerial position; the term here comes from the expression 'managerial effectiveness', which means achieving your output requirements:

- Your EAs should cover all your output requirements, that is the things you are accountable for.
- You should decide the number of EAs that you will have according to the degree of detail with which you prefer to divide up your job. However, each EA should represent an important or significant part of your job.
- All your EAs must be within the limits of authority established for your job.
- Your EAs must not overlap, or underlap, with those of the other managers at your level. Overlap is when two positions are accountable for the same output, and underlap is when no position has been assigned the accountability for an output.
- Your EAs must incorporate those of your subordinate managers and your EAs will be incorporated in those of your superior. This helps ensure that your EAs complement those of other managers.
- Avoiding overlap and underlap, and ensuring that EAs are complementary, is an important part of the regular reviews of your team's job effectiveness descriptions.

**The key to the output-oriented organization: job effectiveness description**

Many organizations are based on hope rather than reality. That is not true for the output-oriented organization. It is designed with high precision, at the job to be done and how best to do it in terms of allocation of authority, roles, effectiveness, outputs, and so on. This applies as much to the multi-national as to the typing-pool. The principles are in fact identical.

A job effectiveness description (JED) is a description of a managerial position using output terms. It comprises a manager's effectiveness areas and the accompanying measurement areas and authority areas. The JED provides:

- *Effectiveness areas* – a list of the areas in which you are required to achieve results through daily work.
- *Measurement areas* – a list of the ways in which outputs are measured in progress reviews and appraisal.
- *Authority areas* – the levels of authority allocated to the position, thus what actions are to be taken and what decisions made without referring to your superior.

The JED is a critical document because it helps the manager to think of the job (and those of the subordinates) in terms of outputs. It is an essential part of the output system because it is the basis upon which objectives are written. Planning starts with the JED.

**How to get managers output-oriented**

A method widely used to increase the output orientation of managers is the 3-D Managerial Effectiveness Seminar, described in Chapter 7. The case studies in this book provide examples of the seminar's outputs; the basic idea concerning outputs which needs to be transmitted is given in Chapter 2. Before you decide on the method to increase your own output orientation, or that of others, it is worthwhile reading the whole book since a variety of ideas and techniques are put forward.

**INTEGRATION OF KEY SYSTEMS WITH THE CONCEPT OF OUTPUTS**

It is possible to place the idea of outputs at the heart of the organization by linking various systems in that organization around the idea of outputs and the job effectiveness description (JED). As you will recall, this document consists of three main elements; the outputs of the position expressed as effectiveness areas, the measurement area for each of these outputs and the statement of authority.

The well-created JED can be applied at the centre of many organization systems. In the same way that the organization output statement drives many aspects of the organization's operations, the JED drives many internal systems. The systems to which the JED may be linked include management information systems, objectives for managers, appraisal, job evaluation, job specification and budgets. All these can be made output-oriented by linking them to the JED. While not a system in the conventional sense, the JED can also assist with team-building and organization design.

Large and small organizations, but particularly the larger ones, tend to be riddled with what might be referred to as competing systems or competing bases of systems. The accountants decide the budgeting systems, the mainframe people design the management information system (MIS), the personnel department designs the job evaluation (JE) scheme, and so on. Too often, they start with completely different philosophies about how the organization is to be run. The concept of outputs gives them a common philosophy, on which all such systems should be based. In short, if you truly want to create an output-oriented organization, then work hard at linking the major systems around the concept of outputs. As you do this, those with a power base built around their particular system will normally resist: they will have to be taught about outputs themselves.

*Integration of outputs with management information systems (MIS)*
The JED contains measurement areas for each effectiveness area. These measurement areas, then, are the most important way in which a manager is actually measured. It should be obvious that the MIS of the organization should be designed around the measurements that managers want. Very often the MIS is designed somewhat independently of what managers want, rather what those in control of the mainframe think they should have. This sets up two competing measurement systems where only one is needed – it is obvious which one. In those organizations with too many so-called 'knowledge workers' one finds that senior management sometimes actually believes these knowledge workers should design the MIS to suit what they would like to know about the managers and their performance. If what they want to know is not what the manager needs to know, and not what the team has reached agreement on, something is wrong.

*Integration of outputs with objectives for managers*
While not clearly enough understood, it is obvious that objectives for managerial positions arise by only one method: this consists of putting agreed numbers on measurement areas. Suppose a manager has an output of 'swimming-pool utilization' and the measurement method is the load factor on the pool expressed in terms of the number of hours when at least twenty people are in it. The objective is obviously derived by agreeing a number of hours of load. In short,

the objectives are thus derived by putting numbers on measurement areas.

In the early, crude attempts at management by objectives (MBO) people again thought this was an independent new system with different ideas. However, this was not so. If one wants to have objectives for managers, or to design any kind of MBO scheme, it must be based on outputs. Objectives can be derived only from the measurement areas associated with those outputs.

## Integration of outputs with appraisal

With an agreed JED, based firmly on outputs, no organization needs a separate set of criteria for an appraisal form. Managers should be appraised on only one thing: the extent to which they achieve the output requirements of their position. These output requirements are clearly expressed by the objectives based on measurement areas which, in turn, are based on effectiveness areas. No one needs to know whether a manager excels in initiative – or whether an army officer sits well astride a horse! The organization needs to know whether or not the manager has achieved the output requirements of the position.

## Integration of outputs with job evaluation (JE)

There are many proprietary and non-proprietary job evaluation schemes. In all, about forty are well recognized by experts in the area. The majority uses criteria which might include the level of responsibility, unsocial hours, number supervised, and so on. Points are assigned to these to indicate relative weight, then each job is evaluated on a point basis, and from this the salary band for the job is derived. One interesting research study compared most of the well-known methods across a wide variety of jobs, and this showed that no matter what the proposed criteria, the rank order of ratings of the job turned out to be rather similar. What this means, then, is that the rating methods, while appearing different, are really not so different.

There is one simple method of job evaluation based on outputs. Essentially, the method involves as many people as possible looking at two job effectiveness descriptions, and based on what those descriptions contain, asking the simple question: 'Which of these two jobs has greater value to the organization?' This leads to a natural rank order of jobs from which the appropriate salary level is derived. While this method is important in itself, the key point here is that the basic philosophy of the method is outputs – and this philosophy integrates with everything the firm does.

*Intregration of outputs with job specification*

The term 'job specification' is somewhat loosely defined, but it is normally taken to mean what the job really *is* and what it involves. However, the last thing that any organization needs is a job specification other than the JED itself. For instance, job specifications are sometimes created for advertisements; they are not needed. The JED, perhaps in slightly rewritten form, is quite sufficient. Would you not have liked it when hired for your most recent job to have had a clear JED in front of you, describing your outputs with precision and how you were to be measured, with your authority clearly specified? Obviously many organizations do this at the moment, but still too many do not.

*Integration of outputs with budgets*

Budgets can be based on an input orientation or an output orientation. Those budgets based on input orientation take the general view that the main point is to keep the organization ticking over. Those based on output orientation deal with the issue of how much is needed to achieve objectives stated in output terms. The change of budgets to output orientation can be a long and difficult task. It is not essential for budgets to be completely output-oriented to still have an output-oriented organization, yet it is obviously desirable. When budgets remain input-oriented, managers tend to ignore them more and more; they see them as independent systems to suit others, not themselves.

*Integration of outputs with team-building*

While team-building is not a system in the normal sense, it can be seen as one, and there is little doubt that the JED helps enormously in team-building. Sports teams and jazz bands have rather clear outputs, measurement areas and authority. Participants enjoy the organization and, most times, do it simply for fun. Why not, then, use these ideas to design our work teams as well? A superb weekend for a team, after they understand what outputs really are, is to derive and agree upon the JED for the top team member, and for all team members, and the team as a whole. A more obvious objective for such an event is to increase role clarification and finish up with JEDs being agreed. However, the latent and far more important objective is to build a team around the concept of outputs.

*Integration of outputs with organization design*

The creation of JEDs may lead on directly to thoughts about reorganization. When one has a one over one situation, it sometimes occurs that the top position has all the authority and the deputy position has essentially none. Often the problem is not only that the deputy is there at all, but also that the job that in fact barely exists is valued highly in monetary terms, when it perhaps could be devalued to the level of a senior secretary. A good rule in thinking about JEDs and organization design is: *if two people are responsible for the same thing, one of them is not needed.* Whenever the JED is constructed on a team basis and the contributions of each team member to the team's output is carefully considered, it should become obvious that a position be eliminated or moved, and sometimes that a position should be added. All of these are organization design issues which the JED can help to highlight.

*Summary*
If one really likes the idea of output orientation, it is a straightforward matter to place the idea at the centre of an organization and design systems, in order to institutionalize it.

## LINKING OF ORGANIZATION, UNIT AND MANAGER OUTPUTS

It is clear that in an output-oriented organization the outputs of the individual manager and the unit of which the manager is a part, and other units and the organization as a whole, must be linked. This is accomplished by a variety of methods.

In structural terms the linking is accomplished by the JED. This document, which is also created for teams as well as individuals, encompasses more and more of the organization as it moves upward. The JED is expressed as reality when teams discuss the output of their teams in relationship with other teams, and the outputs of all individuals on their teams with the outputs of other individuals. It is obvious that one manager's outputs become another manager's inputs. It is the same with teams. A good concept is to see outputs as flows across the system. Managers, particularly at a more senior level, seem to see things that way, and make the necessary changes in order that outputs can be implemented to create effective linking.

### One organization's statement about teamwork

Here is an actual organization statement about teamwork. It may not appear directly to lead to linking the organization unit and manager outputs. However, when one considers that teams are larger and larger aggregates of subteams, then the linking process is seen as obvious and natural:

● We are structured as many interlocking teams. All managers are members of their superior's team, and if they have subordinates, are the top person of their own team.
● Teams are an effective and natural way of:
  – communication;
  – gaining commitment;
  – achieving results.
● One benefit of teamwork is that it improves the performance of all the team members. Teamwork must not be neglected if we are to make the best use of our people resources.
● The basis of teamwork is simple – it is talking with people. Managers are expected to talk with other managers, their subordinates and customers. If we all talk with one another more often, then better communication, understanding and co-operation will follow.
● Much of our communication should take place, and many of our management decisions should be made, in team meetings. Managers are expected to contribute actively to their teams.

For good linking to take place, it must be obvious that a high degree of candour is necessary. The most important thing to be candid about is one's own perception of one's level of effectiveness and one's perception of that of others, and of how either might be improved. Invariably these things are not talked about, yet they should be if we desire team work and linking. As with trust, one really cannot expect to receive any degree of candour unless one also gives it.

Some form of team training is crucial in helping effective linking. A suggested team meeting to achieve this is described on pp. 129–31.

### Linking of outputs at Honeywell

The following is an example of how Honeywell approaches the linking of outputs and objectives:

The process begins each spring with a memorandum from the chairman, setting forth some general goals of the corporation for the next three years; suggesting certain areas of interest; and indicating roughly the contributions the various divisions might be expected to make to attain these ends. On the basis of this document the division managers prepare their own three-year plans in fairly great detail.

Then, in the autumn, these same officials begin planning for the fiscal year that begins on 1 January. The managers within each division prepare a planning book, the first chapter of which details specific goals for the division in terms of profits, volume, return on assets and new products. Subsequent chapters of the book present specific goals for each of the division's major functional units, with cross-references indicating how the goals of one function will support those of other functions. While the individual goals of each manager may not be included in the book, the division's goals are based upon those set by the managers.

The work done in the spring to set forth a context within which detailed planning can take place provides the necessary direction from the top of the corporation. In the autumn, specific goals and objectives can be set at lower levels in the organization with the expectation that they will mesh into the overall plan.

With relatively minor variations, this procedure is widely used in output orientation implementations. The process followed is very similar to that of sound budget allocation and is often done together with it. The important differences are that it is concerned with outputs (objectives) rather than inputs (budgets) and that the initial plan comes from the top down and is based on what the company wishes to achieve.

## The down-up-down linking system

The down-up-down linking system is the name given to the procedure used to get the best set of linked objectives for a company. In essence, it involves draft objectives being passed downward (the 'roll-down'), a formal reaction to and revision of them from below, then being passed upward (the 'roll-up'), and a final passing down of objectives on which all managerial objectives are based and to which they are linked. Without this full cycle installed in this way, output orientation is not being fully utilized.

The first one or two trials are often a little clumsy and much difficulty is experienced in tying all the subunit objectives to the company objectives. This usually leads, in turn, to a dramatic increase in meetings – i.e. for the adjustment period only. What is happening at these meetings is the process of realistically linking objectives. The surface agenda may be 'You can't do that', 'It

cannot work', 'How does that relate to our plans?' or 'Our objectives must have priority', yet beneath all of these comments lies
the question: 'How can we get all our objectives linked together?'
These discussions often uncover basic flaws in organization design
that have not been previously identified – flaws which perhaps
do not simply inhibit, but actually prevent, linking. During this
adjustment period a mechanism needs to be available (usually in
the form of an external consultant) to identify such structural faults
and bring them to the attention of the management.

As the organization gains experience with this process, all
managers tend to plan ahead, so that they may have their own
draft objectives prepared prior to receiving the draft from top
management. This can be most important. A crucial part of the
whole process is the reaction and sorting out that takes place when
the 'top-down' and 'bottom-up' plans meet.

## Linking not automatic

The objectives of one manager must be related to those of other
managers and to an overall plan. Frequently at the beginning of
output programmes it is discovered that one manager's objectives
conflict with those of another. It can be a good thing to discover
this! Without an output orientation programme, such 'cross-
purpose efforts' might not have been found until perhaps too late,
or not at all:

> Prior to introducing output orientation, one company had experi-
> enced losses for three years running during a growth period,
> following several high-profit years. The managers appeared to be
> highly motivated and industrious, had excellent functional area
> experience and knowledge and desired to co-operate fully with
> one another. Analysis revealed that while all departments were
> working hard, they were apparently working towards conflicting
> corporate objectives. The bulk of the engineering department's
> time was spent on maintenance, that of the marketing department
> was on new brand introduction and that of the executive
> committee on overseas expansion, while a key staff assistant was
> spending most of the time predicting political climate in the home
> country. Taken separately, these directions had value but they
> simply did not lead to the formation of an integrated set of linked
> objectives.

Some highly motivated managers set objectives to maximize the effectiveness of their own position, but which if achieved, may not lead to maximizing the effectiveness of others because the objectives simply do *not* link together. This condition is most often seen between such functions as sales and credit, research and production and sometimes production and sales. Output orientation clarifies the need for linking objectives, thus providing a starting-point for it.

## A FLEXIBLE RESPONSE TO ACHIEVE OUTPUTS

Obviously achieving outputs is not always easy. Quite apart from having a clear understanding of what outputs really are, a key problem in achieving outputs is changing what the manager, the unit or the organization is already doing. Output-oriented organizations need to be flexible organizations. Chapter 6, on overcoming resistance within the organization details this.

We know too well the characteristics of the 'frozen' organization: too long in making decisions; no innovation, or innovation coming too late; no market-orientation; lagging technology and resistance to change. Rules and past practice are the main theme and there is some desertion at all levels.

The characteristics of the flexible output orientation include having a wide range of appropriate responses to a changing environment; an unrelenting emphasis on effectiveness first; an acceptance of change at all levels; and a free power flow, in particular across the top team, so that changes can be made easily, flexible resource allocation. This means that budgets change in response to output needs, not input needs, together with a free information flow, so that managers in units can make rapid changes in response to new environments.

### A sound way to increase flexibility

A tested way to increase flexibility in organizations is the 3–D Managerial Effectiveness Seminar (3–D MES), or some version of it, as described in Chapter 7. This seminar is deliberately designed to lower resistance by increasing objectivity about situation and, in particular, about what truly are outputs for the position. Another method – though this should be preceded by the 3–D MES – is the Team Meeting, described in Chapter 8.

**THE CREATION OF YOUR OWN APPROACH TO OUTPUTS, NOT COPYING THOSE OF OTHERS**

In creating the output-oriented organization it is critical that the organization as a whole, its units and its individual managers, feel they own the ideas and methods by which the output orientation will be achieved. This book does not prescribe the method by which an organization is to achieve its highest effectiveness; however, some books do, and these list the characteristics of excellent organizations, the implication being that if other organizations would emulate them, they too would be good. We all seek answers and, at times, are trapped by those who claim to have them. We search for hope rather than reality and those who provide hope with a simple solution are those that sometimes get the most attention.

One of the reasons why this book has been written is that it is easy to describe successful organizations, but it is not so easy to explain how to get there. 'How to be more like me' might be a good title for appraisal interviews, but it is *not* a good way to design organizations.

This book helps you to create your version of the output-oriented organization. It is uncompromising on the definition of outputs, and somewhat uncompromising too on the types of meetings that will help your organization to achieve the kind of outputs that you want and in the way you want. However, this book does not propose that your organization should be thus – rather its message is that you have an understanding of the concept of outputs and then use all your resources to decide on how you will implement the ideas in the best way for your organization, and in its existing environment.


**THE OUTPUT ETHIC**

Output orientation is not a one-sided concept – it is a value that we can embrace and use. Whatever our personal values, objectives, moral philosophy or political stance, output orientation is a lifeline; it says, 'use resources productively, waste less and make work enjoyable and worthwhile'. The question is not 'Should I be nice to people?', or on the other hand, 'What rules should be followed?', but: 'What does it take to be output oriented here?' We are not talking about the 'work ethic', and clearly not about the 'welfare ethic' but about the 'output ethic'. It says nothing about 'more power to the workers!' or 'screw the workers down!' Nor does it argue for higher profit, but simply says: 'Measure managers by the extent to which they achieve the output requirements of their positions.'

# 2  What are outputs?

Let deeds correspond with words.
Plautus

Empty sacks will never stand upright.
G. Torriano

The objective of this chapter is to explain exactly what an output is, and the examples are drawn from individual teams and positions. The basic ideas apply equally well to organization outputs, but a much greater variety of examples can be drawn from outputs of particular teams and outputs of individual positions. The same principles apply across individual positions, teams and organizations.

There is only one realistic and unambiguous definition of managerial effectiveness. It is: the extent to which a manager achieves the output requirements of the position. When seen in this way, effectiveness becomes a central issue in management. It is every manager's job to make the organization more effective. In fact it is the only job. Once this definition is understood, accepted and applied, it leads directly to changes in the self, and can lead as well to changes in personnel policy, methods, management information system and management structure. The emphasis, in this chapter, will be on managerial and team effectiveness, but the concept does apply to the organization as a whole. Using organization effectiveness examples can sometimes lead to deflecting the issue along the lines of something like, 'well, I have no control over that – it is someone else's problem'. By looking at the managerial and team level we are looking at actual outputs at a concrete level that we can all understand and to which we can relate.

## CONCEPTS OF MANAGERIAL EFFECTIVENESS

To understand the nature of managerial effectiveness it is necessary to distinguish the three terms 'managerial effectiveness', 'apparent effectiveness' and 'personal effectiveness'.

### Managerial effectiveness

Managerial effectiveness is not an aspect of personality. It is not something that a manager *has*. To see it that way, however, would be a return to the now discarded 'trait theory' of leadership, which suggested that more effective leaders have special qualities not possessed by less effective leaders. Effectiveness is best seen, perhaps, as something a manager produces from a situation by managing it appropriately. In current terminology it represents output, not input. The manager must think in terms of performance, not personality. It is not so much what managers do, but what they achieve. The following is an extreme example.

Managers' true worth to their companies may sometimes be measured by the amount of time they could remain dead in their offices without anyone noticing. The longer the time, the more likely it is that they make long-run policy decisions rather than short-run administrative decisions. The key decisions in a company are long-term ones and may refer to market entry, new product introduction, new plant location or to senior appointments. The people who make these decisions should not get involved, as can happen with short-run issues. If they do, they have not properly decided on the output measures of the job, nor have they the skill or opportunity to create conditions where only policy issues reach them.

Some managers have narrow views of their jobs. What they do, they may do well, but they leave an enormous amount undone. Some managers let the in-basket define the nature of their potential contribution and the clock its limit. Some managers might view their contribution as simply that of managing a going concern and keeping it on an even keel, while others might see the same job as having within it large components of subordinate development and creative problem-solving. Still others might see their position primarily as a link-pin connecting with other parts of the firm, and thus might take a wider view of their responsibilities.

**Apparent effectiveness**

It is difficult, if not impossible, to judge managerial effectiveness by observation of behaviour alone. The behaviour must be evaluated in terms of whether or not it is appropriate to the output requirements of the job. For example, the following qualities may be crucial to effectiveness in some jobs, while in others they may well be irrelevant: is usually on time, answers promptly, makes quick decisions, is good at public relations and is a good writer.

These qualities might give an air of apparent effectiveness in whatever context they appear; but apparent effectiveness may or may not lead to managerial effectiveness.

Conventional job descriptions often lead to an emphasis on what could be called managerial efficiency: the ratio of output to input. The problem is that if both input and output are low, efficiency could still be 100 per cent. In fact a manager or department could easily be 100 per cent efficient and 0 per cent effective. Efficient managers are easily identified; they prefer to:

| | | |
|---|---|---|
| do things right | *rather than* | do right things |
| solve problems | *rather than* | produce creative alternatives |
| safeguard resources | *rather than* | optimize resource utilization |
| discharge duties | *rather than* | obtain results |

Conventional job descriptions lead to the apparent effectiveness of the behaviour as listed in the left-hand column; a job effectiveness description which emphasized managerial effectiveness would lead to performance as listed in the right-hand column.

Normally conventional job descriptions and management audits focus on the internal efficiency of an organization system rather than on its external effectiveness or its outputs. It would be a simple matter to increase internal efficiency, and to decrease external effectiveness, just as sharply. Usually the paperwork is quite unrelated to effectiveness.

The distinction between managerial effectiveness and apparent effectiveness can be further illustrated by what really happens when a hyperactive new manager brings what appears to be 'chaos' to an organization, but the situation is seen to begin to improve. Unless outputs are the focus of attention, the result can be serious distortion about what is really going on.

**Personal effectiveness**

Poorly defined job outputs may also lead to what might be termed as personal effectiveness, that is the satisfying of personal objectives rather than the objectives of the organization. This is particularly likely to occur with ambitious people in an organization having only few closely defined management output measures. Meetings with these people are riddled with hidden agendas, which operate below the surface and lead to poor decision-making. To illustrate, in a three-day meeting to set corporate objectives for a consumer goods firm, one of the four assistant CEOs in attendance initiated a series of proposals for reorganization, arguing for them with great force.

While all had some merit, it was evident as they were outlined that most would not lead to greatly improved team effectiveness. The other team members quickly saw that all these proposals were aimed, to some extent unconsciously, at improving the assistant CEO's power and prestige. This issue was debated for several hours and the team members, many of whom had previously had intentions similar to those of the assistant CEO, finally decided to turn their attention away from improving their personal effectiveness towards improving their managerial effectiveness and thus their total team effectiveness. The top management structure was modified, but in keeping with market, consumer, competitive and organization needs, not with personal needs.

There is nothing wrong with either personal effectiveness or apparent effectiveness. Most of us prefer to operate on our own terms and we all like to appear effective. The problem arises only when either condition is confused with managerial effectiveness. In a well-designed firm all three kinds of effectiveness might occur simultaneously for any particular manager. This would mean that managers who are indeed effective actually look as if they are (apparent effectiveness), and are rewarded for it (personal effectiveness).

## THE DEADLY SIN OF INPUTS

The first step in helping managers to be more effective is to help them to see their job in output terms. Keeping the concept of effectiveness in mind, we can refer to these outputs as 'effectiveness areas', but they go by a variety of other names. The problem is that too many jobs are described in terms of inputs, not outputs; and in terms of input areas, not in terms of effectiveness areas.

The source of much of the problem which surrounds effectiveness is found in the way job descriptions are written. Usually, lengthy job descriptions, or crash programmes to write or update them, have little usefulness. As C. Northcote Parkinson has pointed out, the last act of a dying organization is to issue a revised and greatly enlarged rule-book. This observation may hold just as well for crash programmes to write job descriptions.

Many, if not most, managerial jobs are defined in terms of their input and behaviour requirements by such words as: 'administers', 'maintains', 'organizes', 'plans' and 'schedules'. Naturally enough, managers never refer to job descriptions like this; once made, they are not very useful as an operating guide. Initially they are often proposed by those who want to use a seemingly scientific technique to justify a widespread change in salary differentials, or a change in the organization structure; they are a negative influence as they focus on input and behaviour, the less important aspects of the manager's job.

**The Training Officer**

While many initial attempts to set effectiveness areas turn out to be a list of activities instead, many attempts can go in the other direction: everyone appears to think they are heading a profit centre. Of any proposed effectiveness area, the question should be asked: 'Why is this being done?', or 'Why is this important?' Training managers, for instance, might go through this kind of process. First, they are asked what is their most important area – to which they might reply, 'To design a management development programme'. When asked why, they reply, 'To put on courses for managers'. Again, when asked why, they reply, 'To improve the quality of managerial decisions'. To further interrogation, they reply: 'To improve profit performance.' The correct area of concern for these training managers would probably be increased managerial skill in problem-solving. It cannot be to 'improve the quality of managerial decisions' or to 'improve profit performance' since both of these are influenced by factors over which the training managers have no control and no authority. On the other hand, the correct area cannot be simply that of programme design or putting on courses, which are clearly inputs. The sole objective of industrial training is to change behaviour, and the effectiveness areas and the objectives of a training manager must reflect this.

Most inputs can be converted to outputs if the position is needed at all. Some examples where inputs are converted to outputs include the following: coach subordinates to subordinate effectiveness; church attendance to Christian values; and farmer education to high-value crop acreages. One should be wary of such areas as communication, relationships, liaison, co-ordination and staffing: these areas usually suggest inputs.


## FROM INPUTS TO OUTPUTS

The following examples of improved effectiveness areas show both the first and second attempts to establish them. Most often, the first attempt was the result of private work, without consultation; the second attempt showed how first attempts were improved after small-group discussion. Such before and after changes as these are typical. They demonstrate what an imperfect view many – or even most – managers have of their jobs, and how easy it is to change this view, given the appropriate method and conditions. None of the second attempts is claimed to be perfect for the job in question and, in any case, this would be impossible to determine without much more information. The point here is that the second attempt clearly is better than the first.


### Chairman of the board

A full-time chairman of the board of a 6,000-employee company produced these two sets of effectiveness areas:

*First attempt*:
1   improve value of board;
2   assure good executive meetings;
3   provide useful counsel to company officers;
4   maintain effective remuneration and personnel policies for senior executives;
5   develop high-level corporate image and public relations;
6   initiate sound long-range planning
*Second attempt*:
7   board decision quality;
8   national corporate image;
9   corporate strategy.

The realization that the second set of areas was really the chairman's job led to many changes, particularly in time allocation. Areas 1 (improve value of board) and 2 (assure good executive meetings) could be replaced by area 7 (board decision quality); area 3 (provide useful counsel to company officers) was seen as meddling; area 4 (maintain effective remuneration and personnel policies for senior executives) should be given to the CEO; area 5 (develop good high level corporate image and public relations) was the chairman's job, but on a national scale, as expressed in area 8 (national corporate image); and area 6 (initiate sound long-range planning) was best replaced by 9 (corporate strategy).

## University director of physical education

A newly appointed university director of physical education with a staff of about ten produced the following as first and second attempts:

*First attempt*:
1  character-building;
2  health;
3  sports activity;
4  maintenance;
5  staffing;
6  future programmes
*Second attempt*:
7  utilization of facilities;
8  readiness of facilities;
9  quality of facilities;
10  programme innovation rate;
11  growth of facilities.

This director came to see that there could be only partial influence on areas 1 (character building) and 2, (health) and that there was no practical measuring device for the former (character building); areas 3 (sports activity) and 4 (maintenance) were best expressed as 7 (utilization of facilities) and 8 (readiness of facilities); and area 5 (staffing) was an input, and area 6 (future programmes) could be more clearly worded as 10 (programme innovation rate). Unlike some such managers, there was some control over the growth of facilities and it was thought appropriate to include area 11 (growth of facilities).

**A food-processing company CEO**

The CEO of a 5,000-employee food-processing company initially produced the following sets of effectiveness areas:

*First attempt*:
1   profitability;
2   planning;
3   top-team quality;
4   profit growth;
5   reputation growth;
6   growth momentum;
7   trade relations;
8   industry relations;
9   government relations;
10  board and employee relations;
11  capital employment;
12  return on investment;
13  management succession plan
*Second attempt*:
14  profitability;
15  planning;
16  reputation in industry;
17  company climate;
18  customer/top management relations.

This CEO decided to retain areas 1 (profitability) and 2 (planning) as areas 14 (profitability) and 15 (planning); area 3 (top team quality) was identified as a common area; area 4 (profit growth) could be included as a subobjective of 14 (profitability) by using a longer time span; area 5 (reputation growth) was changed to 16 (reputation in industry) – this was kept as this marketing-oriented CEO spent much time on customer and industry visits; area 6 (growth momentum) moved to 14 (profitability); area 7 (trade relations) moved to part of 16 (reputation in industry); and area 8 (industry relations) became more specific as area 18 (customer/top management relations) was changed to 17 (company climate); areas 11 (capital employment) and 12 (return on investment) were given to the deputy CEO of finance; and area 13 (management succession plan) was seen as an area belonging to the deputy CEO of personnel.

## JOB OUTPUTS ARE ALWAYS MEASURABLE

If a so-called effectiveness area or objective is not measurable, we can forget it, for no one will know anyway. The most stern but necessary test of effectiveness areas and objectives is measurability. The rule, then, is: if you cannot measure it, ignore it.

In the left-hand column of the following table is a list of qualitative objectives which are used as an illustration in one popular MBO textbook to suggest that such qualitative objectives must sometimes be used; but this has been found to be incorrect. In the right-hand column are my own conversions which show that such qualitative objectives are usually unnecessary:

| *Actual suggested qualitative objectives in standard management by objectives textbook* | *Conversion to illustrate that qualitative objectives are found to be activities* (By asking the purpose of the activities, quantitative objectives are derived) |
|---|---|
| Conduct monthly management development sessions for superintendents in techniques of standard cost programme. | Have 50 per cent of superintendents using standard cost programming techniques on at least two projects by end-July. |
| Prepare a programme for patent productions. | Have no patent loopholes in our patents discovered by our own staff, independent agents or competitors during the year. |
| Prepare and distribute an internal public relations manual. | Obtain average 75 per cent unaided recall by all non-managerial employees of 50 per cent of the key corporate activities or accomplishments of the prior month for each month next year. |
| Improve statistical reports to reduce time lag between production and publication dates. | Without decreasing usable content, reduce by average of four days time spent distributing the following reports by end-September. |

| | |
|---|---|
| Prepare quality control manual for supervisors. | Eighty-five per cent of first-line supervisors to know eight of the ten key points in company quality control practice by end-December. |
| Improve appearance, packaging and design of products. | For each item in product line design a package which receives more consumer jury votes than any competing product by end-November. |
| Undertake to ally research efforts more closely with production needs. | Have at least 80 per cent of proposals to production manager accepted during the year. |

Most of the above conversions from inputs to outputs involve a broader view of one's job, a greater responsibility for the staff function and a higher cost of measurement.

## Measurement of knowledge workers

It is a popular myth that the effectiveness of many knowledge workers cannot be measured; but look at the following disarmingly simple set of effectiveness areas, all of which are capable of measurement if the associated objectives are worded correctly:

1  Consulted in area of competence.
2  Advice accepted.
3  Advice acceptance leads to improvement.

The first area obliges the knowledge worker, not the manager, to ensure that the knowledge worker is consulted. Too many knowledge workers, like some university professors, see themselves as information reservoirs with no responsibility to provide a 'tapping' facility; and usually this is sorely needed. Knowledge workers, more than managers, have the opportunity to develop a relationship such that their advice is sought when appropriate. Industry has no place for knowledge workers who do not themselves create consultative conditions.

The second area reflects that it is all too easy to give advice that is not accepted. Knowledge workers must be evaluated on their effectiveness in giving line managers the advice that they can use.

Area 3 records that just as it is too easy to give advice not accepted, it is all too easy to give advice that leads to a 'a poorer situation developing'. Knowledge workers have a responsibility for the success of their advice. Personal competence is not listed as an effectiveness area, it is an input; and in any case, if the knowledge worker were not competent, the advice would not lead to improvement.

While the measurement problem can usually be solved with imagination, the cost of the measurement problem may remain. To measure the impact of a training course on behaviour necessitates, at least, many telephone calls and questionnaires, and preferably a field survey. The outputs of a public relations position are hard to measure without some kind of formal survey. Here one needs to ask whether the function is important enough even to have a rough measurement of its effectiveness; if not, then the function is eliminated. However, if it does, then allocate ten per cent of total appropriate budgets to measurement. Conventional wisdom may well insist that a particular activity is a 'good thing', but measurement is the only way to test it.

It seems difficult for some managers to accept our philosophy, that: if you cannot measure it, forget it, because no one will know. Yet accurate measurement is central to good management. Some managers see their job as having vague, pervasive and very long-term effects, claiming that it is impossible to measure their performance by normal methods. If such managers also say that they understand what managerial effectiveness really means, then they occupy a position that is unneeded or they have no authority to do their job or they are avoiding responsibility.

As a simple example, the 'good relationship' is often proposed as an effectiveness area. This is not measurable, except by highly subjective methods. A sales manager who once proposed this area later claimed that it was not only non-measurable, but an input as well; effectiveness in this area could be equally well measured by short- and long-term sales.


## IS THERE A JOB AT ALL?

If two people are responsible for the same thing, one of them is not needed.

Some supervisors who misunderstand their jobs believe their task is to ensure that subordinates do what they are supposed to do. This view, if taken to its natural conclusion, means that the sole function of all levels of management is to make sure that the workers get on with it. Logically this would mean that all levels of management existed only to see that workers at the lower levels worked. While this may be true in some technologies, it is hardly true of many. We simply cannot say that superiors' jobs are always well represented simply by a collection of their subordinates' effectiveness areas, or their objectives as the following example shows.

An assistant CEO supervised four managers of profit centres, as show in Figure 2.1. The assistant CEO knew the difficulty in determining effectiveness areas: one area could not be profit because this was an area of each of the subordinates, and there were no resources such as capital to allocate among them; in fact the assistant CEO did not have a job, and at a meeting held for the unit this became clear. The team recommended that, as a unit, it be dissolved. The four profit centres became attached to other parts of the organization and the assistant CEO assumed another role which had previously been filled only nominally.

Clearly, for every position effectiveness areas must be identifiable. Typically what happens is that, in their first attempt, these managers accept the fact that all their effectiveness areas are really those of their subordinates. While apparently left with nothing to do, the managers know that they are filling a useful role. With further thought, they come to see their unique contribution only dimly perceived before. With their real job thus identified, they get on with it rather than with the jobs of their subordinates.

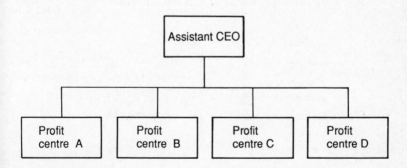

*Figure 2.1* The team that did not exist, it looks very important but is not needed

**The Personnel Manager**

One personnel manager listed effectiveness areas as: training, wage and salary administration, employment, staffing, safety and security, and industrial relations, as shown in Figure 2.2. The personnel manager was then asked to draw the unit as an organization chart and to identify all the effectiveness areas, starting with those of subordinates and not duplicating any; the result is shown in Figure 2.3. The effectiveness areas ran out before the personnel manager's own position was reached. This meant that the position was seen as having no unique responsibilities. The personnel manager's job, as defined, was either doing the subordinates' work or making sure that they did it. This was a narrow definition of the responsibility. The job was seen in broader terms than that and, surely, the personnel manager has more to contribute.

The following questions were asked: 'What is your unique contribution?' 'What is the biggest thing which could go wrong?' 'What do you, or could you, do that the managers do not, because (1) they do not have the ability or experience, (2) they do not have the time or (3) they do not have the information?' 'Why was your position created?'

This personnel manager came to see that the unique contribution was in the areas of: personnel policy, working conditions, organization development and managerial effectiveness. The personnel manager could not accept full responsibility for all of these areas, but was responsible, as any staff person, for giving acceptable advice. When we compare the first set of effectiveness areas with the revised set, a greatly enlarged view of the job is apparent, together with a preparedness to allow subordinates to 'get on with it'.

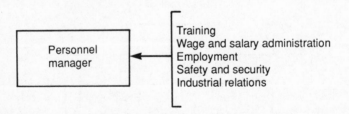

*Figure 2.2*   A personnel manager's view of the effectiveness areas (at first glance, this appears to be an accurate description but is not!)

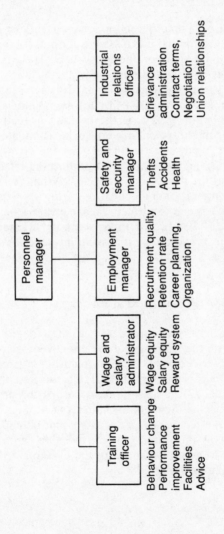

*Figure 2.3* What is the job of the personnel manager (when your subordinates share all your effectiveness areas with you, what are you left with)?

As the subordinates were fairly experienced, they could be allowed to work with full authority in their respective positions. If a position in the structure or a key subordinate were lost, the personnel manager might temporarily cover the effectiveness areas of the position concerned.

## How to select effectiveness areas

Here is a list of simple questions for managers to ask themselves and to develop an initial list of effectiveness areas for their position to test both on the superior and co-workers. There is much overlap, and essentially all the questions really ask: what is the job?

However, some managers find that ideas are triggered when the question is asked in a variety of forms. 'What is the position's unique contribution?' 'Why is the position needed at all?' 'What would change if the position were to be eliminated?' 'What will change if I am highly effective in the position?' 'How would I know, with no one telling me, when I am performing effectively?' 'What authority does the position really have?' 'What do the job description and the organization manual say?' 'How do I spend my time?' 'How should I spend my time?' 'What would I be most likely to concentrate on over two or three years if I wanted to make the greatest improvement in my unit or in my superior's unit or in the organization as a whole?'

## Guides to testing effectiveness areas

When effectiveness areas are identified, they should satisfy six tests which check on the adequacy of the effectiveness areas, both individually and collectively. Each effectiveness area should: (1) represent output, not input; (2) lead to associated objectives which are measurable; (3) be an important part of the position; and (4) be within the actual limits of authority and responsibility.

In addition, effectiveness areas as a whole should: (5) represent 100 per cent of the outputs of the position; and (6) not be so numerous as to avoid dealing with the essence of the job, nor so few as to make planning difficult.

**Flexibility of effectiveness areas**

Managers at the top of any unit usually have some flexibility in the choice of the effectiveness areas that they decide to associate with their own position. This freedom is most marked when they have the ability to create a subordinate and can assign part of their own work to that subordinate. Under these conditions the top persons' areas become fully flexible and they can make them what they want to be. For instance, they could become an 'outside' person with an emphasis on liaison with other organization units or customers. The newly created subordinate could be the 'inside' person concerned with managing the unit. The reverse situation is equally feasible. This demonstrates that, within broad limits, managers who can create a subordinate and can design their subordinates' effectiveness areas have an extensive range of different areas which they can associate with their own job.

It is impossible to look in isolation at the effectiveness areas for a particular position. Such areas are best seen as sets of areas which link together several positions. It is quite possible that if the set of areas for one position changes a great deal, sets of areas for other positions may change as well, and so they should. When setting areas, the question is not 'what are they?', but 'what could they best be?' Clearly, the output orientation is intimately related to both organization design and organization flexibility.

After three years on the job, the plant manager may decide to change the effectiveness areas established, and indeed may have trained one or more subordinates to assume some of them. The important thing is that effectiveness areas should not simply be applied to an existing organization design and then considered to be relatively permanent. Instead the assigning of effectiveness areas should be used as a basis for inducing organization flexibility and ensuring that it is maintained. Normally the effectiveness areas are subject to change when a new manager is appointed; co-workers change; a manager's skills are increased; power and decision levels move; management by objectives (MBO) is implemented; or any major organization change occurs.

## MAKING OUTPUT ORIENTATION OPERATIONAL

Output orientation should be linked directly to organization philosophy, induction training and organization development (OD). In this way, it becomes the firm's central value induced by training and OD. Effectiveness areas should be the basis of describing jobs and of linking one job to another – i.e. system design. Measurement areas form the basis of job specifications in determining what kind of manager is required. In manager selection: is this the person we want? In training plans: how do we obtain desired behaviour? And in job evaluation: how much should we pay? Objectives form the basis of the link between corporate strategy and managerial appraisal.

So to make the concept of output orientation operational for an organization, it must be linked with objectives. This is easily done by use of following (linked) ideas:

1 *Managerial effectiveness*: the extent to which a manager achieves the output requirements of the position.
2 *Effectiveness areas*: general output requirements of the managerial position.
3 *Measurement areas*: the way in which an effectiveness area is measured.
4 *Objectives*: effectiveness areas and measurement areas which are as specific, time bounded and as measurable as possible.

While the concept of objectives is central in output orientation, the other three ideas (managerial effectiveness, effectiveness areas and measurement areas) form the foundations of any objectives that are set; and only with an understanding of these will the objectives be sound.

**Managerial effectiveness**

A sound implementation of output orientation must be preceded by the acceptance of managerial effectiveness as the central value or philosophy in management. Unless this is given a primary importance, output orientation will be no more than a highly sophisticated managerial-level work study. A small, or even a large, firm can have values built in which counter the idea of managerial effectiveness. Such values may seriously interfere with - or completely prevent – the implementation of output orientation.

**Effectiveness areas**

The second idea, effectiveness areas, is based on the view that all managerial positions are best seen in terms of the outputs associated with them. However, surprisingly few managers see their positions in this way. Effectiveness areas spring primarily from the strategy of the firm as made operational by the organization structure. To a lesser but significant extent, they depend on the top management's views on the best locus for decision-making.

## Measurement areas

Measurement areas are sub divisions of effectiveness areas, which incorporate measurement criteria explicitly or implicitly. An effectiveness area of 'sales' might be conveniently broken down into one or more of the following sets of measurement areas:

existing products – existing markets; existing products – new markets; new products – existing markets; and new products – new markets.

or unit sales by area, product and customer;

or sales of product A, product B and product C;

or sales of product A, gross margin of product A and profitability of product A.

One of the above four sets of standards, or some combination of them, would suit most situations. The set of measurement areas chosen is that which best covers the total job in output terms.

## Objectives

Essentially, objectives are specific measurement areas with time limits and numerical values attached to them. Thus, for the effectiveness area 'sales', we have seen that one measurement area might be: sales revenue from product A. The associated objective might then be: increase sales revenue for product A by 15,000 for the period 1 January to 31 December. The concepts are related in this way:

*Effectiveness area*
Product A.
*Measurement areas*
1   Sales revenue increase for product A.
2   Gross margin increase in percentage on product A.
3   Profitability increase per unit in money product A.

*Objectives*
1   Increase sales revenue for product A to 400,000 during . . .
2   Increase gross margin of product A to 22 per cent by decreasing
    distribution cost to 1.10 money units per unit during . . .
3   Increase profitability of product A to 0.22 money units
    during . . .

For each measurement area there is usually one objective, as shown
in the above example. All this is relatively straightforward, but it
may well be worthless if the effectiveness areas do not represent
outputs from the beginning.

## THE JOB EFFECTIVENESS DESCRIPTION

A job effectiveness description (JED) is needed which describes a
managerial position almost exclusively in output terms. It contains
first a list of the effectiveness areas of the position. Together with
each of the measurement areas, managers develop a specific objective (usually annually), and measure their degree of attainment of
the objective by the established measurement area also contained
in the job effectiveness description. For most managers this can be
put down on one side of a piece of paper.

The only additional content of the job effectiveness descriptions
are specific statements of the authority vested in the position. These
statements may refer to authority to enlarge or decrease staff, use
overtime, change the product or service, rearrange the work flow
or modify a production programme. In constructing these job effectiveness descriptions great care is needed to ensure that the authority is sufficient for the specified measurement areas and the objectives derived from them. Either the authority is found, or made
sufficient, or the effectiveness areas and measurement areas are
passed upwards.

The job effectiveness description is prepared for each managerial
position, and for each unit, which include a manager and all the
subordinates. Thus managerial objectives are formally linked to
team objectives.

Now that the notion of outputs is clearer, we move on to look
at your part of the organization, or the organization as a whole, to
consider what needs to be changed in order to increase output
orientation. Some organizations are highly input-oriented, it is their
way of life! Asking them how to change things leads to more ideas
on how to improve on their inputs. That is why discussion of outputs

must precede Chapter 3 which asks, 'What is needed to create your output oriented organization?'

# 3  Achieving output orientation

The task of administration is so to design the environment that the individual will approach as close as practicable to rationality (judged in terms of the organization's goals) in his decision.

Herbert A. Simon

Structural relationships are not once and for all prescriptions but are 'rules of the game' which are adaptable to changing situations and the changing desires of the participants.

Ogden H. Hall

What people often mean by getting rid of conflict is getting rid of diversity and it is of the utmost importance that these should not be considered the same. We may wish to abolish conflict but we cannot get rid of diversity.

Mary Parker Follett

This chapter is designed to help you think about your own part of the organization and to consider what needs to be changed in it so as to achieve output orientation. It might be, for instance, that you think nothing can be accomplished without reorganization or that you think the key point would be increased candour or that you think moving decision levels upwards or downwards is called for. Or indeed that you need better teamwork. A reasonably complete list of possible changes is provided here, although you may have other ideas of your own to add. These criteria are presented in order to guide your selection of the change objectives for the change targets that you wish to influence. In addition to listing these possible change objectives, this chapter provides criteria for selecting them.

More and more managers are setting what have come to be called *planned change objectives* for their part of the organization. This involves the identification of change targets, for example, the organization as a whole or parts of it such as the regional structure. The setting of planned change objectives might range all the way from reorganization to improved job satisfaction. The application of strict measurement areas for these objectives achieves greater clarity about what is being sought. Finally, we present a plan to achieve these objectives. Here the purpose is to explain the method and provide ideas for possible planned change objectives which can lead to greater output orientation.

## THE PROCESS OF SETTING PLANNED CHANGE OBJECTIVES

The process of setting planned change objectives is quite straight-forward. The following issues need to be addressed:

- can we change?
- what are the change targets?
- who decides the objectives?
- what are the criteria for selecting the objectives?
- agreement of possible objectives
- selection of objectives
- agreement on the measurement areas for objectives

### Can we change?

The technology is now available for facilitating change in large systems. Twenty years ago it was difficult to talk, with any degree of certainty, about plans to centralize, decentralize, remove a layer of management, introduce participative management, build teams or unfreeze an organization. Advances in behavioural science are such that many such changes can be planned and implemented with a high degree of certainty of success. This book is intended to facilitate this in total systems or subsystems or, if you like, whole organizations or parts of organizations.

We all know the story of the traveller who asked a local for directions to a neighbouring village. The local thought for a while and then said, 'You can't get there from here!' This exactly describes the unconscious approach of some managers. They think that change is impossible. So before we address the issue of objectives for planned change, we must consider the more fundamental issue of whether or not the managers involved believe that change is possible. This may take one minute or it may take longer. Similarly, management must agree that it wishes to become more output oriented before embarking on any of the activities described in this book. Here is the big problem – but keep reading!

**What are the change targets?**

When the decision is made that change is possible and that management wants to become more output oriented, the change targets need to be decided. These will include such things as a normal production system, the organization as a whole, the top team as a unit or the various functional areas such as production, marketing and finance. There may be some common objectives across all these areas, or the sets of objectives for each may be completely different. There is nothing wrong with having only one change target, such as the organization as a whole, or with having many. It will depend upon the system and its needs. Change targets may well be differentiated by level, for example, the top team or those reporting to the top team or middle management and supervision. If manufacturing facilities are dispersed and have a reasonably low rate of interaction and different technologies, then the change target might be that of each remote plant taken independently of one another.

**Who decides the objectives?**

Who should decide the change objectives? The obvious choice, if one is interested primarily in improving organization effectiveness, is the top team of the unit under consideration. Normally this is in fact what happens. The main alternatives for who chooses the objectives are the top team of the organization, the top team of the particular change targets, the top team of both the organization and the change target together or an individual such as the chief executive (CEO) – or you alone. All can work.

**Criteria for selecting the objectives**

There are five criteria for selecting planned change objectives:

- measurable;
- attainable;
- within control;
- cost/benefits;
- priority/sequence.

*Measurable*
It is absolutely essential that one or more clear measurement areas be applied to every objective selected: if this is not done, then one

will never know whether the objective is achieved! For instance, a very poor objective would be 'delegation' – try to define it. A far better one would be 'move decision levels downwards' – one can ask what decisions in particular? How far down? How soon?

A bank decided that it wanted to move decision levels downwards. In banking an important decision concerns loan limits. Here they moved loan limits from where the top team approved every loan of over 1 million to where the top team saw no loans under 20 million. A clear objective needs a clear measurement area. Such objectives as 'improved communication' are incomprehensible unless measurement areas are applied. Does one mean more communication, less communication, communication upwards, communication downwards, or more or fewer memos? In short, the measurement areas define what exactly we do mean.

*Attainable*
The planned change process does not deal with 'blue sky' ideas. The central issue is rather that it is likely the objective will be achieved. Assuming that this is not known in advance, the question really becomes: is there a decent probability of attaining the objective?

*Within control*
Is the capacity to achieve the planned change objective within control? This process is not concerned with issues that are not in control of the group trying to make the implementation. Moaning about others is easy but does not make one more effective. The moaning issues can be left to one side as they are outside of control.

Deal with issues that the group is involved with and can deal with directly. For instance, in organization restructuring, one always needs to ask the CEO whether or not it is reasonable to assume that the proposed new structure could be sold to the board or whoever has to agree. Sometimes it lies completely in the CEO's hands, so there is no problem. But sometimes there *is* a problem. The issue needs to be addressed before the planned change objective is agreed.

*Cost/benefits*
Obviously there must be agreed presumed cost/benefits to any planned change objective. Otherwise why bother? As it happens, the biggest cost of all is the management time cost to implement a change. Managers do not realize that, in the process of change, they have really made an addition to their existing jobs. Change takes time.

*Priority/sequence*

Some planned change objectives have to be achieved before others can be started. For example, if the organization needs restructuring, and this will naturally lead to power being moved, then anything concerning decision-making, such as moving decision levels downwards, must come after it. If managers are highly demotivated because they have no real authority and their operation can be changed on a week-to-week basis by personnel, then it would be better to tackle that issue directly rather than trying to start first with job satisfaction. Some top teams (who do not really know what they are doing) simply bring in a 'communication' consultant, who no doubt gives an effective series of presentations but who fails to get down to the basic issue. All concerned have not grasped the nettle.

It is not unusual to get a letter requesting, 'Please will you introduce output orientation within three months'. This may turn out to be completely impossible because of such things as the poor management information system, the incompetence of some managers, the lack of interest in profit as the organization has become 'fat and happy', the weak basic organization structure or that there are no line managers. So any intelligent person does not start with output orientation; it may be good to end with, but not to start. Other things come first.

## Agree possible objectives

Quite obviously, possible objectives can be many and varied. There are some forty possible objectives that have been used by companies large and small, and each has been found useful. By all means add more of your own to a preliminary working list or allow others to arise naturally in discussion. The list has been proven to be a very good base to start with in selecting objectives.

## Select the objectives

The process of selecting change objectives usually takes about a day when done by a team; and it is best done in the context of the process described in Chapter 9, outlining a total planning method where the top of the unit in the primary change target makes a complete plan to implement changes leading to the output-oriented organization.

The best way of starting a meeting on planned change objectives is to list the change objectives for the first change target selected, then to put them all up on newsprint in the front of the room where the whole team can see them and, then, agreement is sought. In the discussion many issues will arise which most probably constitute key factors hindering achievement of the output-oriented organization. If all this were to be done by an individual, it could be completed in one or two minutes, yet, that may not make it any more cost-effective, for in choosing planned change objectives there are many considerations, such as overcoming resistance, what is meant by managerial effectiveness and what time and money resources can be afforded, and perhaps disagreements on the general issue of how to make any system more effective.

**Agree the measurement areas for the objectives**

At some point, it will be necessary to select measurement areas for the change objectives. At times this is difficult, but it can and must be done. What it does is to reduce overly high principles such as 'reorganized' to the more manageable 'exactly what do we mean by that?'

One of the hardest groups of objectives for which to set measurement areas lies in the area of communication. What should it mean to have 'improved communication?' Does it mean more memos, no memos, public-speaking courses, better writing courses, or an internal newspaper or suggestion box? Many people would scoff at many, or all, of these possibilities. The problem of meaning may be best approached by remembering the question: 'when we have achieved the objective, exactly how will things be different? One can see that the exercise is difficult, but it does bring things into the context of reality. (If you cannot set measurable objectives, then forget them because no one will know anyway.) Never let anyone argue that such-and-such cannot be measured, or it is too difficult to measure. Simply, everything that exists is measurable. The reason some people claim that some measurements are impossible to make is that they are not clear about what measurement is to be made.

# PLANNED CHANGE OBJECTIVES

Naturally there are an unlimited number of possible planned change objectives, together with unlimited ways of attempting to categorize them. Here is a list that has been used for many years and has been found to useful; it provides a reasonable and comprehensive starting point.

**Classes of planned change objectives**

There are eight identifiable classes of planned change objectives, as follows:

1   structural objectives;
2   effectiveness objectives;
3   decision-making objectives;
4   interface objectives;
5   communication objectives;
6   flexibility objectives;
7   individual objectives;
8   climate and style objectives.

A summary of what each means follows.

*Structural objectives*
These refer to things that deal with reorganization. This might be moving power around through clarifying roles, or reorganization as such.

*Effectiveness objectives*
These deal with outputs of individuals or the organization. The objective might relate to improved corporate strategy or, very broadly, improving organization effectiveness. This objective does not mean much unless the measurement areas are attached to it: it might be service to clients or profits.

*Decision-making objectives*
The nature of decision-making is critical in any organization. Should it be centralized or decentralized or should power be moved laterally, or is it just that people need to listen more to one another when talking about decisions?

*Interface objectives*
These objectives deal with relationships between organization parts. The most obvious one is production and marketing, which sometimes do not co-operate as much as they might.

*Communication objectives*
One problem with communication objectives is that everyone must agree that it is a good thing to improve it. The other problem is: what exactly do we mean? The objectives proposed in this section try to clarify these.

*Flexibility objectives*
Is it the organization that needs to be more flexible? One way of doing this is to facilitate easier changes of power and resources. Or, instead of organization flexibility, is it managers who should be made more flexible? These two approaches are absolutely different. Thus one needs to be clear about what kind of flexibility is envisaged.

*Individual objectives*
There is a class of objectives which might be termed 'individual'. Generally these relate to personal or interpersonal needs. One is improved job satisfaction, and another is improved candour.

*Climate and style objectives*
Organization climate and managerial style make a lot of difference to the degree of output orientation that is obtainable. Should one have a bureaucratic style of company, for there are many bureaucratic companies which are doing well. Or perhaps one should have a rather dedicated, production-oriented company? At the present time, many of these companies are also doing well.

**Particular planned change objectives**

What has just been described are the eight classes of planned change objectives. They are so broad that, as they stand, they are perhaps not useful for planning purposes. The following presents the particular change objectives that fit within each of the eight classes. In thinking of a change target it is these particular objectives that should be considered, not the class. That is, not 'structural objectives', but one or more of its subcategories such as 'add layer of management' or 'remove layer of management'. Read over this list and then look at the short explanations of each one; in most cases, the term itself describes the objective quite adequately, but some phrases may be unfamiliar.

1  *Structural objectives*
    (a)  role clarification;

       (b)   reorganize;
       (c)   flatten pyramid;
       (d)   add layer of management;
       (e)   remove layer of management.

2 *Effectiveness objectives*
       (a)   improved organization effectiveness;
       (b)   improved managerial effectiveness;
       (c)   improved profit planning;
       (d)   introduce or improve MBO;
       (e)   improved corporate strategy.

3 *Decision-making objectives*
       (a)   improved teamwork;
       (b)   introduce participative management;
       (c)   move decision-making downwards;
       (d)   centralize;
       (e)   improve problem-solving climate.

4 *Interface objectives*
       (a)   optimizing system;
       (b)   improved horizontal communication;
       (c)   improved interfunctional co-operation;
       (d)   improved HQ-field relationships;
       (e)   facilitate a merger.

5 *Communication objectives*
       (a)   improved upward communication;
       (b)   improved downward communication;
       (c)   increase output new ideas;
       (d)   increase use of new ideas;
       (e)   create greater unit autonomy.

6 *Flexibility objectives*
       (a)   improved organization flexibility;
       (b)   improved manager flexibility;
       (c)   management revitalization;
       (d)   improved marketing orientation;
       (e)   facilitate system introduction.

7 *Individual objectives*
       (a)   improved climate;
       (b)   improved candour;
       (c)   improved job satisfaction;
       (d)   serve individual needs;
       (e)   increase individual autonomy.

8 *Climate and style objectives*
       (a)   increased separated managing;
       (b)   increased related managing;
       (c)   increased dedicated managing;

(d)   increased integrated managing;
(e)   increased matrix managing.


## Meaning of the objectives

Here are some general comments on each of the above objectives. The measurement areas that you apply to any objective that you choose defines precisely what you mean.

*(1a) Role clarification:* This refers to being clearer about authority and therefore responsibility. It refers also to specifying in some detail not only the authority, but the outputs for the change target, the measurement areas for the change target and probably the plan. In other words, to make sure that those in the change target have a sharper idea of what their job actually is in output terms. This is only hindered by initiating a programme to create greatly enlarged job descriptions.

*(1b) Reorganize:* This term is used in the conventional sense. Essentially, it means moving various positions around. It may involve adding positions or removing positions. Often when one approaches this as a change objective, one is not quite sure how it will end up or whether it is needed at all. It has been found best to approach this objective with the general proviso that 'we're not sure whether we need to reorganize but we should at least look at it'.

*(1c) Flatten pyramid:* Normally, flattening the management pyramid involves increasing the span of control, and by this means removing one or more layers of management.

*(1d) Add layer of management:* To some, this may seem an unusual objective, but it is often a good one. Suppose a company has grown by acquisition, and it is not that uncommon, the chief executive (CEO) finds twenty units reporting directly to the CEO position. Clearly, there is a need for an assistant-CEO level.

*(1e) Remove layer of management:* This term is used in the conventional sense: as organizations grow, layers are often added quite unconsciously and this issue needs to be addressed. Removing a layer of management does not have to apply simply to the CEO and assistant-CEO levels. It can apply equally well to supervisor and assistant-supervisor levels.

*(2a) Improved organization effectiveness:* This is a rather broadly stated objective, but it can easily be refined when one puts measurement areas against it. For some organizations it might be lower costs, for others it might be improved service to clients.

*(2b) Improved managerial effectiveness:* In some situations planned change is best looked at on the basis of the organization as a whole. In other situations it is better to look at it based on the individual manager, as this objective suggests.

*(2c) Improved profit planning:* Some organizations are well structured, with managers reasonably motivated. The problem is that they do not have a good planning cycle, do not have sharp pencils and do not spend enough on profit planning or any real planning at all!

*(2d) Introduce or improve management by objectives (MBO):* Some organizations have had good experiences with MBO, some have had poorer ones. This objective reflects a well-planned introduction, or what may amount to a reintroduction of an MBO that did not work as well as was expected.

*(2e) Improve corporate strategy:* Corporate strategy is used in the conventional sense i.e. 'what business are we in?'. It does not refer to selling plans for one or two years, but rather to a more fundamental issue of the organization as it fits into the environment.

*(3a) Improved teamwork:* This objective does not only refer to relationships orientation improvement but this is certainly one component; it also means making more decisions on a group basis, with the emphasis on the quality of the decision and the commitment to it.

*(3b) Introduce participative management:* This objective has an associated problem: very few people agree with what it means! Some people think it means lower levels getting more involved in their work directly, and some think it means lower levels getting involved more in the work of senior levels. Here, again, the measurement areas attached to it will clarify what the term really means.

*(3c) Move decision-making downwards:* Many organizations talk about the desirability of doing this, but use rather general terms such as 'decentralize', 'participation' and 'delegation': the term as

worded here is probably better because it clearly states what is intended and leads naturally on to the questions of 'what decisions?', 'how far down?' and 'when?'

*(3d) Centralize:* This is an extremely broad objective. One can centralize some areas, while leaving many others uncentralized. Again, the measurement areas will specify what is meant.

*(3e) Improve problem-solving climate:* this refers to improving the quality of decisions and commitment to them.

*(4a) Optimizing system:* Organizations consist of positions and aggregates of positions which are called 'units'. Sometimes the positions connect well with each other and the units connect well with each other, sometimes they do not. In short, the interfaces do not run. Optimizing systems means getting the organization to work as a whole rather than thinking exclusively of getting the individual units or positions to work at improving their own effectiveness and not thinking so much about improving the effectiveness of others.

*(4b) Improved horizontal communication:* Most people think all communication problems are vertical, but some are horizontal.

*(4c) Improved interfunctional co-operation:* There may be some specific functions (e.g. production or marketing) which do not co-operate as well as they might. This objective helps to deal with these issues.

*(4d) Improved HQ-field relationships:* Sometimes level A does not work well with level B. This objective deals broadly with that issue. Obviously it could be expressed as relationships between divisions and branches, managers and supervisors, and so on.

*(4e) Facilitate a merger:* It is well known that the key problems in a merger are not financial ones, but rather the human ones. Often a merger results in a combined balance-sheet but no real combination of effort.

*(5a) Improved upward communication:* Sometimes the issue is that those at the top are not listening enough to those at the bottom.

*(5b) Improved downward communication:* Some senior managers think that this is always the problem. Sometimes it *is*, but not always.

*(5c) Increase output new ideas:* Essentially, this is creativity but it says it more clearly; it leads directly to better measurement areas than the term 'creativity' might.

*(5d) Increase use of new ideas:* Many organizations have high output of new ideas but for one reason or another seem unable to use them. Plans are everywhere but they do not seem to get implemented. Here this objective is better than that referring to increasing the number of ideas, much better to use the ones already in existence.

*(5e) Create greater unit autonomy:* Sometimes organizations are combinations of discordant parts. Great efforts may be spent making the parts work together when in fact a different organization structure should be created.

*(6a) Improved organization flexibility:* some organizations grow old too soon. They lose their power to adapt. Broadly, this objective relates to making the organization respond better to external forces. Among these are competition, government legislation and new technology.

*(6b) Improved manager flexibility:* In some organizations managers tend to display a high degree of resistance to change. Increased manager flexibility is the key to lowering resistance.

*(6c) Management revitalization:* This is a rather broad, but useful, objective. It refers to getting managers to rethink what they are and should be doing.

*(6d) Improved marketing orientation:* In short, this is getting the organization to think more of the market than their own production system.

*(6e) Facilitate system introduction:* It is quite common for new systems to be introduced in organizations with little thought on the human side; this system might be a new budgeting system, a new management information system or a new computer system.

*(7a) Improved climate:* organizations have climates, sometimes called 'cultures'. What they amount to is: 'the way we do things around here'; possible climate objectives, in group 8, are specific.

*(7b) Improved candour:* In some organizations people do not talk frankly to others about the right things.

*(7c) Improved job satisfaction:* Obviously this means arranging the situation, so that the individual whistles on the way to work rather than whistling going home!

*(7d) Serve individual needs:* Some organizations want to do a better job at integrating the needs of the individual with those of the organization. Sometimes this is very difficult, but it can on occasion be done.

*(7e) Increase individual autonomy:* This can relate to such things as job enrichment; in essence, it means letting the individual 'get on with it', without being told as much as before.

*(8a) Increased separated managing:* This refers to increased emphasis on systems orientation and procedures.

*(8b) Increased related managing:* An increased emphasis on people.

*(8c) Increased dedicated managing:* An increased emphasis on getting the work done with reference both to cost and quality.

*(8d) Increased integrated managing:* An increased emphasis on both people and teamwork.

*(8e) Increased matrix managing:* An increased emphasis on the use of project teams, even to the extent where the whole organization is designed on a project-team basis.

## AN EXAMPLE OF PLANNED CHANGE OBJECTIVES

Here is an example of planned change objectives, set by an organization wishing to improve its output orientation.

### Electrical products manufacturer

A heavy electrical products manufacturer with about 1,000 employees had recently grown by making several acquisitions in the same general field. The rather rapid growth by acquisition had created many problems, and these appeared to be leading the organization to lower effectiveness. The forty most senior managers met together for two days and created the following planned change objectives to increase their output orientation:

- improved role clarification;
- improved organization effectiveness;
- improved MBO;
- improved horizontal communication;
- improved interfunctional communication;
- improved downward communication;
- improved organization flexibility.

The last four objectives all touch on aspects of getting the new organization to work better. The word communication is often used. The choice of these objectives generally indicates that the group did not think that the various parts of the organization were linking well enough. They chose role clarification primarily as a means to becoming clearer about who had authority for what. In its rapidly changing situation power had to be moved around. A rigorous approach to effectiveness areas, measurement areas, and authority to achieve the outputs can help deal with this issue. The two objectives of improved organization effectiveness and improved MBO generally refer to getting better in the service of increasing output orientation.

## A SHORT CASE STUDY

Here is a case study designed to improve your understanding of setting planned change objectives. It will be used again in Chapter 8, when you will be asked to propose a method of achieving the planned change objectives. An organization chart is given, together with a brief description of the characteristics of the organization. You are asked to propose what planned change objectives you think are best. Proposed solutions are given on pp. 61–2.

### Case study: the farm machinery manufacturer

A farm machinery manufacturer has the organization structure shown in Figure 3.1.

The founder of the organization and the family which owned all of the shares sold out about six years ago. The company is now publicly owned and quoted. Appointed as chief executive officer was a professional manager with stock options who had been in that position for four years. The five divisional managers had been with the company from two to fifteen years. They are seen as knowledgeable, committed and hard-working, but only moderately

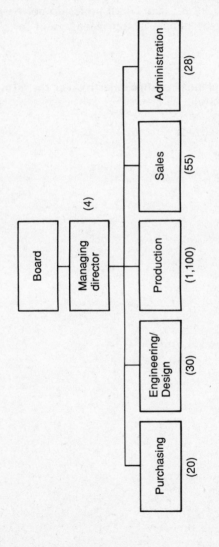

*Figure 3.1* Case study: the farm machinery manufacturer

innovative. The managers at the third level, those reporting to the five division managers, were seen as good to excellent. The organization is moderately profitable now, but the board wanted growth in profits. How this might be obtained was open to question, but it was believed that a revitalization of top management thinking was needed.

The view was that the top management was satisfactory, but it had many 'old ideas'. The board preferred no reorganization and no change in the people in top management for a few years, at least.

**My proposed planned change objectives for the farm machinery manufacturer are:**

*(See list on pp. 51–2)*

1

2

3

4

5

6

**Proposed solutions to case studies**

This case study is a real-life example. These proposed planned change objectives are not necessarily the 'right' ones, but they were a product of a great deal of work by the managers involved, who did end up being committed to them. They appeared to have the desired impact on creating the output-oriented organization. That is not to say that other objectives might not have done as well or better.

**Proposed planned change objectives chosen by the farm machinery manufacturer**

The issues facing the farm machinery manufacturer in its attempt to become more output oriented are not too difficult to determine.
   In this case the objectives decided were:

- Role clarification
- Improved organization effectiveness
- Improved managerial effectiveness
- Improved profit planning
- Introduce MBO
- Increase output of new ideas
- Increase use of new ideas
- Management revitalization.

The most important objective dealt with improved management revitalization and most of the other objectives were designed to impinge on that in one way or another. In this firm there did seem to be a need for improved profit planning, which means in essence sharpening a pencil and thinking about the job.

**SUMMARY**

In creating the output-oriented organization change targets need to be identified. These change targets might relate to level or function, or other things, depending upon the nature of the organization. For each change target planned change objectives should be decided. There is little doubt that these planned change objectives are best decided on a team basis as this serves to improve both the quality of the decision and commitment to it. Clear criteria have been given to aid you in selecting the planned change objectives;

these should have measurement areas attached, in order to clarify precisely what is meant.

# 4 Climate

> The beginning of administrative wisdom is the awareness that there is no one optimum type of management system.
>
> Tom Burns
>
> All living organisms adapt or they cease to exist.
>
> Louis E. Davies
>
> Life is not long, and too much of it must not pass in idle deliberation how it shall be spent.
>
> Samuel Johnson

This chapter helps you to decide what climate your own organization should be moving towards. Eight different types of organization climate are explained; four are more effective, and four are less effective. For the more effective ones a guide is given for your information. The eight organization climates can be directly related to eight managerial styles (these are described in Chapter 5).

Organization climate is attracting much attention these days. Increasingly it is coming to be seen as having a great influence on effectiveness and outputs, and that it can be managed. The main function of changing climate is to improve effectiveness. This seems to be the short way round to improve things. If we want a highly motivated and integrated response organization-wide to the pressing issues in the organization, we must develop a culture around outputs.

Obviously there is great difference between organization climates. Production organizations tend to be task oriented; educational organizations tend to be people oriented; and banks and administrative systems, such as life insurance companies and lower levels in government organizations, tend to be systems oriented. While analysis must start with the identification of the climate we have now, the important question remains: what climate should we have in order to become more output oriented?

## THE NATURE AND ORIGINS OF ORGANIZATION CLIMATE

The organization climate comprises all those factors which influence behaviour in an organization and which are common to essentially unrelated positions in that organization. In a nutshell, it describes how organizations – taken as a whole – differ from one another in their typical behaviour. Such differences are influenced by, and expressed through, such things as standard operating procedures, overall organization structure and other often unwritten but powerful guides to behaviour.

There are four basic types of organization climate: systems, people, production and the team. Managers need to be sensitive to their own organization climate as it is difficult to change, dangerous to violate to any degree and has a powerful impact on subordinate expectations.

The typical organization environment is a complex one. While the organization chart appears quite clear, and the standard operating procedures are well established, much of importance is not written down. In all organizations there exist expectations about what is appropriate behaviour, and there are often some aspects of behaviour or dress that are almost sacred while others may be safely ignored. That there are differences among organizations is apparent when one compares the basic climate of a defence force, the public service, a university, a life insurance company and a typical factory. Some organizations have a very clear and powerfully expressed climate, others do not.

### Influences on organization climate

Organization climate is shaped from the top, and from the past. The primary influences, not in order of importance, are the following.

*Top person's styles*
This is the way in which the top people think the organization should be run, reflected in the way they act with their team members.

*Founder style*
The impact of the founder can carry on for many years, even for ever. This is particularly noticeable in religions, but it is also clearly present in secular types of organization.

## Dominant group
The top management of some organizations comprises the dominant group; primarily one of the following: marketing types, actuaries, engineers, accountants, alumni of another firm, playboys, MBAs or even college dropouts. A concentration of any one type in positions of power will influence organization climate.

## Dominant family
Families, as well as individual founders, can exert a profound influence on climate, particularly but not necessarily, if the firm is small.

## Technology
To a degree, organization climate is dependent on technology, but to a degree it is independent of it. The precise degree to which one is dependent on the other can be seen by comparing a group of car plants with a group of bank offices. The technology within each group is similar and so, to a large extent, is the organization climate. However, suppose we compare the two most different car plants with the two most different bank offices. We may find that one of these car plants is closer in organization climate to one of the banks than to the other car plant.

## Other important influences
Other important influences on organization climate are:

- Size of organization
- Ratio of workers to managers
- Objectives and corporate strategy
- National importance and visibility
- Legislative control
- Degree of external control
- Location/isolation
- Physical structure in which organization is housed.


### Sensing organization climate

Organization climate can be sensed very quickly or deduced from the answers to the following questions:

- What kind of manager gets ahead?
- What behaviour is most likely to be rewarded?
- What is considered to be a reward?
- What behaviour is discouraged?

- What is considered to be a punishment?
- How wide are status differences between levels?
- How are mistakes handled?
- How is conflict handled?
- How are decisions made?
- What is the communication network?
- What is an acceptable level of performance?
- Do people trust each other?
- How easy is it to change things?

In some organizations no one ever gets fired, while in others the standing quip is; 'I wonder who is my boss today?' In some organizations any innovation must be cleared by the top of that organization, in others each level is given wide freedom. In some, outstanding performance is rewarded, and in others it is ignored. Managers, particularly those who have recently entered the organization from a quite different one, have little difficulty in diagnosing organization demands in terms of being one or a combination of system orientation, people orientation, production orientation or team orientation.

## FOUR BASIC ORGANIZATION CLIMATES

The four organization climates which you need to know are derived from two climate dimensions. These dimensions are task orientation and relationships orientation:

*Task orientation* (TO): Task orientation emphasizes productivity, getting the job done, initiating, organizing and directing.
*Relationships orientation* (RO): Relationships orientation emphasizes people as evidenced by listening, trusting and encouraging.

These two orientations lead on to four basic types of organization climate, that is the climates low on both, high on one or the other, or high on both (Figure 4.1).

## CHARACTERISTICS OF THE FOUR BASIC ORGANIZATION CLIMATES

There are a total of twenty-three characteristics differentiating the four basic organization climates (Figure 4.2). Look at the first

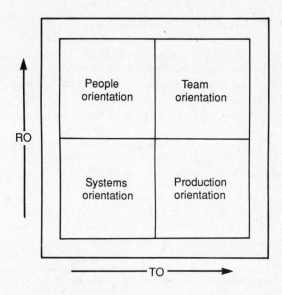

*Figure 4.1* The four possible combinations of task orientation (TO) and relationships orientation (RO) lead to four basic types of organization climate

two. The interactional mode of the system orientation climate is correcting. The interactional mode of the people orientation climate is accepting. The production orientation climate tends to emphasize domination and direction. The team orientation climate wants to join others in the service of work. The preferred method of communication for the system-oriented climate is in the written form as this involves less relationships orientation and may also involve lower task orientation as well. The people-oriented climate emphasizes conversations as its main mode of communication. The production-oriented climate emphasizes verbal directions as this helps domination. And the team-oriented climate, rather obviously, is characterized by its use of meetings.

## How to identify your organization climate

It is an easy matter to recognize one's basic organization climate by use of Figure 4.2. For each of the twenty-three factors, circle

| Factor | Systems orientation | People orientation | Production orientation | Team orientation |
|---|---|---|---|---|
| 1 Interactional mode | Correcting | Accepting | Dominating | Joining |
| 2 Main mode of communication | Written | Conversations | Verbal directions | Meetings |
| 3 Direction of communication | Little in any direction | Upwards from subordinates | Downwards to subordinates | Multi-way |
| 4 Time perspective | Past | Unconcerned | Immediate | Future |
| 5 Identifies with | Organization | Subordinates | Superior and technology | Co-workers |
| 6 Systems emphasis | Maintains procedural system | Supports social system | Follows technological system | Integrates sociotechnical system |
| 7 Subordinates judged on | Who follows the rules? | Who understands people? | Who produces? | Who wants to join the team? |
| 8 Superiors judged on | Brains | Warmth | Power | Teamwork |
| 9 Team mode | Clarifying, guiding and channelling | Supporting, harmonizing and coaching | Initiating, evaluating and directing | Setting standards, testing and motivating |
| 10 Typical work situation | Administration, accounting | Managing professionals, training and co-ordination | Production and sales management | Interacting managers |
| 11 Unlikely work situation | Non-routine | Low personal contact | Low power | High routine |
| 12 Employee orientation | Security | Co-operation | Performance | Commitment |
| 13 Reaction to error | More controls | Pass over | Punish | Learn from |
| 14 Reaction to conflict | Avoids | Smothers | Suppresses | Utilizes |
| 15 Reaction to stress | Withdraws and quotes rules | Becomes dependent and depressed | Dominates and exploits | Avoids making decisions |
| 16 Positive source of control | Logic | Praise | Rewards | Ideals |
| 17 Negative source of control | Argument | Rejection | Punishments | Compromise |
| 18 Characteristic problem of subordinates | Lack of recognition | Lack of direction | Lack of information | Luck of independence |

*Figure 4.2*  Characteristics of the four basic organization climates

| Factor | Systems orientation | People orientation | Production orientation | Team orientation |
|---|---|---|---|---|
| 19 Punishments used | Loss of authority | Loss of interest by manager | Loss of position | Loss of self-respect by subordinates |
| 20 Undervalues | Need for innovation | Needs of organization and of technology | Subordinates expectations | Need for independent action |
| 21 Main weaknesses | Slave to the rules | Sentimentality | Fights unnecessarily | Uses participation inappropriately |
| 22 Fears in general | Emotionality softness and dependence | Rejection | Loss of power | Uninvolvement |
| 23 Fears about others | System deviation irrationality | Conflict | Low production | Dissatisfaction |

Figure 4.2 (*concluded*)

one or two items under the four climate headings. This chart does not give you a measure of levels of effectiveness, but rather indicates what *is* the basic climate. For instance, if you circle most of your items in systems orientation, it is rather clear what is your organization's basic climate.

## THE FOUR BASIC CLIMATES IN SUMMARY

Using the ideas contained in Figure 4.2, a clear description of the four basic organization climates may be derived.

### System climate

The system-oriented climate is characterized by managing prudently and therefore also by being very concerned about the correction of deviations. There is a tendency to write more than talk, and partly because of this, there is relatively little personal communication in any direction. The time perspective tends to be directed to the past and on 'how it was done last time'. The climate fosters identification with the organization as a whole rather than with individual members of it. Because of the desire to keep things on an even keel, interest is taken in the rules and procedures and people are naturally judged on how well they adhere to them. Intellect is valued in senior managers, but not necessarily in others. Committees tend to use a subdued procedural style, attempts are made to clarify positions, members work through the agenda and most communications are channelled through the chair.

This system climate is obviously well suited for units working in administration, accounting, statistics and engineering design, and for some government departments and in the control departments of head offices.


## People climate

The main characteristic of the people climate is a recognition of the individual. This does not mean that effectiveness is not recognized, or that people do not sometimes get annoyed with one another. This is no dreamy system living on impossible assumptions, it is a system that recognizes the individual. People, then, tend to talk to one another more in this climate. Because of this emphasis on communication, there is usually a good linkage up and down the organization and across it. Members of the organization tend to identify with other members; usually these are team members, superior and subordinate.

A primary method of judging people in this organization climate is how well they get along with and understand others. These are of course cardinal virtues. Senior managers are judged by the warmth they show to subordinates, and by their understanding of the subordinate's point of view. Committee work tends to run smoothly. The ideas of others are given a hearing, differences are harmonized rather than rejected. Informal coaching is a widespread practice in the service of helping others to become better or to feel better.

This climate is particularly suited for managing professional workers, for some kinds of training and development work and for co-ordinating the activities of several diverse groups. The climate places more emphasis on motivation than appraisal and error correction. There is a degree of dependency, and when stress increases, possibly because of changes or market conditions, any level of employee may become depressed and even more dependent. The positive source of influence is likely to be praised, while the negative source tends to be rejection of ideas. A characteristic of this type of climate is a relatively low level of direction. The assumption is that people either know themselves, or can find out by themselves, rather than being told. The punishment most often used is lack of interest by others.

While it is seen as good to work in a people climate, a characteristic problem encountered is an undervaluation of the importance of the organization's technology for the design of work relationships and overall structure. One of the weaknesses is sentimentality and the fear of being rejected; the thing most feared by employees in this climate is conflict.

## Production climate

The production climate tends to give dominance to the work process. The time perspective is immediate or short term, and the preferred choice is 'do it now'! The climate identifies with superiors and with the technical system of the organization. Where possible, the demands of the technical system are emphasized rather than the human system. The organization judges employees on the degree to which they produce and senior managers on their skill in using power. The employees soon learn that performance is the thing that counts and punishment can be expected if in error. Employees often complain about lack of information. The expectation is for an active part to be taken in discussion, and the general thrust is towards initiation, evaluation and direction. The production climate is well suited for types of production, and for sales units, where directions are needed; but it does not work well in situations where there is little need for the exercise of power, or where it is not normal to simply tell people what to do.

This climate deals with conflict by suppressing it; it deals with other stressful situations by domination. The climate fosters belief that rewards are a good way to influence employees, and that punishments are the best way to stop people from doing the things they should not; and the most severe punishment is loss of position. This climate does not reflect that employees exist as independent entities and thus undervalues the importance of employees' individual expectations. The climate's main weakness is a tendency to allow arguments when matters could be solved by other means. It emphasizes the use of power so much, that the loss of it is greatly feared. The biggest fear about employees is that they will not produce.

## Team climate

The team climate is characterized by interaction between individuals and units. The climate places a high value on communication in group settings and therefore the use of formal and informal meetings. It is not just two-way communication that is above average here, but also communication multi-way, upwards, downwards and laterally. There is less concern than average about power differentials between individuals or units.

Attempts are made to integrate the individual with the organization as a whole, or with the particular technology with which the individual works. Naturally the climate leads to judging people on their willingness to join and work with the team and their general skill in teamwork. In this climate work is not regarded in an easy way, it is tough. Teams set performance standards both for the teams and for individuals; team members are tested for their commitment and purpose and are motivated to achieve. Obviously this climate is most suited to work involving a high level of interaction, and it is less suited to work in technology where there is a high level of routine. Errors are dealt with as opportunities to learn; they are not simply punished. When conflict arises, it tends to be looked at closely with a view to determining the cause and getting to that issue rather than the apparent issue of the conflict itself.

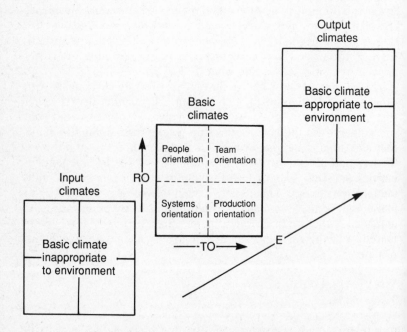

*Figure 4.3*   Basic climates embedded in environments

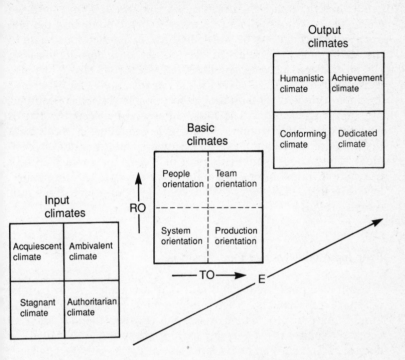

*Figure 4.4*  Four basic organization climates, when effectiveness is also considered lead to four input climates and four output climates

Some negative characteristics in this type of organization include a tendency to postpone decision-making, an equal tendency to give wider control when it is not needed and the acceptance of a compromise rather than the single best decision. Individuals sometimes feel a lack of independence. Ultimately the need for independent action in this climate may be undervalued or participation used inappropriately.

## WHAT ABOUT CLIMATE EFFECTIVENESS?

As there are four basic organization climates, and each of these may be appropriate or inappropriate to the technology or broader environment, it is clear that there are really eight organization climates when effectiveness is considered as well, that is four more effective and four less effective climates.

So while the four basic organization climates deal with the issue conceptually without direct reference to the environment, the real organization climate to be considered is the one that does relate to the environment, leading to the notion of eight organization climates. When one thinks of effectiveness in broad terms, one may consider that there are two types of organization. One is termed an 'input-oriented' organization, the other is termed an 'output-oriented' organization. The main difference between the two is whether or not the strategy, climate and operational methods meet the needs of the technology, the customers and the wider environment. The various combinations of high and low on each of task orientation, relationships orientation and effectiveness orientation lead directly to eight types of climate, four input-oriented and four output-oriented.

## Four input climates and four output climates

These four input climates and four output climates, then, parallel the four basic climates. When used in an inappropriate setting, the basic climate of production orientation is called the authoritarian climate. When it is used in the appropriate setting, it is called the dedicated climate. Figure 4.4 repeats Figure 4.3, with the labels for the input climates and the output climates included.

In summary, the climate types are:

| Basic climate | Associated input climate | Associated output climate |
|---|---|---|
| Systems orientation | Stagnant climate | Conforming climate |
| People orientation | Acquiescent climate | Humanistic climate |
| Production orientation | Authoritarian climate | Dedicated climate |
| Team orientation | Ambivalent climate | Achievement climate |

These eight climates which incorporate effectiveness will be the main focus of the rest of this chapter, and they will be your main concern when thinking of climate in your organization. As you read about these eight climates, you should consider which ones best represent your organization today – and which ones should and might.

## THE STAGNANT CLIMATE

The stagnant climate is one which reflects a low task orientation and a low relationships orientation in an environment where such orientations are inappropriate, thereby creating an input orientation and less effectiveness. The climate is perceived as highly insular, uncreative and having low involvement; as resistant to change, with low concern with errors except to cover them up; and working to rules, with too many people making things difficult for others.

*Stagnant climate indicators*

- Working to rules as general practice at all levels
- Barely acceptable outputs
- General avoidance of involvement/responsibility
- Few volunteered suggestions/opinions
- Too many managers are uncreative/unoriginal/narrow-minded
- Apparent theme is to make things harder rather than easier
- Resistance to change
- Low concern about errors/quality
- Typical manager seen as uninvolved
- Low co-operation.

## THE ACQUIESCENT CLIMATE

The acquiescent climate is one which reflects a low task orientation and a high relationships orientation in an environment where such orientations are inappropriate, thereby creating an input orientation and less effectiveness. The climate is perceived as an organization which is pleasant, kind and warm; as somewhat passive, with low initiation levels and unclear directions given, and unconcerned with outputs and standards, and very good at smoothing over conflict.

*Acquiescent climate indicators*

- Disagreement avoided/smothered
- Maintained atmosphere pleasant/kind/warm

- Human relations high precedence
- Organization intent is easier, not harder
- Low initiation, passive
- Few directions given
- Unconcerned with outputs
- Social activity emphasized
- Typical manager seen as pleasant/kind/warm.


## THE AUTHORITARIAN CLIMATE

The authoritarian climate is one which reflects a high task orientation and a low relationships orientation in an environment where such orientations are inappropriate, thereby creating an input orientation and less effectiveness. The climate is perceived as critical, threatening, suppressing conflict, mainly downward communication, with much acting without consultation; with many managers feared and disliked, and an emphasis on day-to-day productivity rather than on the longer term; and with a low performance level maintained primarily by threats.

*Authoritarian climate indicators*

- Mainly downward communication
- More orders less consultation
- Superior seen as critical/threatening
- Short-term, not long-term, productivity emphasis
- Suppressed disagreements
- Immediate action/results required
- Typical manager seen as quick decision/no consultation.


## THE AMBIVALENT CLIMATE

The ambivalent climate is one which reflects a high task orientation and a high relationships orientation in an environment where such orientations are inappropriate, thereby creating an input orientation and less effectiveness. The climate is perceived as accepting grey acceptable decisions, with some encouragement of ideas and high performance; with low support and not much response even when good performance is delivered; there is much yielding and giving in to pressures, and too much use of inappropriate participation.

*Ambivalent climate indicators*

- Ambiguous about overall purpose
- Emphasis is try but not too hard
- Unclear about strategy/structure/policies
- Acceptable/grey decisions are the rule
- Ideas encouraged but poor follow-up
- Unmonitored plans
- Typical manager seen as good face-saver.

## THE CONFORMING CLIMATE

The conforming climate is one which reflects a low task orientation and a low relationships orientation in an environment where such orientations are appropriate, thereby creating an output orientation and more effectiveness. The climate is perceived as highly concerned with orders, rules, and procedures; as supporting good systems, where details are watched, and written communications are preferred; and the typical response to disagreement and conflict is to refer to rules and procedures.

*Conforming climate indicators*

- Established system maintenance
- Details/efficiency watched
- Written communication prevalent
- Rules reference preferred
- Reliable/dependable/uncreative
- Concern with orders/rules/procedures
- Large rule-books
- Typical manager seen as logical/fair/follows rules.

## THE HUMANISTIC CLIMATE

The humanistic climate is one which reflects a low task orientation and a high relationships orientation in an environment where such orientations are appropriate, thereby creating an output orientation and more effectiveness. The climate is perceived as having a high level of shared understanding and co-operation, with much trust and openness, high involvement in planning and productivity; with talents reasonably well developed; and open communication channels.

*Humanistic climate indicators*

- Talent development emphasis
- Supportive in success/failure
- High co-operation
- People listen
- Teamwork decisions
- High communication upward/downward/horizontal
- Typical manager seen as others-interested.


## THE DEDICATED CLIMATE

The dedicated climate is one which reflects a high task orientation and a low relationships orientation in an environment where such orientations are appropriate thereby creating an output orientation and therefore more effectiveness. The climate is perceived as having high levels of initiative. energy and industry, committed to finishing well, highly evaluative of quantity, quality and time, results oriented, ideas that arise tend to be implemented, efficiency and productivity valued.

*Dedicated climate indicators*

- Heavy emphasis quantity/quality/time
- Highly conscious costs/sales/profits
- Results-oriented
- High level industry/energy
- Strong top-down emphasis
- Productivity valued above all
- Typical manager seen as putting productivity first.


## THE ACHIEVEMENT CLIMATE

The achievement climate is one which reflects a high task orientation and a high relationships orientation in an environment where such orientations are appropriate, thereby creating an output orientation and more effectiveness. The climate is perceived as having a high level of achievement of objectives, with mutual encouragement for high performance; high co-ordination of people in work; and much use of teamwork in decision-making.

*Achievement climate indicators*

- Output orientation stressed
- High unit co-ordination
- Commitment to organization purpose
- Higher performance continually encouraged
- Emphasis on people-work balance
- Decision-making balanced individual/team
- Typical manager seen as having high standards for self/others.

## Is there single ideal basic organization climate?

Organizations desiring to become more output-oriented will need to address one question closely. Is it true or not that one of the four basic organization climates is generally good for all organizations? It is very easy to be lured to the easy way out, which is really a trap, and to decide that there is an ideal basic climate which is common across all organizations.

Managers who think this way are living in a world of hope rather than reality. Many theorists propose a particular ideal climate and advocate that all organizations adopt it: some of the well-known names are Weber, who proposed systems orientation as the best; McGregor, who proposed people orientation as the best; Odiorne, who proposed production orientation as the best; and Blake and Mouton who proposed team orientation as the best. Each believed their ideal climate to be correct most of the time; a better belief is that any of these may be right, at times, depending on the environment and technology.

A great deal of organization effectiveness research has been conducted, and the conclusion strongly emerges that no single climate is naturally more effective than others. Clearly, the climate must be appropriate to the situation in which it operates. The situational elements include such things as the technology – i.e. the type of work being done; and the demands of the broader environment – e.g. of the customers or the community or clients, or, if such is the organization, it may be other departments with which a particular department must relate. Obviously the effectiveness of the climate will also depend on the nature and expectations of the workforce at all levels.

Some managers are not sure whether a system orientation climate in an organization can lead to an output-oriented organization. Certainly, it can if the main outputs of the organization are achieved by a system orientation. Some organizations produce systems, other organizations such as power and water utilities are designed to maintain systems – and not much more. A system orientation, then, is appropriate and leads to an output-oriented organization. Obviously, in a selling or production orientation, a system orientation would be highly inappropriate and would lead to an input rather than an output-oriented organization.

# 5 Management styles

I will pay more for the ability to deal with people than any other ability under the sun.

John D. Rockefeller

People move in the course of their daily work from a role in one system to a different role in another system; and it is essential that this be recognised and that behaviour appropriate to the role be adopted if trouble is to be avoided.

Wilfred Brown

The average human being learns, under proper conditions, not only to accept but to seek responsibility.

Douglas McGregor

This chapter encourages you to think about your managerial style, and that of others, and to what extent the revealed styles might be modified for creation of the output-oriented organization. There is a wide variety of more effective styles, just as there is wide variety of less effective ones. Style can be linked to both effectiveness and climate and examples of this are given.

While organization climate is most important to bear in mind when creating the output-oriented organization, so is the issue of managerial styles. Climate is important too. Organization climate exerts an influence on managerial styles, but managerial style also influences organization climate, particularly if one considers the style of the top person of the organization or the top team as a whole. The top person could be the chief executive officer (CEO) of a multinational company or an office pool supervisor. In terms of style there is little difference, for the same labels apply.

Managerial styles can arise from situational differences such as climate and technology, or individual differences such as personality. Sometimes situational differences have the most impact, sometimes the individual differences do. Whatever the causation, the fact is that all managers have one or more styles that they consistently use. These may be more effective or less effective, and

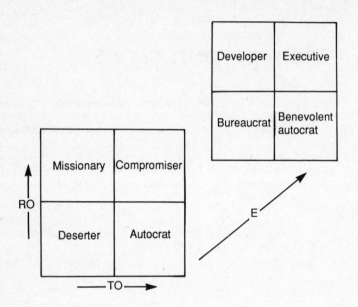

*Figure 5.1*   The 3D managerial style model – four styles are less effective,
and four styles are more effective

an understanding of them can help managers to become more
effective and more output-oriented.

## EIGHT MANAGERIAL STYLES PARALLEL THE EIGHT ORGANIZATION CLIMATES

They arise in much the same way from a combination of task
orientation, relationships orientation and effectiveness orientation.
The four less effective styles are referred to as the deserter,
missionary, autocrat and compromiser styles. The four more effective styles are referred to as the bureaucrat, developer, benevolent
autocrat and executive styles. The eight managerial styles parallel
the eight organization climates as follows:

| *Organization climate* | *Managerial style* |
|---|---|
| Stagnant | Deserter |
| Acquiescent | Missionary |
| Authoritarian | Autocrat |

| Ambivalent | Compromiser |
| Conforming | Bureaucrat |
| Humanistic | Developer |
| Dedicated | Benevolent Autocrat |
| Achievement | Executive |

*What's in a name?*

The eight managerial style labels were deliberately chosen to suggest, if somewhat dramatically, that the style is good or poor. This greatly facilitates the model's use. Certain of the eight style labels, such as 'deserter' and 'autocrat' may jar on some people; they were selected because their use in helping managers to think about change made clear labels appropriate. If anyone should find that any style label is ambiguous or troublesome, they are welcome to change it for their own purposes; it is the idea not the name that is important.

## CAPSULE DESCRIPTION OF THE EIGHT MANAGERIAL STYLES

In brief, the eight managerial styles may be described as follows. The style definition, the indicators and the kind of things each style might say, and what others say about the style, taken together will give you a good sense of the eight styles. As you read, you should think about your own style, the style of your team members and of your top member, and also the styles you would perceive in your subordinates. Think about whether any of these styles needs changing in a quest for the output-oriented organization.

### Deserter

The deserter is a manager who is using a low task orientation and a low relationships orientation in a situation where such behaviour is inappropriate and who is, therefore, input oriented. This manager is perceived as uninvolved, passive or negative.

*Deserter indicators*

- Works to rules/minimum output/gives up
- Avoids involvement and responsibility
- Gives few useful opinions or suggestions
- Uncreative/unoriginal/narrow-minded

- Hinders others/makes things difficult
- Resists change/uncooperative
- Shows little concern about errors and usually does little to correct or reduce them.

Some things the deserter might say include:

'The boss is asking about that report and is getting heated about it. I don't know why – it's not that important.'

'If you don't understand it, forget it.'

'If at first you don't succeed, give up.'

'I love my job; it's the work I hate.'

'Mistakes are bound to happen, particularly when I give them a little help.'

'Think – there must be a harder way to do the job.'

'Let's refer the whole thing back to a committee.'

'I really cannot give an opinion on that.'

'I really enjoy work. I can sit and watch it for hours.'

'There is no reason for it – it's just some company policy.'

'I don't know and I don't care.'

Some things that others might say about deserters include:

'They have a great labour-saving device – tomorrow.'

'They've stopped drinking tea or coffee in the morning because it keeps them awake the rest of the day.'

### Missionary

The missionary is a manager who is using high relationships orientation and a low task orientation in a situation where such behaviour is inappropriate and who is, therefore, input-oriented. This manager is perceived as being primarily interested in harmony.

*Missionary indicators*

- Avoids conflict
- Pleasant/kind/warm

- Seeks acceptance of self/dependent
- Makes things easier
- Avoids initiation/passive/gives no direction
- Unconcerned with outputs and standards
- At first sign of conflict attempts to smooth things over.

Some things the missionary might say include:

'The boss is asking about that report. I hope that it won't inconvenience you to let me know how it is coming when you have the time.'

'Fringe benefits should always be increased rather than profits.'

'Look after the people and the organization will look after itself.'

'Argument and conflict never solved anything.'

'The best company is a harmonious company.'

'Harmony leads directly to higher morale and productivity.'

'Conflict is a negative human quality.'

'Day by day, in every way, people are getting better and better.'

'I changed my mind to minimize the chance that someone might be hurt.'

'Keep people happy and they will look after the rest.'

Some things that others might say about missionaries include:

'Their remarks are always more candied than candid.'

'They like to do things the herd way, not the hard way.'

'They treat subordinates with great kindness and consideration.'

'They allow subordinates to set their own objectives according to their needs and accept them even if somewhat unsatisfactory.'

'They believe that if an error occurs, it should be corrected in such a way that no one will be upset.'

## Autocrat

The autocrat is a manager who is using a high task orientation and low relationships orientation in a situation where such behaviour is inappropriate and who is, therefore, input-oriented. This manager is perceived as having no confidence in others, as unpleasant and interested only in the immediate task.

*Autocrat indicators*

- Critical/threatening
- Makes decisions
- Demands obedience/suppresses conflict
- Wants action and results immediately
- Downward communication only
- Acts without consultation
- Feared/disliked
- More interested in day-to-day productivity than in long-run productivity
- Performance maintained through subtle threatening situation.

Some things the autocrat might say include:

'The boss is asking about that report, and is heated about it and so am I. Get on the ball and let's get some action here.'

'Stop talking while I am interrupting.'

'Let me have your ideas, even if it costs you your job.'

'My mind is made up, don't confuse me with the facts.'

'Let me have your opinion – I haven't had a good argument in days.'

'Be reasonable – do it my way.'

'In case you think this is merely a suggestion, folks, you might bear in mind the source.'

'Don't do as I do, do as I say.'

Some things others might say about the autocrat include:

'The rough exterior covers a heart of flint.'

'Some call them a pain in the neck and some people have an even lower opinion of them.'

'They think they are big shots just because they explode.'

## Compromiser

The compromiser is a manager who is using high task orientation and high relationships orientation in a situation that requires a high orientation to only one or neither and who is, therefore, input-oriented. This manager is perceived as being a poor decision-maker, as one who allows various pressures to influence the situation too much and as avoiding or minimizing immediate pressures and problems rather than maximizing long-term production.

*Compromiser indicators*

- Overuses participation
- Yielding/weak
- Avoids decisions
- Produces vague, acceptable decisions
- Idealist/ambiguous
- Sometimes encourages new ideas but does not always follow up on them

Some things the compromiser might say include:

'The boss is asking about that report. Are you busy now? Can you try to get something down on paper as soon as you have the time?'

'You can convince some of the people some of the time and that's usually enough to get by with.'

'Any plan is really a "best fit" or simply a balance among the conflicting demands of the organization.'

'I want all my people to think my way but only after they have really understood and accepted it.'

Some things others might say about the compromiser include:

'They are always trying to save both faces.'

'That manager has three hats: one to cover the head, one to toss in the ring and one to talk through.'

'They're real decisive types, you'll always get a definite "maybe".'

**Bureaucrat**

The bureaucrat is a manager who is using a low task orientation and low relationships orientation in a situation where such behaviour is appropriate and who is, therefore, output-oriented. This manager is perceived as being primarily interested in rules and procedures for their own sake, as wanting to control the situation by their use and as conscientious.

*Bureaucrat indicators*

- Follows orders, rules, procedures
- Reliable/dependable
- Maintains system and going concerns
- Watches details/efficient
- Rational/logical/self-controlled
- Fair/just/equitable
- Prefers to write out communications with others
- Responds to disagreement and conflict by referring to rules and procedures.

Some things the bureaucrat might say include:

'The time is getting near for that report. Is it in good order and on schedule?'

'If we each know and carry out our own particular duties, not much can go wrong.'

'I think we should try to exercise a little more creativity around here. Where is that memo on creativity from Head Office?'

'I like to stay within the bounds of past practice, this keeps everything on an even keel.'

'The really good thing about this company is that everything is laid down for you.'

'Look after the rules and regulations and the company will run itself.'

'Going through the right channels is the mark of the effective manager.'

'Follow the rules and you'll never go far wrong.'

'Let's see how we did it last time, that is usually the best way.'

'Clear rules and procedures are the basic elements of efficiency.'

'I believe that formal meetings are a perfectly sound way to produce new ideas.'

'Decide what is best and then make sure it is followed closely.'

## Developer

The developer is a manager who is using a high relationships orientation and a low task orientation in a situation where such behaviour is appropriate and who is, therefore, output-oriented. This manager is perceived as having implicit trust in people and as being primarily concerned with developing them as individuals.

*Developer indicators*

- Maintains open communication channels
- Develops talent of others/coaches
- Understands others/supports
- Works well with others/co-operates
- Trusted by others/trusts/listens
- When responsible for planning, involves many others.

Some things the developer might say include:

'About that report, do you need any assistance from me in order to do a good job?'

'My job is to tap the creativity and ingenuity of my subordinates.'

'The fewer direct controls on individuals, the greater the likelihood of motivation and quality production.'

'If employees do not grow to accept new responsibility, it is often the fault of the boss.'

'Leaders are best when people barely know they exist.'

'People want to work: my job is to create the situation where they can.'

'My main interest is in finding better ways to coach my subordinates.'

'Managers should be judged by their subordinates' growth.'

**Benevolent autocrat**

The benevolent autocrat is a manager who is using a high task orientation and low relationships orientation in a situation where such behaviour is appropriate and who is, therefore, output-oriented. This manager is perceived as knowing what is wanted and how to get it without creating resentment.

*Benevolent autocrat indicators*

- Decisive/shows initiative
- Industrious/energetic
- Finisher/committed
- Evaluative of quantity, quality and time
- Costs, profits and sales conscious
- Obtains results
- Both develops and proposes many new ideas
- Shows that efficiency and productivity are valued.

Some things the benevolent autocrat might say include:

'The boss is asking about that report. Let me have a memo immediately on its current status, your problems, if any, and your anticipated completion date.'

'I like to walk fairly softly but still carry a big stick.'

'I prefer to make up my own mind but will sometimes ask my subordinates for ideas.'

'The best managers are those who work their way up and learn about the best ways of achieving production from the mistakes they made in being tough at times.'

'A good manager keeps a clear eye on the output of all the subordinates.'

'Promotion and pay rises should be based exclusively on output.'

'A tough-minded disagreement with a fellow manager over how best a task is to be done is a sure sign of productive decision-making even though feelings might get hurt.'

**Executive**

The executive is a manager who is using a high task orientation and a high relationships orientation in a situation where such behaviour is appropriate and who is, therefore, output-oriented. Perceived as a good motivating force, who sets high standards, treats everyone somewhat differently and prefers team management.

*Executive Indicators*

- Uses teamwork in decision-making
- Uses participation appropriately
- Induces commitment to objectives
- Encourages higher performance
- Co-ordinates others in work.

Some things the executive might say include:

'I aim for true involvement, and by it obtain commitment to optimum output.'

'In some situations, I announce my decision after hearing ideas: in other situations, the team works for consensus.'

'High output standards, clear quality controls and high subordinate motivation and commitment are the marks of a good manager.'

'I want my subordinates to produce at their optimum which, I realize, may vary widely from one to another.'

'My job is to obtain the best thinking of all and to get everyone to translate this into optimum production.'

'Optimum production involves both an understanding and utilization of the human and the task variables.'

'A good manager can always make the standards known without impairing the subordinates' approach to their jobs.'

'True team management, in the long run, is the most effective.'

'To obtain optimum production, managers sometimes have to treat everyone somewhat differently.'

**Summary**

There is a connection between managerial style and effectiveness and output orientation. Four managerial styles are input-oriented and may be seen as serving one's own needs rather than situation needs. These four styles are that of the deserter, missionary, autocrat and compromiser. Four styles are output-oriented, and therefore serve situation needs rather than personal needs. These four styles are bureaucrat, developer, benevolent autocrat and executive. Any of the four more effective styles can be effective at times, depending upon the situation.

Managers need to think about their situation and what they are trying to achieve in it and consider which one or more of the four more effective styles they might use. It might be if the situation has sufficiently diverse elements that they use all four more effective styles with different elements of the situation or different people in them. The thrust of this chapter, however, has been to show that there are four more effective styles, and the manager who wants to be effective should be aware of them and attempt to use them as appropriate.

# 6 Overcoming resistance

In 1789 Ben Franklin wrote to a friend, 'But in this world nothing is certain but death and taxes'. He neglected to mention a third certainty . . . change.

A. Judson

There is nothing more difficult to take in hand, more perilous to conduct, or more uncertain in its success, than to take the lead in the introduction of a new order of things.

Machiavelli

The primary task of management is to arrange the situation so that people co-operate readily of their own accord.

Mary Parker Follett

This chapter helps you understand the nature of resistance to change in organizations. You will then be better at using the ideas in the following Chapters 7–9 which show you how to overcome resistance in creating the output-oriented organization.

The truly effective company must be capable of making adaptation to changing conditions; it must be flexible when appropriate. A company that can make appropriate changes in its procedures, structure or products, as they are required, is well equipped for the continuing search for effectiveness. The larger company often has difficulty in maintaining this flexibility. Good ideas are not always accepted or even recognized, and divisional rivalry sometimes impedes change. Emphasis tends to be on operating well today rather than superbly tomorrow. This situation can be modified, so that productive change can be achieved.

## THE FROZEN ORGANIZATION

The frozen organization is input-oriented. Its orientation is to the self rather than to the environment. Using the ideas contained in this book, one may change the frozen organization into an unfrozen one, that is from an input orientation to an output orientation.

The frozen organization has the following characteristics:

- Long decision-making
- Low/late innovation
- Not environment/client/marketing orientated
- Technological lag
- Change resisted
- Rules/past practice
- Some desertion.

Look back at the decisions that your organization as a whole, or your particular unit, has made in a past time period; depending on the nature of your organization or unit, the time period may be anything from six months to five years. Then ask the question: 'Were the decisions made at the optimum time or were they made too late?' If you are at divisional or corporate level, you might think about new market entries, adding new products, hiring a new person or changing the organization or any major decision. Quite apart from whether the decision was right or not, when was the best time to make it? If you keep finding there has been long delay in decision-making, this could indicate a degree of frozenness.

Related to this point is a low level of innovation or that which comes too late. When you look at similar units to your own, do you then think your innovation rate is too low or too late?

Probably the essential characteristic of frozen organizations is that they fail to relate to the environment: they want to maintain themselves, or they are not client- or market-oriented. They want to maintain the status quo.

The frozen organization has a technological lag. As perhaps an extreme example, take the methods to deal with a detected white-collar embezzler. The person may be put in gaol; this can be expensive. Another method is simply to put a bracelet around the ankle which is monitored by local police, so that the embezzler may not move from home more than 100 feet without risking being checked. This second method is now in operation in some places. While this book is not about penal reform, it is about using the technology currently available to improve output orientation. A characteristic of the frozen organization is that change is resisted, that rules and past practice are the guidelines and desertion is obvious. All organizations of course have some degree of frozenness over some things.

## Indicators of the frozen organization

Here are some indicators of the frozen organization. The list is by no means exhaustive, but it is the best that can be created considering that organizations have such different purposes and such different designs. Quite definitely, exceptions can be found for any or all the indicators, but taken as a whole, they indicate the existence of the frozen organization. If many apply, this would clearly indicate that the organization under consideration is indeed frozen; the indicators you think apply may give you a guide to what planned change objectives you might select from Chapter 3. It is always best to review these characteristics on a team basis. The procedure is, first, to go through the list to see which ones apply to the unit or the organization as a whole, if that is what is being considered, and then to evaluate in terms of the presence or absence of each characteristic.

*Indicators of a frozen organization*

- Low skill in dealing with change
- High levels of desertion
- Following of past practices too much
- The use of clumsy, instant, unannounced change
- Heavy top-down authority
- Conflict is handled by suppressing it or smothering it
- Poor communication generally
- Poor interfacing across functions, subsystems or teams
- Frequent operational traumas
- High levels of resistance to change generally
- Resists change in working environment
- Lack of confidence in self, others and the organization
- Low trust
- Low candour
- Apparent fear of relearning
- Feelings, probably disguised, of low security
- Reluctance to share information
- Little interest in colleague effectiveness
- Lack of downward communication
- Lack of upward communication
- Lack of horizontal communication
- Belief that change is virtually impossible
- Belief that change is very unlikely.

The following indications apply primarily to organizations as a whole which market products:

- Market followers
- Technological followers
- Not marketing oriented
- Stay with traditional markets
- Stay with traditional customers
- Stay with traditional product range

## THE FLEXIBLE ORGANIZATION

A direct outgrowth of the unfrozen organization is the flexible, output-oriented organization.

Here are the indicators of a relatively unfrozen organization. Obviously one could simply reverse all the indicators of a frozen organization, and this is quite open for you to do, but here are a few further ideas. As with frozen organization indicators, not all will apply to every organization. If you are on the top team of a small or large organization, then most will apply. If you are on the level-three team in a particular function, such as production or marketing, then only some will apply. You may wish, first, to decide which ones will apply, and then rate only those.

- Commitment to outputs
- Commitment to improvements
- Appraisal based on outputs and effectiveness
- Relatively high rate of change in systems and operating procedures
- High level of communication up and down
- High level of communication across
- Enthusiasm for the work
- Willingness to engage new learning experiences
- Good understanding of managing change
- High level of interdepartmental communication
- Good level of critique with view to making things work better next time
- High loyalty up and down
- High training and development budget
- Openness to managerial rotation
- Some new blood regularly appearing
- High generation of new ideas

A flexible organization is one with a range of appropriate responses to a changing environment. Outputs are high and probably increasing, with a large amount coming from products or services not available five years previously. In a government department or other non-profit-making concern flexibility is shown in increasing effectiveness and lowered cost of the services provided, and in increasing internal use of advanced organization and management techniques.

The characteristics of a flexible organization, are:

- Emphasis on effectiveness, so that this value is the most important consideration in changes affecting individuals, units or the organization itself.
- Acceptance of change, so that decisions may be easily implemented at all levels.
- Free power flow, so that decisions are more likely to be made in an appropriate area, not simply where they have been made before.
- Flexible resources allocation, so that people, money and materials are shifted to where they may do the most good.
- Marketing orientation, so that the market defines the organization.
- Technological orientation, so that new technological devices are investigated for their appropriateness.
- Free information flow, so that within limits imposed by the restraints of commercial intelligence, all parts of the organization have a larger frame of reference with which to see their own potential contribution to effectiveness.
- Project teams, so that fresh approaches have a way of being generated.
- Focus on outputs, so that the test of a manager's action is not 'what did the manager do?' but 'what was produced?'

Many organizations are moving towards having many or all of these conditions now; all organizations could obtain them.

## AIDS TO UNFREEZING THE ORGANIZATION

An important step in creating the output-oriented organization is to increase the level of unfrozenness. For this a planned approach is needed. Our three proven methods to unfreeze the organization and to create the output-oriented organization are as follows:

- Training managers in outputs (see Chapter 7).
- Putting theory into practice (see Chapter 8).
- Planning the output-oriented organization (see Chapter 9).

By applying the above three methods, your organization can become output oriented, and if it is output-oriented already, it will become even more output-oriented!

### Training in outputs

Chapter 7 on training managers in outputs makes the point that the key step in creating an output-oriented organization is to have a formal training programme which teaches all managers exactly what outputs are all about and how to apply outputs to their own situation. This output seminar is called the 3-D Managerial Effectiveness Seminar (3-D MES). Some naïvely think that an output-oriented organization may be created by passing out copies of a textbook or by giving a couple of one-hour lectures or by the chief executive officer (CEO) giving a talk or sending a memo. Some think that a two-day training course using colourful video tape will help. However, all that this method does is to ravish the retina while leaving the mind untouched. What is needed is an approach which enables managers to believe in, to understand and be able to use the notion of outputs. This is easy to achieve, and Chapter 7 provides some tested ideas; and you may well design your own in-company training course based on these ideas.

### Putting theory into practice (teamwork)

There are many wrong ideas about teamwork. Some think it is 'group think' and a way of blurring decisions. Obviously, if badly handled, it can be just that. Chapter 8 on putting theory into practice provides guidelines for using the ideas in this book at all levels and in any kind of organization. It presents five highly practical methods of changing organizations – all of which may be used, or only one or two depending upon what are the change objectives (as derived from Chapter 3). A good way to change a team, and thus help change an organization, is to get the team away for two or three days and to discuss: the outputs of the team, the outputs of the team members, how team members can help one another, the things left undone that should be done and many other things; it really should be preceded by training in outputs.

**Planning the output-oriented organization**

To use this book well, one should think along the lines of planned change, that is exactly how we want to change the organization and how we will do it, and what is the time frame. Chapter 9 gives clear guidelines on how the top team can use all the ideas in this book to plan to make changes; it is in fact an outline workbook. It raises the important questions arising from the key chapters which the teams at the top of units need to answer and plan for in order to create the output-oriented organization. The term 'top team' is not meant to suggest a board of directors of a multinational company, though it might be so. It applies just as well to the team of a remote factory or the top team of an internal service station.

A good way to help unfreeze the top team is to get them together for a few days to discuss important issues. This may be easy to advise, but hard to arrange, yet hundreds of companies have done just this.

## UNDERSTANDING RESISTANCE TO CHANGE

Resistance to change, rather than always being seen negatively, might be perceived as normal, natural and appropriate. We all have some of it! The issue is 'how high is high?' or 'when is it that we have gone beyond reasonable limits?' To some degree, resistance occurs in all normal organizations, and in both managers and employees. It can be lowered when people are encouraged to think about effectiveness and outputs and their own style. Resistance is the way people kill organizations, simply that! Sometimes organizations kill people! Some resistance is acceptable, but not too much.

Depending on our orientation, we may think resistance occurs primarily at the top of organizations or at the bottom of organizations or somewhere in the middle. The truth is that every level resists change to about the same degree, and our view of where it occurs least or most, probably reflects only our prejudices. Perhaps the major problem with resistance to change is that we think others have it more than ourselves, yet as most people think this the idea is nonsense. Good managers who want to be more effective, or wish their organizations to be more effective, simply have to recognize that one of the major elements of resistance to change in their situation is themselves.

Many approaches exist to lowering resistance to change in organizations. While some ideas will be given here, our thrust is not so much overcoming resistance to change as how to understand it. It is misunderstanding resistance to change that causes most problems in introducing change. As we have stated, the first thing to accept, and for some this is difficult, is that resistance to change in life as well as in work is normal, natural and appropriate. Sigmund Freud showed that healthy individuals resist change in order to protect themselves from an environment that they cannot easily handle. The same is true of managers: we do not see things that are there, we distort the things we do see and get up to all kinds of antics to avoid addressing the situation. Clearly, a mark of an effective manager is to see the situation for what it contains, not what one might wish it contained. Similarly, we should recognize our own resistances and try to overcome them and, at the same time, understand that resistance in others might arise for very natural reasons. For it is nonsense to claim that all those who resist change are necessarily the ones driving an organization to less effectiveness, while those who want change are directing it to more effectiveness; often this may be true but not always. On every good top team there are 'red light' managers, 'green light' managers and others; all are needed.

Kurt Lewin, the German-American psychologist, who might well be called the founder of organization development, had many highly creative ideas concerning change. One of these ideas was based on three words: unfreezing, change and maintenance. His idea was that, in terms of change, we can think of social systems in the same way as we think of physical systems. If you want to change a block of ice you first unfreeze it, then change it to a new shape and refreeze it to maintain the new shape. Lewin in fact did not use the word 'maintenance' but the word 'freezing' instead. Many managers clearly do not like the thought of being 'frozen' again, prefering the use of the term 'maintenance' or 'flexibility maintenance'. So we use it.

This notion of unfreezing change and maintenance applies equally well to change in organizations, and certainly to change in individuals. Of course, some companies and some individuals are not frozen at all; indeed the opposite might be the case. Often newer companies with newer technologies and with younger management and active markets, are relatively unfrozen. However, one must not make sweeping generalizations, and perhaps should sometimes refine the analysis to 'unfrozen about what?' Most organizations which exist to trade stocks or commodities are well designed, are flexible about trading methods and give traders an enormous amount of autonomy. So far, it appears they are highly flexible indeed. However, when government tries to introduce change in these systems by suggesting anything, from better self-regulation or government regulation, watch the barricades go up! So a further refinement becomes, 'what is most and what is least resisted?'

Once the organization is unfrozen, then change more easily can be introduced. Usually this change takes one of two forms: a change in system which leads to changes in behaviour, or no changes in the systems but with change in behaviour. Suppose one installs a new management information system, a new reporting system, a new planning system, or a new organization structure, all these are systemic changes which lead directly to obvious changes in behaviour. However, change may simply be improved candour, or better teamwork, which do not involve systemic or structure change, but do involve changes in behaviour.

Many management development programmes and planned change efforts have a common fault of 'fade out'. That is, heat is generated in many concerning a change, but a few months later they seem to forget it. It is observable that in many management development activities the participants return to their work high in enthusiasm and wanting to make changes in themselves, in others and in the system. For a variety of reasons, and the most common is a hostile company climate, they meet with rebuffs and, in a few months, their enthusiasm has waned. Much the same occurs in poorly planned change on an organization-wide basis. A method often used to secure and maintain change is reorganization. Another is a vastly improved planning system. A well designed – repeat, well designed – management by objectives system could also achieve this.

Much light can be thrown on the nature of resistance by referring to carefuly controlled experiments. What follows may be seen, by some, as an extreme or unusual example. It is neither. However, it precisely mirrors what happens concerning resistance in organizations, large and small. The experiment involves a fish-tank with a glass partition in the centre, a big fish on one side and small fish on the other (see Figure 6.1).

In this experiment the big fish is separated from the small fish by a glass partition: it can see them but cannot get at them. What happens, quite routinely, is that the big fish attempts to get closer to the small fish but continually bumps into the glass partition. After doing this a few hundred times, the fish gets rather sore and stops doing it. So far what has happened is rather obvious; what happens next is not. The glass partition is removed, the small fish surround the big fish and the big fish makes no attempt to eat them. The big fish in fact dies of starvation in a sea of plenty. It has learned only too well that the small fish are unavailable, and that

*Figure 6.1*    Unfreezing is needed here

if you try to reach them, pain will result. It has great difficulty in unlearning what it has already learned so well. The fish has been conditioned to be unable to learn, or respond to a new situation.

This experiment reflects what may be routinely observed in planned change programmes. Management thinks it is a good idea to 'remove the glass' – this may be their wish to introduce a new climate or new methods in the organization. Other managers in the organization (most having been around for a long time with a different system) have learned only too well not to 'go after the smaller fish'. Top management may initiate training courses, wave flags or give speeches concerning the fact that they have removed the glass, but the middle managers simply do not believe it and do not respond. Their problem is that they have some unlearning to do because their prior learning was so good! In short, they need 'unfreezing'. They need to be able to see the reality of their current changed situation rather than what used to be there.

Several times I have been in a situation where I was quite convinced that the top team had made many actual changes, and intended to make many more and would carry them through. 'But when meeting with those who report to the top team, one finds that, in the first year or so at least, level three do not believe a word of it! Consequently, planned change programmes need a maintained effort and a substantial amount of work on unfreezing and getting managers to accept a new reality.

# WHY RESISTANCE OCCURS

Many people believe that resistance arises from irrational motives. To understand resistance, and how to deal with it, at least equal weight needs to be given to the opposite assumption. It is a relatively simple matter to make the point that resistance is often intended to be helpful and arises from quite logical reasons. Once understood in this way, one may develop better skills in dealing with resistance.

Resistance may arise for a variety of reasons, as follows:

1   No direction to change.
2   No skills to change.
3   No pressure to change.
4   Known is safer.
5   Personal effectiveness.
6   Shell-shock.
7   Prior learning.
8   Personal defences.

These eight factors need always to be dealt with, or avoided, in order to lower resistance with the view to creating the output-oriented organization.

## No direction to change

Resistance to change often arises simply because the type of change desired is not clearly enough specified. It helps little to ask, implore or demand others to change if you are not clear on the exact nature of the changed behaviour required. Often the unwritten desired direction is: 'Change to whatever I want at the time.' In some settings this might be useful, but in most it is ineffective. As an example, the change request to 'improve communication' contains no information on the direction of change. Does it mean: more talk or less talk; more memos or less memos; communication upwards, downwards, or laterally; listening; more speed reading courses needed; more basic language courses needed, more use of the telephone or less use of the telephone; or longer or shorter meetings? Other examples of quite useless direction for change concern such statements as 'Let's make the organization more participative or more 9.9 or more Theory Y'. These statements contain no useful information. All this is why planned change must start with the notion of planned change objectives, and how to measure these objectives. Change must be given direction, a high degree of specificity. Without this planned approach, change must stop dead in its tracks because people lack agreement on what changes are being considered.

## No skills to change

Change sometimes fails because managers are not provided with the skills needed to implement the change. Perhaps the new corporate planning scheme requires that managers have an increased ability to make a plan. It may well be desirable to arrange that every manager has a one- or two-day course on planning which might include such things as being competent at Critical Path Analysis (CPM) or the Programme Evaluation Review Technique (PERT). Performance appraisal schemes often fail because they are introduced simply as a form which is distributed and managers are told essentially, 'get on with it'. Rather there should be a formal one-day course, using video tape feedback, which enables them to practise appraisal and all that it entails, on strangers before they use it on their team members. If one needs to make an organization more participative, it might well be a good idea to offer managers a short one- or two-day course in listening skills or in participative meeting skills, again, to give them an opportunity to learn in a neutral environment before applying their skills on the job.

## No pressure to change

In addition to directionality and skill level, the successful implementation of change requires pressure of some kind. In its starkest terms, it might be financial rewards for correct behaviour change and financial punishments for incorrect behaviour change. More common, the pressure will arise from a message from management that they want the change and are quite determined to see it implemented. Other pressures for change may be created by talks, meetings and system changes. The single best pressure always is that top management is seen to be supportive of the change and, as it applies, to be directly engaging the change itself.

## Known is safer

It is quite common for an effective manager to resist change because of the danger that, in making a change, present good levels of effectiveness might be decreased. The simple truth is that change introduction often results in a short-term decrease in performance while the new skills are being learned or while errors in introducing the change are eliminated. Think of your own situation and some skill that you acquired too late. Perhaps you waited too long to become computer-familiar, or you thought that time taken to learn would lower your effectiveness on other things? Perhaps you took too long in becoming able with a dictating-machine for similar reasons? It is important to understand that a manager who is effective and who resists change may be doing so simply out of fear of lowering the present good standards of performance.

## Personal effectiveness

While the approach so far has taken a fairly understanding view of resistance to change, the crude fact remains that it can sometimes arise from purely selfish motives. If one is primarily interested in personal effectiveness, that is meeting one's own personal rather than organization objectives, one may indeed show resistance towards proposed changes. If one is overly concerned with one's own position, power, possible career route, size of office, work arrangements, numbers supervised, etc., and puts these first, then it would be natural to expect a higher resistance to reasonable changes which would improve organization rather than personal effectiveness. The best way to deal with this issue is to raise it with the person or persons concerned, preferably with their colleagues also being present. A question that comes naturally is: 'Are you objecting to this change because of managerial effectiveness or personal effectiveness reasons?' This is a routine question in organizations with good teamwork and candour.

## Shell-shock

Shell-shock, in military medicine, applies to a psychological malfunction wherein the individual cannot cope with the existing unthreatening reality because of lingering feelings about an earlier shocking reality which it was found impossible to handle. Things are not quite that bad with most organizations, but they sometimes occur; otherwise why would people involved in change frequently have heart-attacks, ulcers or become alcoholics? All of these can be seen as aspects of shell-shock. Some companies pride themselves on being abreast of every new idea in management. Obviously this can be healthy, it depends on the extent to which it is carried. But if in an organization one year it is job enrichment, the next year quality control circles, the next year management by objectives and the next participative management, one could reasonably expect that the amount of change would be so great that it would be impossible for most managers to deal with it, let alone integrate such variety. This is an understandable reaction. Planned change should involve a single comprehensive set of ideas over a period of time long enough for them to be integrated into the ongoing life of the organization.

**Prior learning**

This refers back to the fish experiment in Figure 6.1. Some people cannot change because they have learned the wrong things too well. This is sometimes called 'trained incapacity'; and the fish experiment shows the need for unfreezing.

**Personal defences**

As we have said, Sigmund Freud is credited with developing the notion of defences, the idea that normal people have unconscious defences which they use to protect themselves from certain situations. The result is that they remain blind to parts of that situation, the parts that are most worrying or threatening. As a function of intelligence, one might favour one defence over another; it takes some brains to rationalize really well, it takes fewer brains simply to deny reality.

**METHODS OF OVERCOMING RESISTANCE IN ORGANIZATIONS**

Three broad methods of overcoming resistance in organizations have been proposed on p. 97; they are the subject of Chapters 7–9. Here we list seven techniques by which resistance to change in organizations may be overcome. The methods are easy to learn and just as easy to use. Most of them amount to commonsense, and all of them are well tested. Through a well-designed output orientation programme, all managers should get 'hands on' experience with each of the following techniques:

1 Diagnosis;
2 Mutual objective setting;
3 Group emphasis;
4 Maximum information;
5 Discussion of implementation;
6 Use of ceremony/ritual;
7 Resistance interpretation.

The first three techniques above are specifically designed to give those affected by change the opportunity to have some influence on its direction, nature, rate and method of introduction. Giving those affected by change some control over it enables them to become involved with it, to express their ideas more directly and to be in a better position to propose useful modifications in the proposed change if it should appear necessary to them.

## Diagnosis

Resistance to change may be reduced if a diagnosis of the situation is first made by those affected by the change. The process of making the diagnosis leads to an increased awareness of what is wrong and this, in turn, leads naturally to steps to change the situation. The diagnosis may be in the form of a workteam discussing the question: 'What are the major problems we could solve if we worked together to solve them?' This kind of question has been used repeatedly with success at all levels of management. It is not only the ultimate diagnosis that the question produces that is important. The actual process of making the diagnosis itself leads to a profound unfreezing of the people concerned, in that they are brought together to discuss things about their department that they have not discussed before. Often in such discussions people gain new perspectives on old problems. They may sometimes come to perceive that they themselves are the prime cause.

The diagnostic, or scientific, problem-solving approach allows for mental double declutching! It does not require a direct switch from one point of view to another, it provides a period 'in neutral' when there is an openness to facts, and therefore, a willingness to consider an alternative view.

**Mutual objective setting**

Resistance to change is reduced with the use of objective setting by those instituting the change, and by those directly affected. Much resistance is simply based on a misunderstanding, or a disagreement, about ends. Once ends have been set and agreed upon, there is usually a straight road to their achievement.

Objectives set by those directly affected are usually more ambitious than those set by persons not so involved.

In one application of objective setting, a group of girls asked to (and were allowed to) set their own speed on machine paced work. Before this the girls had failed to meet the required pace. By using a specially installed dial, the girls established their own speed which they varied by the time of day. Their average output was 30–50 per cent higher than expected, and the girls reported that their work was easier.

Bargaining is a lower, but often necessary, form of mutual objective setting. It is a frank exchange such as 'we will do this if you do that'. It is particularly useful and may be the only method to use with union militancy or in situations where hostility has led to poor communication. Bargaining is not necessarily a display of weakness; it may be an acceptance of reality.

Bargaining often leads to compromise. At its worst, bargaining leads to obstinacy on both sides and a consequent win-lose approach to the final decision. But conditions can at times be created where it leads to a better decision than either side has previously considered.

**Group emphasis**

Management training is now moving more and more towards a group or team emphasis. It is clear that the individual group member, in isolation, can have little influence without the whole-hearted co-operation of the others. The best way of obtaining such co-operation is to train the managers as a team, so that all ideas are team ideas to which the team is committed as a unit. Some managers say that the first thing to do with an idea is to separate it from the manager who first thought of it – i.e. make it group property.

Resistance to change is reduced if the group, rather than the individual, is made the focus of change. Group decision-making exerts a powerful control over the deviant member, who is holding up the others, because groups develop both standards for conformity and the means of enforcing them. In the same way that a group can set up work norms to inhibit change, it can set up norms which facilitate it.

As with any technique, there are times when group decision-making is appropriate and times when it is not. For example, it should never be used when management has (or already should have) made up its mind. In fact it can be used only when both sides have something to gain. Also it operates only when a group, or potential group, actually exists.

These first three techniques of diagnosis, mutual setting and group emphasis all involve participation in different aspects of the change. The word 'participation' has not been used as there is so much misunderstanding and disagreement about what it means. In the three techniques no promise can be made that management will accept all the ideas suggested, and there is no need for such agreement. The techniques can be used quite successfully when management says, in effect: 'This much is decided. What are your thoughts on the rest? We will consider all your proposals but cannot guarantee to accept them.'

The success of such methods as these depends on the extent to which they are seen as legitimate, honest and likely to be successful. Although it can be done, it is difficult for a company to start too suddenly to use these techniques in situations where they have never been used before. A certain degree of trust is important; a certain degree of skill in implementation is crucial; and some form of unfreezing, such as the 3-D Managerial Effectiveness Seminar, is useful. Needless to say, managers cannot use these techniques if they have already settled on a course of action. To do so is dishonest and folly – 'You can fool some of the people . . .', and it takes only one to tell the rest. Pseudo-participation is time wasted for everyone, and clearly inappropriate if a degree of meaningful participation might have been used instead.

## Maximum information

When involved in change, management will go through four distinct steps:

1  Recognize change needed.
2  Decide on ideal state.
3  Design method of implementation.
4  Implement change.

These should each, in turn, lead to four appropriate announcements:

1  That a change will be made.
2  What the decision is and why it is made.
3  How the decision will be implemented.
4  How decision implementation is progressing.

Each of these announcements may produce a particular resistance:

(a)  to thought of any change;
(b)  to decision itself;
(c)  to method of implementation;
(d)  to changed state itself.

When analysing a change in process or when planning a change, these twelve elements in turn should each be considered. In particular, management should consider how well it is conveying the four separate elements of information required. There is a tremendous fear of incomplete information, and people usually believe the worst.

The first piece of appropriate information – that a change will be made – is often omitted or left to rumour; the second – what the decision is and why made – is often made too tersely; the third – how the decision will be implemented – is often omitted, or not well enough thought out, let alone communicated; and the fourth – how decision implementation is progressing – is seldom communicated, particularly when there is little that is good to communicate.

Maximum information is usually a sound policy after change has been announced, and sometimes (but not always) before it. Testing the wind with a hint about forthcoming change can sometimes provide useful pointers on the state of resistance or acceptance to that change. On the other hand, it can simply raise the level of anxiety and lead to wild rumours. Prior announcements should be clear-cut as far as they go, but they do not have to be complete.

Vague prior announcements are harmful – e.g. 'Some organizational changes are coming'. A precise prior announcement is most helpful: 'A reorganization to the top two levels of our A division will be announced, by 1 September, by the executive committee. The changes will be carried out during the following two months. The basic function of the division will remain unchanged.'

Once a change has been announced, the maximum possible information should be distributed about it. Resistance to change is almost always lower if the objectives, nature, methods, benefits and drawbacks of change are made clear to all concerned.

Face-to-face announcements are better than the printed word. Not only do they personalize what may be seen as a depersonalized action, but they also allow anxieties to be expressed and, perhaps, dealt with on the spot.

## Discussion of implementation

Discussion of implementation is a component of giving the fullest possible information. It calls for distinct treatment; however, it is a most important step often overlooked.

Resistance to change is reduced if there can be agreement on the rate and method of implementation. It is as effective to have discussions on the way a change is to be introduced as it is to discuss the nature of the change itself. Such discussions will cover what the first steps should be, what the rate of change should be, what the appropriate sequence of changes should be and who should be involved in what elements of the implementation. When this method is used successfully, it sometimes happens that the unit undergoing the change says to management: 'Leave us alone. Come back in two weeks or two months and the changes will be in.' A wise manager accepts that kind of offer.

## Use of ceremony/ritual

Breaking a saucer can eliminate in-law trouble. In some wedding ceremonies in the east a saucer is broken by the bride's father. This act dramatically symbolizes that he no longer considers the bride part of his household. She is now essentially a daughter of the groom's mother. With crowded living conditions, it is important to know who is boss in the kitchen. The broken saucer clarifies the daughter's new role to everyone, especially to her. She is still a daughter but in a different family.

In precisely the same way the 'golden handshake' or gold-watch presentation of western business society is a method of marking a change of status from employed to retired. One problem with the ceremony is that it is essentially one of departure. Only those whom the retired person is leaving are present. This hardly facilitates entry into the community of the retired.

Life consists of a series of periods lived under different statuses. Most of us follow a similar pattern. We are first infants, then schoolchildren, then lovers, then adults, then marriage partners then parents. Some degree of ritual surrounds the passage from one status to another. The more important the status distinction the more elaborate the ritual.

Where there is established progression from one status to another, change becomes easier to accept. One knows that many people have done it before, what are the progressions, and is prepared for the future and the behavioural demands that the next status will make. One also knows the conditions for entering the status and for remaining there, and the meaning and use of the various status symbols which might range from a wedding ring to a big desk or a fitted carpet.

Some of the particular uses of ceremony and ritual for managers are:

- passing on status, competence, power
- preparing individual or group for change
- providing a clear end and a new beginning
- providing for orderly change
- making change legitimate
- emphasizing individual responsibility to organization.

A few of the many occasions when one or more of the above are accomplished, and where ceremony and ritual are therefore useful, are in the situations of:

- retirement
- promotion
- new co-worker
- new superior
- new subordinate
- new job
- start of new system
- reorganization

Ceremonies well used by a manager can serve to focus the importance of the ongoing institution and to underline the importance of individual loyalty to the institution and the positions within it.

Clearly, managers need to learn how to use ceremony and ritual. Both can facilitate adaptation to what otherwise might be a painful adjustment.

## Resistance interpretation

Usually when people understand why they have been resisting a change, their resistance decreases or, at least, becomes more rationally based. Interpreting resistance with those who are resisting is a key step in psychoanalysis and in organization – change agentry.

Resistance has been seen as a symptom of something else, perhaps fear of the future or an unwillingness to give up something. Invariably the form the resistance takes is an indicator of the true nature of the resistance. Seldom is the real reason openly stated. Uncovering these reasons, and discussing them, can get at the real cause of the problem.

Such interpretation of resistance is preceded or followed by some manner of 'blowing off steam'. This may be in the form of a private or public 'beef' session.

## Common errors

Most of the possible errors in output orientation have been discussed or implied already. However, some occur much more frequently, and are more serious, than others; they are:

- Human aspects only
- Technical aspects only
- No information about change
- No planning of introduction
- No benefits
- Seen as personal.

Exclusive emphasis on the human aspects of change may lead to the changes being distorted from the original plan, or lead to no change at all. Overemphasis on the human side is sometimes induced by human relations training courses. Managers then become either over-participative or guilty about the methods they need to use.

At the other extreme is a sole emphasis on the technical aspects of change. Engineers and systems department managers are among those who have been most guilty of this in the past. Such an emphasis might lead to the most extreme personal resistance of all – leading to still more impersonal pressure, to compromise or to an abandonment of the project.

When a firm has a history of resistance to change, it sometimes resorts to the strategy which might be called 'no information', 'no warning', or 'earthquake'. It can employ these strategies, to some extent, in a heavily technical system, or in a situation where payment can be made for compliance and where direct coercion is possible. The negative effects of such an approach are varied, but are often intense. They include 'grapevines', anxiety and suppressed or overt hostility. Eventually the pool duplicator turns out résumés for those seeking work elsewhere.

A widespread error, and one capable of a simple solution, is lack of planning of the method of introduction. A new method might have cost several million to design and purchase, yet not even a single employee-year, nor even a month, is spent on ensuring smooth implementation. But how much time *should* be spent? What is an appropriate situational management design budget percentage? In most firms it is zero. They think that a plan on paper is a short step from a plan implemented. It is not.

All change has associated benefits for the worker, manager or organization as a whole. In the long run those working in the organization will gain if the organization gains. The benefits of some change may simply be survival, but benefits, in some form, are always present. Even though they may not be individual benefits, they should be stressed rather than ignored.

Sometimes change is resisted simply because it is seen as a result of a personal whim. This kind of objection is unlikely to be raised about the manager at a top of a profit centre. It is very likely to be raised about staff who are seen as empire-builders or of very ambitious managers who appear more interested in personal than managerial effectiveness.

## The suppression of resistance

No normal manager prefers to use coercive means to suppress resistance, yet most managers have and know they will again. There is no argument for suppression unless all else has failed. If absolute time limits are near, and if others may suffer because of increased danger or the possibility of adverse economic consequences, then the method may be condoned.

Suppression methods are familiar to all and include threats of punishment, offers of bribes and threatened termination and cancellation of concessions already offered. These methods are not recommended unless others have failed, or unless special conditions prevail, because they can easily lead to increased resistance. When they must be used, they can lead to increased respect if handled properly.

It is unwise to interpret deep resistance as an attack on the manager, or on the changes the manager wants to implement. The resistance may simply be an instinctive or learned reaction to something new and strange. If so, it is unwise to meet force with force because what may simply have been an initial objection may become a lasting resentment.

## Rate of change, not introduction of change

Very few social systems remain unchanged over long periods. Changes may be small and introduced slowly, but they do take place. Therefore, discussion of change should not be solely concerned with the introduction of change itself, but also with the rate of change.

In deciding whether to introduce change rapidly, the following questions should be considered:

1  Is time important?
2  What will be gained by speed?
3  What is past custom?
4  Will speed increase resistance?
5  Can acceptance be sacrificed for speed?
6  How would speed be interpreted?
7  Are other changes still being assimilated?
8  Must other changes be integrated?

General arguments exist both for slow and rapid change. The arguments for slow change are:

- Usually produces less resistance
- Allows for gradual acceptance
- Will be seen as evolutionary
- Allows for greater understanding
- Allows for skill acquisition
- Changes can blend with others
- Changes and modifications in the proposed change itself will be easier
- Changes and adjustments to the method used will be easier.

The arguments for rapid change are:

- Less time taken to reach ideal changed state
- Shorter adjustment period

- Only one basic adjustment required
- Less basic plan modification likely
- Adds impression of resilience.

The speed of change is an important part of any complete plan for reducing resistance. It should be considered carefully along with the methods to be used.


## LEARNING HOW TO SAIL

Thinking clearly about the necessary elements in learning a skill is helpful in thinking about the logical steps you need to take to overcome resistance in your unit. As a particular example which obviously has a general application consider the elements needed in learning how to sail. To approach the learning situation well one must believe in all the following:

- Sailing exists
- I know what it is
- I cannot sail now
- The coach has skills to teach
- I have the ability to learn
- I will obtain benefits from sailing.

The above list is self-explanatory. Apply it to those in your unit who are learning how to become more effective, or teaching others how to become more effective. Or teaching virtually anything and getting others to change their behaviour. Many planned change efforts are stopped cold at the first line: 'There is something called . . .' There is in fact nothing existing called participation, communication or ideal styles. The words may be used, but they mean little. These terms, widely used, are completely incapable of an acceptable definition as they have so many meanings.

Planned change objectives which have clear measurement areas attached are essential if we are to encourage managers or workers to change. Let us convert the above list concerning sailing to a similar list concerning output orientation. All of these conditions must be created if that is the variable you wish to influence:

- There is something called output orientation which is clearly defined in terms of what everyone can accept and understand.
- I personally know what is meant by output orientation. The definition is completely clear to me.

- I am less effective now or I am capable of a higher degree of output orientation.
- The organization planned change programme in its various aspects provides me with all the opportunities needed to learn the skills of output orientation.

I am personally competent to learn about managerial effectiveness and to improve my output orientation.

When I become more effective I will obtain benefits from being more effective.

This example is not in the least extreme; it is simply logical thinking about learning.

## SUMMARY

In creating the output-oriented organization resistance will have to be overcome. Several tested methods have been described, and these include some form of unfreezing activity, a variety of meeting types and a top-team planning session. These are the subjects of Chapters 7–9. Resistance can be viewed positively. It is part of the natural human condition. The organization has a degree of it and so does every individual.

Some organizations are extremely resistant and can be described simply as frozen. It is to that type of organization, in particular, that this entire book applies. However, a healthy organization that is responsive can still improve its effectiveness and output orientation by using the ideas in this book.

# 7 Training managers in outputs

A student of business with tact
Absorbed many answers he lacked.
But, acquiring a job,
He said with a sob,
How *does* one fit answer to fact?
                                        Anon.

No man can reveal to you aught but that which already lies half
asleep in the dawnings of your own knowledge.
                                        Kahlil Gabran

What we need is not the will to believe, but the wish to find out,
which is the exact opposite.
                                        Bertrand Russell

One's education consists of what is left after one has forgotten the
facts.
                                        A. N. Whitehead

This chapter describes an effective method of training managers in
output orientation. An essential part of this process is to help
managers lower their resistance to change. The method used is the
3-D Managerial Effectiveness Seminar (3-D MES).

The 3-D MES relates to the three dimensions of the underlying
theory. This theory, known as the 3-D Theory of Managerial Effectiveness, is based on the three dimensions of the manager, the
situation and effectiveness. Further details on this theory may be
found in my *Managerial Effectiveness* (McGraw-Hill).

For over twenty years the 3-D MES has been used to introduce
output orientation. This chapter describes the objectives, design
and effect of the 3-D MES both on the manager and on the organization. It should be particularly useful for those who know that a
successful output orientation implementation will have to involve
overcoming resistance in individuals and in the organization as a
whole. This is in fact how the 3-D MES has been used to introduce

outputs. There are consistent reports to the effect that with the 3-D MES being used as a first step, the output-oriented organization has far more certainty of being achieved.

This seminar is conducted by W. J. Reddin & Associates. It has worldwide acceptance and has been used by many organizations, large and small. The seminar is highly experiential. The ideas in his book are carried in the seminar not simply cognitively, that could be done by reading the book. The seminar attempts to help managers experience the ideas elaborated in this book and to relate them to their personal situation and also to make some action plans concerning it. Books can help, as can seminars.

Some of the many reasons why the 3-D MES is useful for creating an output-oriented organization are as follows:

- The basis of the seminar is managerial effectiveness.
- Each participant receives a thorough grounding in what is meant by outputs and effectiveness areas.
- The seminar stresses change as an absolutely necessary part of the manager's job.
- The seminar in its various activities stresses measurement of outputs.
- Teamwork and team objectives are given very high priority on the seminar.
- The seminar puts teams into a team appraisal mode at least once a day, sometimes this internal team critique will last for several hours.
- Non-evaluative feedback is formally taught and much practice is given.

The seminar makes salient these ten questions for the individual manager:

1  What are the true effectiveness areas demanded by my position?
2  Should I accept these effectiveness areas as a basis for my outputs in the future?
3  What are my best measurement areas?
4  What are my objectives?
5  How can I improve my effectiveness generally?
6  How will I become more flexible?
7  How will I work to change what should be changed in my situation?
8  How can I improve my superior's effectiveness?
9  How can I improve my co-workers' effectiveness?

10   How can I improve my subordinates' effectiveness?

The theme running through the seminar is that managerial effectiveness is the central issue in management. It is the manager's job to be effective. It is the only job. In fact the seminar carries the issue further, to point out that it is any manager's true social responsibility to be effective. The pens used on the seminar have 'Any manager's true responsibility' printed on them.

## THE 3-D MANAGERIAL EFFECTIVENESS SEMINAR DESIGN

The 3-D Managerial Effectiveness Seminar is a six-day, residential, instrumented seminar. It starts at 5.30 p.m. on the first day, and ends at 12.30 p.m. on the sixth day. This time span normally covers Sunday evening to Friday noon. Hours are long. Each morning starts promptly at 8.00 a.m. in the main room. Teams frequently work from then until past midnight. About 80 per cent of the seminar takes place in team rooms with four to eight managers, which approximates the usual span of control. Participants with close working relationships, such as superior to subordinate or co-worker to co-worker, may attend the same seminar, but are not placed together on the same team.

The 3-D MES confronts the teams with a wide variety of problems to solve, generally related to methods of achieving managerial effectiveness through the recognition of the reality of a situation and the best approach to it. Teams solve problems in their team rooms, then meet with other teams in the main room to report on their decisions and to compare their effectiveness both in making and reaching them.

Organizations introducing output orientation need a specific and tightly defined language, which everyone involved in output orientation uses. It is obviously true that managers who talk and work together need a common set of concepts which they share and agree on. Often, without such a set, objectives are hard to arrive at and are ill-connected as they are based on different ideas. Disraeli spoke for many when he said, 'If you want to converse with me, define your terms'.

Three kinds of effectiveness are clearly distinguished: managerial, personal and apparent. Some managers may learn a great deal from having this pointed out to them. They never saw effectiveness as having three sides before. The 3-D terms provide a conceptual language to make discussions and analyses more precise. The concepts are the fewest possible needed to consider styles, situations and effectiveness. They are used to improve situational sensitivity because they force a focus on elements, activities or outcomes that might otherwise be ignored or misinterpreted.

The result of the 3-D MES is an internalization of the skills, knowledge and beliefs of the output orientation of managerial effectiveness, in such a way that it becomes part of the manager's day-to-day working life. The participants are provided with one central objective for the seminar in the opening minutes: 'The objective of this seminar is to help you become more objective about your situation so you can engage it better and therefore become more effective.' In short, overcome distortions to engage reality.

The seminar is carefully designed, so that while participants will perceive some of the issues raised as mildly stressful, no participant will be unduly frustrated by the experience. No adverse effects have been observed over the more than twenty years the seminar has been conducted. The 3-D MES fosters independence. The manager is required to confront the situation and to decide to engage it and become more effective.

## DESIGN YOUR OWN SEMINAR?

For a variety of reasons some organizations have difficulty in accessing the 3-D MES. Their recourse, then, is to design their own seminar, or to proceed with the five meeting types described in Chapter 8 without first 'unfreezing' the organization and the managers within it. These are not desirable alternatives, but in some cases they reflect the only reality.

The common errors made when attempting to design a 3-D MES equivalent are the following.

- Seminar is too short. It really is impossible to lower resistance and increase output orientation and teach output orientation in a couple of days.
- Not starting at the top. What happens is that the top asks the training section to design a seminar. For middle managers, what has happened since the 1950s is that top managers thought the lower levels were the problem. The trainer who takes on this kind of contract is, inferentially at least, assuming that the existing input-oriented organization was some kind of malfunction of middle and lower managers.
- Rewriting the book. A widespread error in introducing Management by Objectives (MBO) was for the internal adviser or trainer to take one or two textbooks and from those create

the organization's own 'Company MBO Manual'. This is pure nonsense, rewriting something with the company's logo on the front does not internalize the ideas. In many cases, it has helped somewhat – but only when the true nature of outputs have been accepted by senior management.

Thus, while some organizations will continue to try it, it is not really the best solution to design and conduct a 'do-it-yourself' 3-D MES. The 3-D MES has been designed and redesigned for many years. If a single seminar has been around for a long time and the most sophisticated organizations in the world use it without redesign, there must be something right about it. There is no problem at all with 'do-it-yourself' activities, and this book has a lot of ideas about this point. However, 'do-it-yourself' is probably not a good approach in attempting to design a sophisticated seminar to teach outputs and to unfreeze individuals and organizations.

If 'do-it-yourself' is absolutely essential, then focus your attention on the team meeting and the large group meeting both described in Chapter 8, the planning meeting described in Chapter 9 or teaching the whole concept of outputs described in Chapter 2.

## IN-COMPANY USE OF THE 3-D MANAGERIAL EFFECTIVENESS SEMINAR

As with the public 3-D MES the typical in-company 3-D MES starts on Sunday evening at 5.30 p.m. and ends on Friday at 12.30 p.m. It is normally held at a rural hotel, which most or all participants would not know. The seminar size depends upon the organization design but often is six teams of about seven people each, although it might be as small as two teams of five participants each. The head of the unit may well be on the first seminar as a participant but if not attends, in any case, on Friday at 10.30 a.m. and submits a problem concerning the organization for the teams to present ideas about.

Usually the problem concerns improving productivity, but it might be that of introducing change or how best to introduce a systemic change such as organisation redesign, or to increase output orientation in the organization. The comments of all of the teams at the seminar are distributed to all the managers of the organization. This feedback is used as raw data for diagnosing the ills and opportunities for increasing the effectiveness of the organization. The top person always finds the experience enjoyable, and realizes it must be done much more in a variety of other ways.

## Internal staff

Most 3-D MESs are run by company staff members. Sometimes these staff members are drawn from the personnel and training departments or staff functions and sometimes from the line. As a general rule, we find that our post-seminar reaction forms show higher results when the seminars are conducted by internal staff, even though they were never trainers. One bank trained fifteen staff members to conduct seminars and all of these staff members had been branch bank managers at one time in their career. They all started off as cashiers. They were excellent trainers.

## The use of the MES across levels

The seminar has a demonstrated effectiveness at all managerial and supervisory levels. General Motors, for instance, uses the seminar from plant CEO level down to general foreman level. When the seminar is used as part of an organization development programme, then all levels of management and sometimes supervision attend the same seminar. In some companies it is common for several different levels to be attending the same seminar. The reason that all this is seen to work is that the seminar teaches basic truths about management, which simply have application to all management positions. The concepts apply broadly.

## Low in-company seminar costs

Seminar costs are low compared to most management seminars of similar length for a variety of reasons.

- The optimum, not maximum, number on the seminar is 42. The maximum is 72. The reason that this high number can be accommodated is that 80 per cent of the seminar takes place in team rooms. Lecturing is nominal. Teams teach themselves.
- For even the largest seminar, a maximum of only two staff members are needed.
- The seminar is quite highly structured, and this makes it reasonably easy for client staff to conduct the seminars.
- Some organizations purchase the seminar design outright for use within their organization, and this clearly leads to a lowering of average unit cost.

## FIVE STAGES OF LEARNING

The seminar can be seen as providing five stages of learning, as follows.

### Prework

Each participant receives a prework kit. This consists of three texts, wall charts and a seminar workbook. The basic text is my *Managerial Effectiveness* (1984). This explains the 3-D Theory, and shows how it is applied to improve effectiveness. The general seminar workbook contains questionnaires, style tests, effectiveness inventories, seminar tasks, case studies, team diagnosis instruments and other learning aids. Depending on the participant's prior knowledge and individual capacity and dedication, seminar prework generally takes from 50 to 100 hours to complete.

### Days one and two

This is concept mastery. Participants work in teams to deepen their understanding of the basic concepts relating to effectiveness, styles, situation and managerial behaviour. Teamwork skills are also learned during this period. Regular reviews of individual and team effectiveness are made.

### Day three

This is case-study application. Effectiveness concepts are applied to case studies, so the practical application is demonstrated and learned. This day transfers theoretical learning into practical application. Team-building skills are continually practised and reviewed.

### Days four, five and six

This is application to self. The entire second half of the 3-D MES applies effectiveness concepts to the participants' actual work situation. Day four is spent on effectiveness, day five on managerial behaviour and day six on situation management. The last three days are highly involving for all participants. These three days end up with a detailed back-home action plan for each participant. Day four of the seminar is spent solely in each team reaching agreement on the effectiveness areas of each team member. Most managers on this day discover that there is more potential for contributions in their job than they had considered. They experience a new and rewarding understanding of how to be effective; they develop an increased awareness for assessing job demands; they learn to apply what they have learned at the seminar to their actual work situations; they enjoy their work more; they understand it better; and they are more effective.

Participants receive a number of printed and conceptual tools to help them apply effectiveness concepts to their actual work situations; these include:

1   A rating of the manager's effectiveness by their seminar team as well as by seminar instruments.
2   A draft job effectiveness description (JED) which serves as a basis for clarifying the manager's role in the organization. This job effectiveness description contains effectiveness areas, measurement areas for each effectiveness area and the authority vested in the position.
3   An effectiveness improvement plan with month-by-month progress checks.
4   A management style profile, which provides an assessment of style strengths and weaknesses as well as a guide to desirable future behaviour.
5   A situational analysis of the manager's actual work situation.
6   A team skill diagnosis test, which provides an assessment of team skills as well as a guide to sound team operation.

So by the end of the seminar, managers are usually highly conscious of themselves as key figures in situations where effectiveness could be increased. They are usually more open to change. They see themselves, rather than others, as keys to greater effectiveness. They are capable of applying an increased number of sound output orientation principles and techniques to achieve effectiveness.

**Post-seminar**

This covers the job application. After the 3-D MES, managers use the conceptual and printed tools that the 3-D MES has provided. They may use them to redefine their position in output terms, to work with subordinates, co-workers and their superior on objectives and also to change their less effective behaviour.

It has been determined, quite conclusively, that the seminar effects are magnified when the actual workteam meets in the months afterwards to apply the seminar ideas to the workteam itself (see pp. 129–31). The whole point in management training is what is called 'transfer of training', and the transfer is greatly facilitated when a superior and all immediate subordinates, after participating in a 3-D MES, sit down to discuss and agree on any needed changes in their effectiveness areas and any other things that impinge on their managerial effectiveness and the introduction of output orientation.

## WILL THE 3-D MES SUIT YOUR NEEDS?

There is a great deal of evidence that the MES has general applicability across functions, across industries, across types of organizations and across countries.

The MES has been conducted in these countries: Argentina, Australia, Austria, Belgium, Brazil, Canada, Ethiopia, Finland, Guyana, Ireland, Jamaica, Kenya, Mexico, the Netherlands, New Zealand, Norway, Singapore, South Africa, Spain, Sweden, Trinidad and Tobago, the United Kingdom, the United States of America, Venezuela and West Germany.

## SUMMARY

### The 3-D Managerial Effectiveness Seminar

Attendance: All managers and supervisors
Duration: Six days
Main topics addressed:
   Clarification of one's own effectiveness areas and measurement
      areas
   Development of skills to create change in oneself and others
   How to improve one's output orientation
   How to become more effective
   How to increase one's objectivity about situations
   How to decrease one's resistance to change
Main outcomes:
   Improved team operating skills
   Improved output orientation generally
   Improved effectiveness

Greater clarification about the outputs of one's position – role
  clarification
Lowering of resistance to change
Greater openness with others
Increased situational sensitivity, style flexibility and situational
  management skill
Much greater style awareness
Improved conflict management
Better at giving and receiving feedback

# 8 Putting theory into practice

There is nothing so practical as a good theory properly applied.
K. Lewin

Unapplied knowledge is knowledge shorn of its meaning.
A. N. Whitehead

This chapter is intended to give you some practical ideas on just how to create the output-oriented organization. These ideas are based on a single concept, that in creating the output-oriented organization people need to talk to other people about the right things in the right way. While there are many perceptions of what one might mean by the term 'meetings' (some positive some negative), it still seems a good idea to think of the concept of meetings as a way to help things change.

## FIVE TYPES OF MEETING

This chapter outlines five types of meeting, as follows:

1   the Team Meeting;
2   the One-To-One Meeting;
3   the Interteam Meeting;
4   the Corporate Strategy Meeting;
5   the Large Group Meeting.

To create the output-oriented organization you may need only one of these, or all five. You might decide to use only one team meeting or hundreds. You will have a better sense of what you need when you have read through this chapter.

Well-designed meetings are probably the best way of all to improve managerial and organization effectiveness. The objective here is to describe five types of meeting, which are about all the types you will ever need and which can be used in various ways at various times to improve effectiveness. They are all very practical and all focus on the sharp end, namely effectiveness. The primary objective is to give you ideas and encouragement, so that you will try your hand at one or more types of meetings that you have never tried before. This might be taking your team away for a weekend. It might be getting the top three or four levels in your organization into one room for a day or two to come up with a total plan for reorganization. This has been done several times, with good effect, using the method given here.

## THE TEAM MEETING

The objective of the team meeting is to build a team round common outputs and to improve both team and team member effectiveness. Obviously it is attended by the full team of one superior and all the immediate subordinates. Commonly it lasts about three days and is held off-site.

Team training is a relatively new and powerful managerial training technique. In the three-day Team Meeting, the top person and all the team members discuss and decide how best to improve the way they work together. The Team Meeting, more than any other meeting, looks at technology and the possibilities for modifying it. The Team Meeting has been described as situational management for a team and also as a work-study conference for a team. Each of these descriptions reflect the essence of the design. The emphasis is not on personality or subordinates' rating of their superior, but rather on individual and team outputs.

*Topics for team meeting*
The topics for a team meeting will vary somewhat from team to team; however, there are some fundamental topics from which most teams get value. A sound technique is to complete prework for a reasonable range of topics, and then at the meeting the team decides how much time to spend on each. This is sometimes difficult to determine in advance.

*Suggested topics for Team Meeting*
- Effectiveness areas of the team.

- Effectiveness areas of the top person.
- Effectiveness areas of each of the team members.
- Perceived effectiveness of team, top person and team members.
- Improvements in management style that might be made by the top person and each team member.
- How the team now makes decisions, and how it should.
- How the team now meets, and how it should.
- Outstanding problems that could be solved if the team decided to solve them.
- How the team might be reorganized.

A discussion of effectiveness areas is crucial. This starts with a discussion of the effectiveness areas of the team as a whole, then the top person and then, in turn, each team member. Be absolutely strict about the four words concerning effectiveness areas which should be put on newsprint. Is it an OUTPUT? Is it MEASURE-ABLE? Is it within AUTHORITY? And is it IMPORTANT?

It is a good notion if, at the Team Meeting, the team has a frank discussion about the perceived effectiveness of every team member. This of course includes the top person. This can be done in two ways: either by discussion of the dominant and supporting styles, or after a discussion of effectiveness areas, to assign a high, average or low for each one. This is a tough exercise, yet many thousands of teams have done it and survived. In some companies, in about one team in ten, someone threatens to resign. This, perhaps, can only be a good thing.

Teams should look at their decision-making methods. In essence, what decisions are usually reserved for the top person to make, which are made on a one-on-one basis and which are made by the team as a whole? This is followed by a discussion about how these various decisions should be taken. Some top people believe that team members will want to make all the decisions themselves. This does not happen; normally what happens is that they want to know on what basis decisions will be made, and for two or three key decisions they will normally say something like, 'If you want commitment from us, this had better be on a team basis'. They are usually right.

As part of the prework for a team meeting it can be profitable to ask everyone to draw an optimum organization chart which the team should aim for within a year or so, on the assumption that suitable people could be provided for all positions. For some teams this can be an important exercise. However, as one moves down in the organization, it is less important as the teams become embedded in an existing structure and so less able to make changes.

The 'outstanding problems to solve' assignment has enormous cost-benefits for any team. As part of the prework, team members answer a question along the lines of 'What outstanding problems has the team got to solve which it could solve within six months if all agree they are going to?' At the team meeting all these problems are listed and the most important ones chosen and agreement made that they will be solved, and how they will be solved. Obviously responsibilities and timings are assigned.

The team meeting is attended by a complete team. If, for any reason, one team member cannot attend, then postpone the meeting until that member can be present.

At the first team meeting only, it is almost certain to be cost-effective to bring someone outside the team along who has participated in several team meetings as a consultant/observer/helper; while it is not essential to have such a person present, there is little question that it is indeed cost-effective.

The team meeting leads directly to a clear definition of the team's role within the organization. With this established, team measurement areas and team objectives may be prepared. Often the preparation requires some type of team reorganization, which the team designs and implements. Flexible job trading usually occurs and leads to the talents of individual managers being better utilized through job enrichment. Needless to say, the enthusiasm and commitment generated by this activity lead to the solution of many problems.

The team meeting works best after all team members have participated in the 3-D MES. The seminar induces a readiness to change for which the Team Meeting provides the vehicle.

It is important that the team meeting starts at the top of a reasonably autonomous system. This may well be the top team of the organization, but it could also be the top team of a detached plant that is autonomous. The reason for this is that many problems lower down are simply a function of problems higher up, and there is no way to tackle them until the top team has recognized them and moved towards solving them.

## THE ONE-TO-ONE MEETING

The objective of the one-to-one meeting is to strengthen the relationship between the top person and each team member, in turn. By this, to clarify respective roles in terms of effectiveness areas and to build a better open and coaching relationship. It is not the traditional appraisal type meeting. Nothing like it in fact.

**Topics for One-to-One Meeting**

There are varied possible designs for a One-to-One Meeting. The most conventional design is the appraisal meeting, where the top person explains to the team member 'how to be more like me'. Some in-house version of the appraisal meeting is required, although it is much better to do it on a team basis. The One-to-One Meeting attempts to build the relationship between the top person and each team member, so salary reviews and appraisal meetings will go better. Like the unfreezing meeting, it is a useful first step to enhancing other areas.

*Suggested Topics for One-to-One Meeting*

- Effectiveness areas
- Blockages
- Objectives
- Assistance needed

The topics for the One-to-One Meeting must start with agreement on effectiveness areas: first, effectiveness areas of the team as a whole, then of the top person and then the team member. This, then, helps everyone to become more objective and more equal and so less defensive. The One-to-One Meeting often follows the team meeting, and, therefore some of these issues have already been covered, but it is useful to follow up these points on a one-to-one basis.

The meeting then moves to a discussion of blockages to effectiveness, as seen by the team member. These blockages are listed for each member of the organization as a whole, with the top person and with self. All these are reviewed and a resolution made, where possible. Again, what is being encouraged is the building of openness, trust and also a better view of reality.

It may or may not be possible at the meeting to discuss objectives. It depends upon the rate of change in the organization, the quality of the management information system and many other factors. However, where possible, there should be agreement on objectives, against each effectiveness area or the next period. Finally, and to strengthen the relationship, the team member asks for what assistance is needed from the top person to achieve the objectives. The top person commits to all or some of these requirements. The one that most often arises is: 'I want a bit more of your time.'

**The design of the One-to-One Meeting**

*Who:*  Between a top person of a team and each member of that team separately.
*What:*  A discussion of effectiveness areas, measurement areas, blockages and assistance needed.
*Objective:* To strengthen the relationship between the top person and the team member.
*When:*  Whenever needed; start soon.
*Where:*  In the team member's office or in a conference room, but not in the top member's office.

The design of this meeting and the associated activities involve the following topics.

- The team member's prework
- The top person's prework
- The one-to-one meeting agenda
- The checkpoint meeting
- The one-to-one meeting cycle
- Paperwork and records
- The value of the one-to-one meeting
- A comparison with traditional appraisal.

*The team member's prework*
The team member's prework for the one-to-one meeting requires seven lists, as follows.

1 Effectiveness areas of the unit.
2 Effectiveness areas of self.
3 Blockages to own effectiveness within the company.
4 Blockages to own effectiveness between self and the team top person.
5 Blockages to own effectiveness within self.
6 The team member's objectives.
7 Top person's assistance required.

If the team members have had no prior training in output orientation, and no prior discussion about their own unit's role in the company, carrying out this prework becomes a formidable task. Usually, however, the team members will have participated in the team meeting at which effectiveness areas were established. There will also have been participation in the most important team meeting. At this meeting all the ı  ̣s of the one-to-one meeting prework were discussed at length and now the time has come to pin them down.

The effectiveness areas for the unit should have been fairly well established at the team meeting, and all team members in the unit and the top person should have agreed on a single set. In addition, the set should be seen as flexible, and a constant airing of the effectiveness areas in an attempt to improve them is useful. When a team member is asked to list the effectiveness areas of the unit and the top person, it can be found to be rather difficult.

The next three parts of the prework allow a team member to deal directly with perceived blockages to effectiveness. Without this, team members report, it would be difficult, or even impossible, to clear the air sufficiently such that the one-to-one meeting gets off the ground and is productive. Even a willingness to list these blockages requires a degree of candour and trust not always present in an organization. The 3-D MES and the team meeting lead directly to these conditions being produced.

The team members move on to cast their objectives as soundly as possible, together with measurement areas and programmes of activities. This section will take the most time; it is also the one where some outside assistance may be most needed.

Finally, the team members list the top person's assistance required. At times this space is left blank. The team member has both a clear road and competence, and knows it.

*The top person's prework*
The top person's prework for the one-to-one meeting requires making two lists. The prework is indeed little. This is an important and deliberate part of the meeting design. The responsibility for objective setting is thrown on to the team member, not the top person. The combination of the 3-D MES and team meeting help to ensure that the team member is willing to accept such responsibility.

The two lists are:

1  Effectiveness areas of the unit of which the team member and the top person are part.
2  Effectiveness areas of the team member alone.

In addition, the top person considers the team member's

- past effectiveness;
- blockages to effectiveness;
- potential for effectiveness;
- assistance requirement for improved effectiveness.

This prework will take about one to two hours per team member.

The unit effectiveness areas are usually agreed fairly quickly if the one-to-one meeting is preceded by a team meeting, otherwise this topic may take a long time. However, this is an important question to settle as a team member could not possibly set their own objectives without first having a full understanding of the unit effectiveness areas. When (as often arises naturally) the effectiveness areas of the top person also get worked out and agreed, some team members have a better insight into the blockages they thought existed. Some, on coming to understand the top person's effectiveness areas more clearly, remove many of the blockages that they had intended to bring up. This leads naturally to the discussion of the team member's effectiveness areas. When these are agreed, at least one-half of the important work is done.

When dealing with blockages, both sides should work to eliminate as many as possible, but they should be candid enough to accept those things that cannot be changed. Indeed some company blockages may remain as blockages for ever. And human beings, none of whom are 100 per cent flexible, may have difficulty in changing behaviour which gets them into trouble. First, blockages have to be stated clearly on both sides. Whether or not they can be changed is not the issue at this point, candour concerning them is. The top person is usually able to identify some in the three areas mentioned which the team member did not think of.

## A comparison with traditional appraisal

To understand the one-to-one meeting more clearly, compare it with the usual appraisal meeting:

|  | *Old* | *New* |
|---|---|---|
| Time focus | Primarily past | Primarily future |
| Time taken | ½ to 1 hour | 4–8 hours |
| Role of top person | Judge | Counsellor/helper |
| Role of team member | The judged | The initiator |
| Focus of evaluation | What went wrong last year – personality variables | What will go right next year – performance |
| Objective | Evaluation | Planning |
| Location of meeting | Top person's office | Team member's office |

| Help by top person | None | How help can be given to team member |
|---|---|---|
| Typical use | To reward, punish and, to some extent, career plan | To motivate |
| Communication of appraisal | Sometimes not revealed to team member | Always revealed to team member |

## THE INTERTEAM MEETING

The objective of the interteam meeting is to solve outstanding problems between two functions. Typically this might be production and marketing or it might be design and engineering or engineering and production or headquarters and field. A great deal can be done in one day using this type of meeting.

A crucial step in most effectiveness programmes is the resolution of non-productive blockages between organization subparts. These subparts may be staff-line, union-management, head office-field, production-sales or research-production. At the interteam meeting, each team describes its own objectives and effectiveness. The customary differences between the two sets of statements leads directly to a discussion which has proved to be extremely effective on resolving blockages.

This interteam activity has been particularly helpful in improving effectiveness of the operations of international affiliates. Intercultural misunderstandings are nothing new, but resolving them through behavioural intervention is.

### Topics for interteam meeting

The interteam meeting lasts a day and has a somewhat unusual design.

*Suggested Topics for Interteam Meeting*

- How do you see yourselves?
- How do you see the others?
- How do they see you?
- Why are there differences/distortions?

- What do you want them to do?
- What will you agree to?


Without any advance discussion between the two teams, they are asked to go to team rooms, or opposite ends of the room, and make three lists. The first list is headed: 'How do you see yourselves?'; the second is: 'How do you see the other team?'; and the third list is: 'How do you think they see you?' Teams normally see themselves as embodiment of the ten points of the Scout law: trusty, loyal, helpful, brotherly, courteous, kind, obedient, smiling, thrifty and pure in body and mind. They also help old people across the street. The other team is normally described as rigid, uncooperative, ignorant and sometimes more. Marketing is routinely described by production as 'a bunch of drunks'. This is not always a misperception! In the third list, 'How do you think that they see you?', there is often inaccuracy. Sometimes teams know exactly how they are perceived, sometimes they get it completely wrong. These three lists are then brought back to the meeting-room and read out. They are not discussed, simply read. The person conducting the meeting – and someone *is* needed – then raises the key issue: 'There seems to be a perception problem here', and that is exactly what it is. Teams are then asked to return to their team area and to make a list of why the distortions arose and what is maintaining them. This leads to thoughtful discussion. Again, the teams come back and discuss the distortion. It is the first time they have ever done anything like this. They are being reflective about the problems between them.

The teams are then asked to make a list of what they would like the other team to do for them which would improve their own team's effectiveness, without lowering the effectiveness of the other team. This is a key question. These lists are then exchanged and each team asked what it will do.

This meeting never results in a decrease in interteam effectiveness. At times effectiveness is not increased by very much, but most times it is increased enormously. Teams realize that they have been playing silly games with each other rather than getting on with the issue of output orientation. Obviously this meeting has exceptional high cost-benefits in conflict situations.

It is fairly easy to indentify which teams should participate in this kind of meeting. Make both a vertical and horizontal list of teams or subunits, look at each intersect and put an X where there is a problem. The Xs show the places for the interteam meeting. In some situations it is definitely highly advantageous if all participants have participated in an 'unfreezing' meeting such as the 3-D MES beforehand.


## THE CORPORATE STRATEGY MEETING

The objective of the corporate strategy meeting is to improve company strategy. It is usually attended only by the top team of the organization, but others might be included if they can add to it . . .

Some of the decisions made at the corporate strategy meeting relate to what changes are likely to take place in our technology and our market-place?

- philosophy of management
- what business the company is in
- optimal organization chart
- organization development strategy
- corporate government relations
- corporate five-year goals
- career policy
- product policy
- top team members' responsibilities
- liability resource inventory
- management manpower inventory.

The importance of the decisions varies with the organization as does the work already done on each. Through a variety of structured activities and measuring devices these areas are held up for inspection, and plans are made to modify them if necessary.

*Suggested topics for Corporate Strategy Meeting*

- Where is our organization today?
- How has the environment changed?
- What can we do best?
- What business are we in?
- What business should we be in?
- How do we get there?

Any top team will have considered these questions previously; the Corporate Strategy Meeting provides a longer period and a freer discussion climate in which to arrive at an optimum solution to which all are committed.

This meeting has a profound impact on the organization because important changes usually follow it. An analysis of such changes has revealed that they are often ones that the executive had wished to make for some time but has had neither the opportunity nor time to tackle or think through to an agreed decision. This meeting frequently leads to the decision to establish a series of management project teams charged with casting optimum policies and procedures for the organization.

The issues that need exploring are forthcoming changes in technology and competition and in the environment. The environment might include, for instance, a change of government or a change of government policy or results of a government commission. A powerful question which forces participants to come to grips with some sticky issues is along the lines of 'If we had 100 units of discretionary capital over the next five years to spend in any way we wanted, how would we spend it?' This single question has resulted in what was virtually a 24-hour continuous discussion by the top team of a major fish packers. It was concerned mainly with whether the larger amount should be spent on improving processing plants, improving the trawler fleet, or research and development (R & D). In fact R & D won out, and it was almost certain that this was correct.

It is unreasonable to expect that a firm can go away for two or three days and come back with a complete corporate strategy. The initial meeting should be seen as just that. The key part of the action plan may be headed: 'How will we follow up on this?'

## The precise questions

Here are the precise questions developed for a major oil company for their Corporate Strategy Meeting.

1  *Market developments*
   Rank from 1 to 5 the five market developments which will most affect the organization over the next five years.
2  *Technological developments*
   Rank from 1 to 5 the five technological developments which will most affect the organization over the next five years.
3  *Competitive actions*
   Rank from 1 to 5 the five changes competitors are likely to make which will most affect the organization over the next five years.
4  *Government actions*

Rank from 1 to 5 the five government actions likely to be made which will most affect the organization over the next five years.

5   *Optimum production facilities for the present*
    What should the optimum location, size and type of production facilities for the organization be now?

6   *Executive committee effectiveness areas*
    In what ten ways would the company be different in five years' time if the executive committee were highly effective over the next few years?

7   *Strengths and weaknesses*

    (a)   What are the three major strengths of the company now compared to its competitors?
    (b)   What are the three major weaknesses of the company now compared to its competitors?

8   *Critical areas*
    Suppose the organization does not meet its return on investment, or other objectives, over the next five years. Agree on the reasons which would most probably explain it.

9   *Past decisions*
    For the main decisions affecting the organization over the last five years, agree which were:

    (a)   good decisions but should have been made earlier;
    (b)   good decisions but implementation should have been delayed;
    (c)   good decisions and made at the right time;
    (d)   poor decisions in the light of subsequent events.

10  *Actual past policies*
    Compose short paragraphs stating clearly what the actual organization policy has been for the past five years concerning: marketing, finance, manufacturing, procurement, personnel, research and development, product diversification and acquisition.

11  *Acquisition policy*
    Rank from 1 to 5 the five most important criteria by which an acquisition should be appraised.

12  *Business we are in*
    Compose a short paragraph outlining each of the following:

    (a)   the business the company is in now;
    (b)   the business the company could and should be in in five years.

13  *Product policy*
    What is a desirable product mix, by sales percentage, for five
    years' time?
14  *Proposed policies*
    Compose short paragraphs stating clearly what is the best
    achievable policy for the next five years concerning marketing,
    finance, manufacturing, procurement, personnel, research and
    development, product diversification and acquisition. Add
    others as you wish.
15  *Five-year predictions*
    Create lists on these for five years hence:

    (a)  product line accounting for greatest profit;
    (b)  most profitable product-line accounting for at least 10 per
         cent of profit;
    (c)  sales volume;
    (d)  sales distribution by geographic areas.

16  *Priorities for capital*
    Rank capital priorities based on the return on investment
    potential over five years. Also distribute 100 units of new
    money as it should be allocated over five years.
17  *Finance*
    Identify the feasible major sources of financing and the
    approximate amounts you think obtainable for the next five
    years.

**Corporate strategy meeting – first or last?**

Some senior managers, quite naturally, think that all programmes
to increase output orientation should start with the Corporate
Strategy Meeting. The argument runs that if you don't know where
you are going, why start? While this argument is sound, it is not
always the best way to go. One counter-argument is that before
the top team attempts to build the organization, one should improve
the working of the top team. Suppose the top team is not unfrozen
and its members hardly talk to one another. Surely, the 3-D MES
should come first, to loosen things up a bit? Suppose the top team
is quite unclear about the roles of the top team members, suppose
there are nights of the long knives or suppose the team is really
poor at making decisions. Clearly, the team meeting should precede
the Corporate Strategy Meeting. What tends to happen on the
ground is that many of these types of meetings, or parts of them,
run in parallel rather than in series. Naturally things start with the

3-D MES or a version of it. Then the issue is raised, 'What shall we do next?' It may well be a normal full team meeting. Or, if the team is sufficiently mature and ready to discuss serious issues in a competent way, then it might be possible to move sensibly directly to the Corporate Strategy Meeting.

## THE LARGE GROUP MEETING

The Large Group Meeting is somewhat unusual but always very successful. It might consist of anything from 30 to 300 people, they may or may not be managers. It is highly participative and is not, in any way, the top person making a statement about the future or statements from the floor arguing for narrow and defensive positions. It consists of one to three days' problem-solving and determining what is best for the organization on a particular issue. Typically it is used as an excellent way to reorganize. It might be used to improve personnel policies or improve profitability. The basic idea is to tap the best ideas of a large number of people in a short time.

In most organizations there are seldom more than two levels present at a decision meeting. For most decisions this is normal and appropriate. In an effectiveness programme or in a flexible organization, however, much benefit can be achieved by holding a meeting at which several levels are present to decide the best way to resolve problems for which co-operation from the several levels is essential. The Large Group Meeting is a meeting designed to build strong vertical bonds in the organization and to obtain commitment at several levels.

The meeting has a variety of designs to suit particular purposes. One design had five levels represented by only ten people, including a manager and team, the manager's superior, the superior's superior, and on up to division manager and the chief executive officer (CEO). The formal agenda was a review of the teams' objectives set for the coming year. Having a long vertical chain represented at this meeting ensures that all levels are committed to objectives and that troublesome interlevel blockages are ironed out on the spot. Some companies hold these annually for every district or department, with the five or so levels being represented at this single meeting of ten people. The most common agenda is the lower teams' planned objectives and the impact of organization policies on the likelihood of their being achieved.

## Topics for Large Group Meeting

The Large Group Meeting might have virtually any topic discussed. The limiting factor is that those present must be able to contribute to the discussion.

*Suggested topics for Large Group Meeting*
● Reorganization
● System introduction
● Ideas for change

Widely used topics for the Large Group Meeting would concern reorganization, the best method of introduction of a new system such as management information system or a new company planning system, or simply, ideas for changes. These changes might concern changes that would improve productivity.

One highly creative and effective top person once addressed a Large Group Meeting with this question: 'How can I lower your resistance to change?' The top person got away with it!

## The design of the Large group meeting

The basic design of the Large Group Meeting which has been widely used and found to be effective is as follows:

● Teams of four to five
● Team rooms
● 10′ x 10′ screen
● Overhead transparency
● Session one, 1730–2230
● Overnight summary
● Session two, 0800–1530.

The team size should be four to five as this encourages greater participation. A team size much over seven definitely lowers creativity and participation level. If possible, teams should have team rooms to go to, but if this is too expensive (always a fundamental question), then they might have team areas in a large room. It is useful to have a 10′ x 10′ screen and an overhead transparency projector. Thus each team gives rapid feedback on what they think to everyone else in the room. Teams simply write their outputs on an overhead transparency sheet.

If the meeting is held overnight, the first session usually runs from 1730 hours to 2230 hours. Teams report back at that point. If the matter concerns company reorganization, the period between 2230 and midnight is, to say the least, high drama! Staff make an overnight summary of all team outputs and this is ready for the 0800 start, so that every team has a copy of what every other team proposed. Then, usually, the teams are asked to repeat the task in the light of the first pass. For more complex problems two or three passes might be made.

Here is an example. An organization decided that they wanted to reorganize. They rented a hotel ballroom, 150 rooms for people to sleep in and about 15 other rooms for teams to meet in. There was one item of prework and that was to draw the organization's structure for levels one, two and three which could be achieved in about a year. They worked in teams until 2230 and then came back to the main room with their answer. (If the team does not agree they are told to keep on working.) All agreed and drew their new organization chart on an overhead transparency and presented it to the main group.

One does not get consensus with 150 people very easily, so with failure to agree, the participants go back to their teams and have another go. One makes successive approximations over the duration of the meeting. On the last day the company CEO may say, 'I will appoint a group from level three to look at all the data and ask them, within two weeks, to give me one organization chart which best represents all you've said'.

I am often asked to advise on difficult reorganization issues. The large group meeting is the method that I use. While an outside consultant may well help with the design of the meeting, it should be absolutely clear that the top person is running it. The outside consultant never appears at the front of the meeting. The consultant's job is to help with the design, not with running the meeting.


## A SUMMARY OF THE FIVE TYPES OF MEETING

### The team meeting

*Attendance:*    Each management team consisting of a top person and all immediate team members.
*Duration:*      Three days.

*Main topics addressed:*

- Unit effectiveness areas and measurement areas.

- Top person and team member effectiveness areas and measurement areas.
- Outstanding problems to solve.
- Team organization.
- Team meeting methods.
- Team and team member effectiveness.
- Evaluation of style of team top person and team members.

*Main outcomes:*

- Team operating skills.
- More effective working relationships with the unit.
- Commitment to plans and objectives.
- More effective conflict management.
- Better at giving and receiving feedback.
- Team-building.
- Team reorganization.
- Role clarity.
- Agreement to solve several outstanding problems.
- Appraisal of top person and team member style and suggestions for improvement.
- Appraisal of top person and team member effectiveness with suggestions for improvement.

**The one-to-one meeting**

*Attendance:*  Each top person/team member pair.
*Duration:*  Half to one day.

*Main topics addressed:*

- Effectiveness areas.
- Measurement areas.
- Objectives.
- Plans.
- Blockages.
- Resources needed.

*Main outcomes:*

- Open communications with top person.
- Strengthening of working relationships with top person.
- Setting objectives and making plans.
- Removal of obstacles to effectiveness.

- Commitment to plans and objectives.
- Agreement on effectiveness areas and measurement areas for team, top person and team member.

## The interteam meeting

*Attendance:*   Two units, departments or functions.
*Duration:*      One day.

*Main topics addressed:*

- Perceptions by team of others and selves.
- Greater understanding of why these perceptions or misperceptions were created and are maintained.
- Clarity on what each team wants the other team to do to improve effectiveness.
- Agreement on an action plan for each team in terms of helping one another.

*Main outcomes:*

- Openness and candour.
- Clear perception of reality.
- Understanding of interaction of unit roles.
- Effective working relationships between the units.
- Commitment to plans for mutual support.
- Effective conflict management.

## The corporate strategy meeting

*Attendance:*   Top team.
*Duration:*      Three days.

*Main topics addressed:*

- Analysis of environment and changing environment.
- Analysis of match of organization to environment and changing environment.
- Action plan to match corporate strategy with future environment.
- Frank appraisal of past business decisions.

*Main outcomes:*

- Clear perception of market needs.

- Reappraisal of business decisions.
- Formal and informal structure and organization style reflecting market needs.
- Commitment to corporate plans.
- Improved monitoring of the environment.
- Increased openness across top team on business decisions.

**The large group meeting**

*Attendance:* A vertically reporting chain of managers and selected colleagues.
*Duration:* One day.

*Main topics addressed:*

- (Essentially, any topic can be addressed.)
- Organization change.
- How to introduce change.
- Organization policies.
- Personnel policies.
- Organization structure.
- Ideas for profit improvement.

*Main outcomes:*

- Creativity concerning topic.
- Improved decision-making concerning topic.
- Lowering resistance to change to implementation of ideas concerning topic.
- Increased commitment to ideas created.
- Action plan with responsibilities to implement ideas.
- Creation of open climate in organization.

## LINKING MEETING TYPES TO PLANNED CHANGE OBJECTIVES

The meetings used need to be linked to the planned change objectives decided upon. Here are some abbreviated examples which demonstrate that linking. Also of importance here is the sequence in which the meetings are held. In addition to the five meeting types described in this chapter, the 3-D MES is included.

**Unfreezing the organization – as a planned change objective**

If the planned change objective is unfreezing the organization, and only that, then the meeting to use is the 3-D MES. This seminar may be used for management development alone. The assumption, then, is that the forces in the organization will be such that the ideas transmitted on the Managerial Effectiveness Seminar can be used by the managers involved. It may be that a change in the organization is planned and, perhaps, it is inevitable. The idea then becomes one of how one can best get managers ready to cope with this change. If a particular change is considered, such as some new system introduction, it would be very advisable to consider a large group meeting on the topic of how to help get that system implemented easily and well.

**Management revitalization – as a planned change objective**

Management revitalization is a rather broad objective. Certainly, it would appear to need to start with the 3-D MES. Depending upon perceptions of why the management needed revitalization, the next meeting type could be any of team, one-to-one or large group. If it was felt that teamwork was seriously lacking and top people did not talk enough to team members, then the team meeting would be suggested. If it was felt that objectives, planning, review and appraisal were very poor, then the one-to-one meeting would be suggested if it was felt that this would improve things. If it was felt useful to address the issue such that everybody would realize what was needed, and was willing to work to achieve it, then the large group meeting would be suggested.

**Management by objectives – as a planned change objective**

Whether or not the 3-D MES is used depends on the degree of unfreezing considered necessary. Perhaps the organization is considered to be unfrozen enough already, this meeting type would not be used. Very broadly, management by objectives can be implemented on a one-over-one basis – 95 per cent of the implementations use this method – or on a team basis. The decision will have to be made whether one moves first to a team meeting or first to a one-on-one meeting. As the introduction of management by objectives is essentially a system introduction, it would be most advisable to consider a large group meeting to consider how his new system can be introduced easily and well.

## Developing marketing orientation – as a planned change objective

The meeting strategy used to help develop a marketing orientation depends very much on the analysis of the reasons that the marketing orientation does not now exist. A common reason for lack of marketing orientation is that for one reason or another a firm, and possibly its founder, grew increasingly proud of the technology and spent most time and energy on that rather than on the market. This would lead naturally to high power in production and low power in marketing. At some point, the interteam meeting is suggested, but do not start there. Unless there has been a clear message from the top, 'We will become marketing-orientated', such a meeting would not be very productive. Again, the 3-D MES is without question a good start as a major unfreezing of attitudes is certainly required. Then, at least for the marketing team, a team meeting should be held to give them some strength of purpose in dealing with the takeover of marketing from production. One-to-one meetings would not help with this planned change objective, nor would the corporate strategy meeting. What is being worked on here is not corporate strategy, but relative power across marketing and production.

## Merger – as a planned change objective

The method outlined in this book has often been used to facilitate a merger. The 3-D MES is often used as it provides both groups with a common language and a common management philosophy. This can be critical. It so often happens in merger situations that there are two quite different organization climates, languages, operating methods, and so on. The 3-D MES goes a long way to suggest a common, all-embracing climate language and philosophy which both sides can use. An interteam meeting is a crucial next step. As so many issues are to be discussed, it is better for the interteam meeting to last for three days rather than one. The two extra days are needed for attending to additional detail on the action plan. Usually there are one or two team meetings; one of these is held about six months later when more issues that need to be addressed have surfaced.

**CASE STUDY**

Using the case study, described in Chapter 3, one can improve
one's understanding of the use of the 3-D MES and the five meeting
types to improve effectiveness and output orientation in general.
Given below is the organization chart and the objectives the organization actually chose. You may wish to review the additional detail
on the organization given in Chapter 3, and then make a draft
meetings plan. Your plan should give a general idea of what meetings should be held and the sequence; if the large group meeting
is held the topic should be noted and, where possible, who should
attend the various meetings. Comments on, and suggested solutions
to, the meeting plan for the case study are given on p. 152.

**Case study: the farm machinery manufacturer**

The case study for the farm machinery manufacturer is described
in detail on pp. 58–61. The organization chart is repeated below as
Figure 8.1.
   The planned change objectives selected by the farm machinery
manufacturer were:

- Role clarification
- Improved organization effectiveness
- Improved managerial effectiveness
- Improved profit planning
- Introduce MBO
- Increase output of new ideas
- Management revitalization.

**Your planned meetings for the farm machinery manufacturer**

Indicate what your plan for meetings would be for the situation
described in this case study.

My proposed meetings planned to achieve the planned change
objectives for farm machinery manufacturer are as follows:

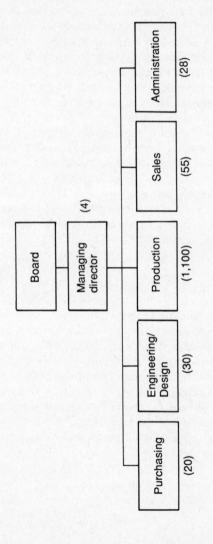

*Figure 8.1*  Case study: the farm machinery manufacturer

### Farm machinery manufacturer – what happened?

This is a conventional production system that needs revitalization
Here there is a well-established approach. First, a decision is to be
made whether or not the 3-D MES, or some version of it, needs
to be used. Then there should be a team meeting for the managing
director and the four people reporting to that position. Further
there would be five more team meetings for the five subordinate
teams. The only exception might be that, in some situations, where
the administration group were largely clerical or almost completely
clerical, then a team meeting might be inappropriate. A corporate
strategy meeting is not needed as it is very unlikely the corporate
strategy will change. There is no evidence that they will move out
of the farm machinery business.

There certainly should be one-to-one meetings, starting with the
managing director and the five subordinates and then flowing down
wards. This would help cause everyone to be rather sharper on
what are the real outputs of the positions. There could well be a
large group meeting on such topics as 'How can we lower costs?'
or better, 'How can we increase profits?' All this is essentially what
happened. They did in fact hold two large group meetings, one on
each of the indicated topics.

### SUMMARY

This chapter has outlined five meeting types. They are not meeting
in a conventional sense. They are really methods of getting people
together to talk about the right things with a shared interest in
effectiveness and output orientation. Not all meetings are needed
for all situations, but normally one or two will be required. There
is no proposed sequence of meetings, again this will depend upon
the situation. Whether these meetings are used with particular
designs proposed is not the real issue. The real issue is that *some
thing* along these lines should be done in your organization.

# 9 Planning the output-oriented organization

> The fundamental qualities for good execution of a plan are, first, naturally, intelligence; then discernment and judgment, which enable one to recognize the best methods to attain it; then singleness of purpose; and, lastly, what is most essential of all, will – stubborn will.
>
> Marshal Foch

> I find the real thing in this world is not so much where we stand, as in what direction we are moving.
>
> Oliver Wendell Holmes

This chapter provides you with a format for an Outputs Planning meeting. This meeting is so designed as to encourage you and your team to think about both your own team and lower-level teams and to apply the ideas presented in this book. Essentially, the meeting is to help you become more output-oriented in your own part of the organization by planning to achieve it. Since you have reached this far in the book you are clearly interested and must think that there is something here that might be helpful to your organization. The issue you should now be concerned about is: 'How can I get others interested too?' You will need to consider whether this meeting is the best approach for your team. It has worked for many teams but it may or may not work for yours.

The main point is to get the team away to discuss the right things. As you read through this chapter, you will need to think about the Outputs Planning Meeting along the following lines:

1 Who should attend?
2 When should it be held?
3 How will we get everyone to do the prework?
4 What should be its duration?
5 Do we need any outside help?

## TEAM CHANGE PROBLEMS

Many problems are common to most teams which inhibit the change process. They arise quite naturally; it is therefore important to understand them:

*Team change problems*

- 'Cannot get there'
- 'Them not us'
- Devalue positive past
- Doubt own capacity
- Overvalue novelty
- Time shortage

*'Cannot get there'*
Some teams believe that certain objectives are completely unattainable. Sometimes this belief arises from ignorance, more often it arises from resistance to change.

*'Them not us'*
Fortunately, it is many years since teams thought the problem was always 'them not us'. This thinking normally leads to courses for supervisors. Teams should heed Pogo's comment 'We have seen the enemy and it is us.'

*Devalue positive past*
To start a programme of planned change and general improvement in effectiveness it is not necessary, at all, to believe that one is less effective. There is no need to devalue a positive past. If an organization survives, it is indication enough that someone must be doing something right. To say that one wants to get better does not mean that one is not so good now. In fact, the truism is that the good companies are the ones most wishing to advance. The better get better.

*Doubt own capacity*
Some doubt their own capacity for change. We all know change is difficult. If change has been relatively unnecessary for several years, then facing change can be a problem. However, people being people, and environments being environments, unplanned change will occur anyway. Planned change is better. Then you are in control.

## Overvalue novelty

Even highly intelligent managers sometimes prefer novelty to reality to help them solve problems. This approach arises from a lack of thought, and might take the form of a new book that sold a million copies or a persuasive speaker, or something that General Motors did last year. But these new ideas might not fit the needs of your system. There are many good ideas around now. The issue is to pick the one that fits your system, not the one that is 'hot'.

## Time shortage

Shortage of time is a genuine team change problem. What is not understood well enough is that change is part of the manager's job. The manager has the operational job and also the change job: two jobs, not one. This will not go away, it is a simple fact and one has to decide whether the extra work – and work it is – is worth the effort. This is a difficult decision.

# FIVE MINIMUM CONDITIONS FOR AN OUTPUT ORIENTATION PROGRAMME

The minimum conditions for success in an output orientation programme are: adequate training in outputs and unfreezing; team commitment; measurable objectives; team training; and a flexible plan. Before you embark on your output orientation programme, reflect on the degree to which your organization has each of these and, as needed, how these conditions might be obtained or improved.

## Adequate training in outputs and unfreezing

Before a social system can be changed it needs to be able to question the past and the present and to be willing to change things that need changing. In social science jargon this is called unfreezing.

## Team commitment

Most output orientation programmes fail because they lack commitment from the whole team.

## Measurable objectives

If measurable objectives for change targets are not developed for an output orientation programme, it is likely to fail as no clear direction has been established. It will often take some time for a team to create a sound programme with a clear set of measurable objectives.

*Team training*
An output orientation programme will produce only minimal returns unless a company succeeds in making the big jump from individual to team training. It is undoubtedly team training that separates average from good change programmes.

*A flexible plan*
It is sometimes difficult to predict the course of an output orientation programme because the company's situation for the years ahead is not always clear. The one anticipated consequence of change is unanticipated consequences. Therefore, it is necessary always to have options ready to present. Alternatives should be available for the total programme and for the various units, especially the teams which are involved.

**Sound planning**
As you will know, planning is difficult. The main problem with planning is that managers do not like to do it, and therefore do not do it. There is little doubt that the more effective firms plan more effectively. Apart from not doing it, there are other errors in planning which you might keep in mind when you are thinking about planning for the output-oriented organization:

1 Planning only two to four activities when many more are needed.
2 Not recognizing that for many objectives several activities may proceed simultaneously.
3 Becoming so fascinated by the plan that its associated objective is seen as secondary.
4 Failure to review a plan when the objective is not met.
5 Omission of key activities.
6 Failure to allow for activities of others that might hinder one's own plan.
7 No review of progress.
8 Stating activities vaguely, so that their completion is uncertain.

**YOUR PLANNING FOR OUTPUTS**

Each of these planning steps essentially encourages you to think about the key ideas in this book and relate them to your organization, or your part of the organization. They can be used for the organization as a whole as well as a subpart of it. The eight planning steps are:

1 Change target planning.
2 Change objectives planning.
3 Change target climate planning.
4 Managerial style planning.
5 Output planning.
6 Managerial Effectiveness Seminar planning.
7 Meetings planning.
8 Staffing planning.

By far the best approach is for each member of the team to answer all of these planning issues as individuals and then meet together to reach consensus on what you collectively agree is best.

# PART II

# Case Studies

## INTRODUCTION TO PART II

The chapters in Part II give actual case studies on creating the output-oriented organizations. None of the eight case studies in Chapters 10–17 were written by the author or his associates, and they had no influence on the presentation format or the facts produced. They were written by client organization staff or by journalists. Chapter 18 contains brief summaries of client approaches to improving output orientation, normally written by the consultant directly involved.

All the case studies show, at least, some success, and a few are without question completely successful. These case studies reflect aspects of what happens when the ideas in this book are implemented.

### Creating higher output orientation in a 35,000-person organization

How does one create change in a large bank? Chapter 10 gives many ideas: this already large bank later merged with a bank about one-third of its size and used most of the ideas in this book in making things work well. Profits went up from $100 million to about $400 million over a four-year period. Profit is not the only measure of organization effectiveness, but certainly things did look much better to all concerned.

### The Chief Executive Officer who changed his organization

The case study in Chapter 11 is an account of how a chief executive (CEO) implemented the ideas of an output orientation into his company, resulting in huge success. Of particular interest to readers is that he did it on his own, with outside help, using the concept of output orientation. Naturally this would be much harder to do for a larger organization, if only for the increased time requirements of the CEO and the consequent delay in moving down level by level. Dramatic change in an organization leading to an enormous profit increase can be traced easily to the top person deciding to implement ideas of output orientation, and then doing it. This case study is an example of just this. The change involved all the best elements of effectiveness, the use of various styles, organization development and management by objectives. We can argue about what these terms mean, but we may know instinctively – this CEO did.

## Change in Falconbridge Nickel Mines

It can be rather hard to create change in a nickel mine of 5,000 people. However, it can be done, and the case study in Chapter 12 supplies many examples of actual effects which lead to improved effectiveness.

## Change in a power commission

Chapter 13 is a detailed account of a comprehensive organization development programme. Some organizations use only part of the output orientation programme. Some organizations use only part of the output orientation approach – normally this is the 3-D Management Effectiveness Seminar (3-D MES). Some use only one or two meeting types. This power commission used all types of meetings.

## Change in a national subsidiary of International Computers Ltd

Chapter 14 shows how insights into management style can greatly improve co-operation and team work.

## Change in John Player & Sons

Chapter 15 concerns change in a 5,000-employee cigarette manufacturing firm. The emphasis is on climate change and management style change.

## Change in Siemens, West Germany

Chapter 16 is concerned with managerial effectiveness improvement in one of the world's leading electrical manufacturers. This multinational organization used the 3-D MES, in part, for the common language it could provide to the managers in several different countries in which it operated.

## Change in Arthur Young & Co.

Chapter 17 reviews this company's approach to team-building, as reported by an employee who not only attended the 3-D MES himself, but also interviewed and spoke with over 70 other participants. The objective of the study was to find out if the seminar had been of considerable use in business and personal life. For the majority the team skills incorporated in the 3-D MES were valuable.

## Other case studies

Chapter 18 contains eight more cases. These are abbreviated case studies, showing a variety of applications. They comprise:

- The use of the 3-D MES for General Motors foremen.
- Improving managerial effectiveness in Ethiopia.
- Introducing output orientation in a government power utility.
- Increased profit in a UK division of an international packaging group.
- Changes in an international petrochemical plant contractor.

# 10 Change in a 35,000-person organization

## A BANK PREPARING FOR ORGANIZATION CHANGE AND A MERGER

- I am committed to the participative style of management.
- Whatever faults we may have had, we were greatly assisted by the high level of trust within the organization.
- Australia is no longer an extension of Europe – geographically it is in the Western Pacific and its future is increasingly bound up with the fortunes of the Western Pacific – and so it was that the name of Westpac was chosen.
- On the first day of the new (merged) bank, the advertising campaign commenced with messages such as:
  - 'The competition is open'
  - 'We are the competition'
  - 'We are changing'
  - 'Normal service will never be resumed. We are rolling up our sleeves!'

This chapter is based largely on talks given by two senior members of an Australian bank which currently has 35,000 employees. The first talk was given by Bob White, chief executive officer (CEO) of Westpac Banking Corporation to a meeting of the International Monetary Conference held in Boston. The second was given by Geoff Thompson, Chief Manager Merger, of the then Bank of New South Wales to the Australian Institute of Management organization development (OD) group in Sydney, New South Wales. (Each talk has been edited, in the main, by omitting sections which deal generally with changes in banking rather than how the bank introduced output orientation.) So far over 1,700 managers from the CEO down have completed the 3-D Management Effectiveness Seminar (3-D MES). There have been about fifty team meetings, starting with the top team and moving downward through the organization, and several Large Group Meetings, addressing such issues as reorganization, changes in personnel policy and how to make the merger effective. As seen by the bank, the environment was changing rapidly and was about to change even more rapidly. A government Commission was expected to propose that foreign banks could enter the market, as it did, and this would produce an even greater need for a flexible response. That, together with a new CEO with deeply held views about output orientation, led to the start of this organization development programme, which has been described as the largest and most successful in the world.

Some minor additions have been made to each article to elaborate on any points made and all of these additions are given in parentheses. The numbers of branches and the numbers of employees vary somewhat as a function of being pre- and post-merger.

At the outset of the programme, the bank's annual profit was $100 million. Some senior managers were somewhat embarrassed at how high it was. After a few years the profit had increased to approximately $400 million. Obviously it would be impossible to attribute a percentage of variance in the change of profit to any particular item. Without question, the critical element was the new CEO. However, there is a widespread view in the bank that the output orientation programme did help a great deal. Looking at the increase in annual profit, it is clear that the cost-effectiveness of the programme bordered on the enormous.

## EXTRACTS FROM TALK GIVEN BY BOB WHITE, CEO OF WESTPAC

When I became Chief Executive Officer (CEO), it was easy to make the decision to change. It was also easy to develop a broad diagnosis. We had to:

- unfreeze the organization;
- become more responsive;
- develop more disciplined planning and objective setting;
- move faster and compete harder.

In addition, we had to do this through 1,300 branches and 25,000 people.

I am committed to the participative style of management, and this influenced me towards the ideas of a Canadian consultant, Bill Reddin, whose speciality can be summed up as: 'how to help any type of organization be successful in a programme of self-directed change.' His methods were used to help the bank's own management team to sharpen up its own diagnosis and develop its own remedies. For us, this approach was much preferred to the overwhelming embrace of any major international management consultant. It was also much cheaper.

And so the bank began a programme of organization development (OD). Reddin's approach appealed to me because he said OD was about getting people together in what, at times, are unusual combinations to talk about what they should talk about anyway, in an atmosphere of candour and willingness to change.

I will dwell on some of the components of this programme because it was so successful in bringing about a change in attitudes, and therefore in bringing about a more ready acceptance of the need for a change in the way we do things:

- A team of bank personnel were trained by Reddin as OD advisers.
- Ultimately over 1,700 managers, from and including the CEO down, attended the six day off-site 3-D Managerial Effectiveness Seminar.
- Managers in administration learned to define their jobs in output terms.
- Managers, as a result of the seminars, developed a clearer sense of their own management styles, of the appropriateness of particular management styles to particular situations, and of the incompatibilities between a particular individual's style and the requirements of the job.
- The seminars provided both self-assessment and peer assessment of management styles – 'am I an autocrat?', 'am I an executive?' or 'am I a missionary?'

At the end of the seminar process, the entire management structure of the bank had a common culture and a common language. The organization had already begun the process of 'unfreezing', and it was ready to address seriously the process of change.

Whatever faults we may have had, we were greatly assisted by the high level of trust within the organization. The level of trust helped to improve the level of candour which was so essential to the process of change.

The next step was a new organization structure – without it, the motivation to continue to change might well be lost. The last such organization change was more than a decade ago and was developed by a few in the top management without consultation, and announced to the network without notice.

We wanted to do it again, but differently. As a starting-point, 80 officers of varying grades of seniority and from right across the bank were invited to a weekend retreat (i.e. Large Group Meeting). They worked in fourteen teams with progressive plenary sessions, and their task was to develop the organization structure they wanted. At this time, some of the traditionalists in the top hierarchy were opposed to the approach being adopted, on the ground that the end-result might not be acceptable. My answer, of course, was that the CEO should be obliged to reconsider his position if he was unable to accept a solution provided by a wide cross-section of 80 of his trusted senior colleagues.

The resulting restructure achieved many of our objectives including the following:

- Moving more power from staff to line positions.
- Removing a layer of top management which permitted line general managers to report direct to the CEO.
- Reducing the numbers in the top team (levels one and two).
- Moving more responsibility downward to as close to the action as possible.
- Becoming more customer-oriented.
- Greater concentration on strategy and planning.

With the new organization structure in place, and again following the same principles, a number of small taskforces were set up within the management to consider the bank's future strategy. The issues identified were:

- maximization of income;
- market share vs profitability;
- international penetration;
- mergers and acquisitions

and so on.

And so it was that the old Bank of New South Wales decided to merge with the Commercial Bank of Australia. The Bank of New South Wales was dominant in New South Wales, but was not strong in Victoria, which was the home of the Commercial Bank.

In searching for the ingredients for a successful merger and for a new national identity, one which would identify easily with the bank's international aspirations, we decided that this was also the time for a change of name. The Bank of New South Wales was the first bank in Australia in 1817 and its history was synonymous with the history of the country, but its parochial name no longer reflected its national character or its international aspirations.

Australia is no longer an extension of Europe – geographically, of course, it is in the Western Pacific and its future is increasingly bound up with the fortunes of the Western Pacific – and so it was that the name Westpac was chosen.

That decision attracted extreme hostility from Australians generally, from customers, from stockholders and from the media. The resulting public discussion and debate was extraordinarily valuable in publicizing the name at home. The staff of the two banks, on the other hand, generally responded with enthusiasm to the name change and to the opportunity it presented to create a new bank with a new image and with a new vision.

The management challenges were now twofold:

1   On the one hand, to implement a successful merger.
2   On the other hand, to create the new bank.

Looking first at the merger, we had two paramount objectives:

(a)   The price had been high – much higher than we had anticipated – and it was, therefore, necessary to preserve the market share which had been so expensive. And that was objective number one.
(b)   Banking is a service industry in which people play a dominant role. Objective number two therefore, was to plan for harmony.

These objectives were achieved and a variety of techniques were used:

● The two boards of directors were combined.
● The composition of the Executive Committee was changed likewise to include the executives of both banks.
● About twenty Merger Committees were set up with representatives of both banks, to plan every facet of the merger - e. g. industrial relations, accounting and tax, data processing, audit, advertising, etc. Their activities were co-ordinated by an Integration Committee. Although this approach was to some extent bureaucratic, it provided an excellent opportunity for key officers of both banks to work together and to get to know one another in advance of day one.
● The off-site managerial effectiveness seminars, mentioned

earlier, were revived to transfer the culture to a wide range of managers from the other bank.

It was easy with this kind of activity to direct the focus to the launch of a new bank. As day one approached, we:

- asked the five leading advertising agencies to bid for the advertising contract, and in so doing, to tell us how to launch a new bank;
- decided to give our 35,000 staff the opportunity to purchase at a substantial discount a new wardrobe, designed by one of Australia's top designers – the theory was that if we made our staff look good, they would feel good; it worked, and the anticipated take up of 75 per cent proved to be 95 per cent;
- installed television receivers throughout the 1,500 branch network, so that I and other executives could talk direct to the staff and so we would have an audio-visual communication for training, new product familiarization, etc;
- instituted a corporate roadshow to introduce the new bank, the wardrobe, the advertising campaign, etc; the biggest movie theatres in every major city in Australia and New Zealand were hired, and every manager was instructed to present him/herself for a half-day programme to see and hear about the new bank; and a fashion show to exhibit the new wardrobe was on the programme.

On the first day of the new bank, the advertising campaign commenced. In the print media, we ran full-range advertisements with such messages as:

'The competition is open'
'We are the competition'
'We are changing'

and even:

'Normal service will never be resumed'

and later:

'We are rolling our sleeves up!'

In retrospect, I am convinced that the theme of our advertising achieved a lot in convincing the public, together with our customers and our staff, that we were serious in our endeavour to change. And, of course, the successful transmission of that message placed great pressure on the staff to respond.

Having achieved the merger at home, and having achieved the objective of a major and balanced share of the domestic market, our attention was then diverted to the international market.

With the growing influence of foreign banks in Australia, and the threat of deregulation carrying with it the certainty of greater competition, both domestic and foreign, it was simple to deduce that our domestic market share would be under challenge. It was then simple to deduce that the international route was the only one available for meaningful growth.

In the retail bank the use of advanced technology to deliver services was inevitable. Plans were set in train to develop a network of street-based teller machines, point-of-sale terminals in retail stores and front-office terminals throughout the huge branch network. Banking is unionized in Australia and there has been strong union opposition to technological change. To publicize their opposition the union recorded a song and distributed the recording widely. One verse went like this:

'Oh technology is great, that's what we hear them say
as unemployment grows with every day
now just stop and count the cost,
of the jobs that we have lost
and you'll see the price the country has to pay.'

In my experience unreasonable union activity can usually be successfully met by direct communication with the rank and file members of the staff who have much less difficulty in appreciating the importance of the latest technology to the longer term security of their jobs. As a result, we now have 500 tellermachines and are moving towards 2000 store terminals.

### EXTRACTS OF TALK GIVEN BY GEOFF THOMPSON, CHIEF MANAGER MERGER

(*This talk was given some years before the one above.*)
Over the past 12 months, I seem to have been engaged in an endless stream of speeches on the merger between the Bank of New South Wales and the Commercial Bank of Australia, as seen from the viewpoint of shareholders, of staff and customers, or as seen by the stockmarket, and especially the latter. But your session tonight

gives me a chance to talk from the perspective of organization change – and this is the perspective which perhaps has the most relevance to the actual pattern of events.

Historically, as I will attempt to demonstrate, the concept and implementation of the merger negotiations and the execution so far could not have taken place without our organization development (OD) programme. In fact our OD programme itself may not have happened if it had not been for the Australian Institute of Management, which is another reason I count it a privilege to be here tonight.

Let me explain. The most convenient starting-point is at the breakdown in the original merger negotiations between the Wales and the Commercial Bank of Australia (CBA) (and incidentally between the National and the Commercial Banking Group of Sydney Ltd (CBC)). The only merger of that era to reach consummation was that between the Australia and New Zealand Banking Group Limited (ANZ) and the English, Scottish and Australia Bank (ES&A).

As a result of the breakdown of the other merger proposals, the CBA made a number of changes, under the influence of McKinseys who, in usual fashion, proposed a fair degree of centralization and some changes in style for that bank. On the other hand, we at the Wales continued to operate much as we had always done. True, there had been reorganization of the top structure and the equivalent of a Corporate Planning Department had been established, but these were measures created by bankers, for bankers. It would be fair to say that there was a certain amount of disdain within the Wales for the ideas of management gurus and a certain pride in our own achievements.

Our market-place and the environment in which we were operating and doing business were changing at a rapid rate and we were not changing fast enough. In effect, the Wales was still the biggest trading bank and still the most profitable, but we were suffering a bit from hardening of the arteries. We were getting good at generating paper, not very good at acting on it.

Power was essentially in the hands of the 'staff'. The 'line' people who dealt with the customers were given a fairly limited say in the decisions about policies and the day-to-day management of their business. Inevitably, in the very restricted environment in which banks operate, a premium was placed on conformity to the rules, on keeping your nose clean, on not making waves, on not incurring bad debts and on letting your customers come to you.

That is not to say that nothing new was tried – on the contrary, there were a lot of positive steps taken – but we were still slower

to respond to the market-place than we ought to have been. And
our weaknesses were beginning to show in the shop-window:

- The Commonwealth Trading Bank was challenging us for the
  top spot as largest trading bank.
- The ANZ was about to challenge us in total profit terms. They
  were already beating us in the measure of return on assets.

A major review was soon put in train by Sir Robert Norman
who at that stage was some five months off retirement as Chief
General Manager. At that time, the bank's management consisted
of the Chief General Manager, two General Managers and nine
Assistant General Managers. These met as an Administrative
Committee – not a decision-making body, but more of an infor
mation meeting. Most of them had risen through the ranks of the
bank and were experts in a fairly limited range of activities. This
Administrative Committee carried out a review, namely looking a
the future and where we were headed.

Three months afterwards Sir Robert retired and Mr White
succeeded him, the Administrative Committee decided on the
Bank's *Corporate Philosophy* – which you now see on the inside
cover of the Wales' Annual Report or on the wall in your friendly
branch.

A series of objectives were sketched out but not finally decided
One of those objectives – and probably the one of most relevance
to us tonight – was to introduce output orientation as a managemen
style into the bank.

Even in this limited brief, there were some constraints or
freedom of action – the Administrative Committee didn't want any
outside consultants of the McKinsey type, and they wanted the
changes in a hurry.

**How we chose the Reddin method**

At that point, the Australian Institute of Management sent round
an invitation to attend a session called 'A Day with Bill Reddin'.

Reddin, as many will know, is a university-based Canadian
consultant offering a system of output orientation – which wa
really OD in disguise. So we were getting the latest in a disguise
that would be acceptable.

It was evident at the first seminar that the Reddin method wa
ideal for our purposes – it was true that his staff were consultants
but they were consultants with a difference, as follows:

1   They did not propose to bring in a bright young team to go all
    over our building to get the ideas of our bright old and young
    people, write them up and sell them back to the bank.
2   The Reddin assumption is that all the ideas are already in the
    bank – what was needed were some techniques to liberate them.
3   The Reddin method would provide the needed techniques and
    train our own people to use them.
4   Moreover, their method wasn't like that of any other manage-
    ment consultants we knew. There was no ideal theory of
    management. We knew a little of McGregor's Theory X and
    Theory Y, and the Blake and Mouton grid and other devices,
    all designed to turn that nasty, mean-tempered autocrat into a
    sweet, docile, yet high-performing executive.

The Reddin method assumes, realistically, that the latter is
nonsense. Human beings are as unchangeable as they have always
been. But they can learn to use their temperament effectively. So,
for example, 'autocrats' can begin to use their personality strengths
to do the job better and so become 'benevolent autocrats'. A
'missionary' can become a 'developer'; a 'compromiser' can become
an 'executive'.

The claim is that there's no inherently bad temperament – even
the bureaucratic style can be an effective way of managing certain
types of business.

Moreover, people who are 'deserters' do not get that way because
they want to be, they are in the wrong job or the job is badly
designed or they are not being properly led.

The job design should be based on outputs – on what someone
produces, not on the inputs – i.e. what they do. There are a lot of
busy people who produce nothing.

As you know, a lot of this is not new – and indeed credit is given
to people like Peter Drucker and to Mary Parker Follett who said
many years ago:

How do we avoid the two great extremes – too much bossism on
the one hand, or practically no orders given. My advice is to
unite people in a study of the situation – to discover its laws and
obey them.

And so we get Reddin's definition of OD:

Getting people together in what at times are unusual combinations to talk about what they should talk about anyway, in an

atmosphere of candour and a willingness to change and a shared interest in effectiveness.

So here is the background:

1   We had a novel consultant method which was saleable to the top team.
2   The method assumes that people can work better and be more effective if they have the right stimulus, the right job structure and the opportunity to air their views.
3   Commitment takes precedence over elegance – i.e. people will do something because they believe in it, even though it may not be the neatest or prettiest way of doing it.

On our part we wanted to manage the bank more effectively, using planning and objective setting. The key element was that the Chief Executive was firmly behind this concept.

**What did he do**

We decided we wanted to try Reddin's Organization Effectiveness Programme (OEP). Thus:

(a)  we carried out a trial run with two questionnaires with all our managers;
(b)  we took 84 of our managers away in two groups to the 3-D Managerial Effectiveness Seminars (MESs) – a week-long 'unfreeze' session at Leura, in the Blue Mountains, run by Reddin consultants;
(c)  we had several team meetings.

Six months later, Reddin visited me. He asked to spend three days with the complete top team and to do his own diagnosis over a period of about two weeks. The last day of the three days with the top team was him presenting his diagnosis. He suggested that we should look at reorganization, and we did. He suggested that all of the top team should participate in a six-day residential MES, and we did. He proposed to us a fairly high staffing need, based on our own internal staff, and we accepted that as well. All through the next year, we applied the Reddin techniques:

1   We trained a team of our own people as OD advisers.
2   In all, about 1,700 managers went through the MES – everyone

from Bob White down to the lowest assistant manager in administration and some branch managers as well. By the time this
ended, we had a common culture, and language and the organization was unfrozen, ready to address change.

3   Managers in administration had defined their jobs in output
terms, and departments were looking at team outputs.

4   Everyone who went through the process had a clear idea of
their management 'style', how it related to their job and how
they could deal with incompatibilities between their style and
the requirements of the position.

5   We reorganized the bank from the top down, in an entirely
different way. In the old days, the Chief General Manager's
Assistant would have drawn up an organization structure and
had the boss adopt it. This time we took the top 80 people away
for a long weekend.

The participants split into teams and came up with a remarkable
degree of consensus. As a result, the organization structure was
radically altered:

1   Power went from staff to line (from those in the backroom to
those in the front).

2   We removed one layer of top management and reduced the top
team size from 13 to 8. To reflect its new role it became the
Executive Committee, not the Administrative Committee.

3   We delegated responsibility, moving power from the Board
down through layers of management to the point as close to the
action as we could.

4   We began to get a marketing orientation to our business – i. e.
focusing on the needs of the customer, not on those of the bank.

5   The top team of 8 began to address strategy and policy and
began to become generalists, leaving the level-three Chief
Managers to deal with operations.

6   But whatever the design, the important feature was that this
structure had commitment from the people who had to make it
work.

7   Later we had a look at all our personnel policies – not in
head office, but by getting in 100 people, from Chief General
Manager to young tellers and branch assistants, and taking them
for another long weekend at an hotel. All had been 'unfrozen'
at an MES.

8   Many of our policies were overhauled, for example, a much
greater commitment of resources was made to the training func-

tion, so that branch managers could receive ongoing training
business practices were reviewed, and so on.

### Result

We became a much more flexible organization, better able to dea
with the changes going on around us. We put much more logic inte
the way we approached problems, in the way in which we approvec
budgets and set guidelines.

### Evaluation

There is no question that, on the whole, the OD exercise ha
greatly helped the bank's move towards modern management. The
process is not yet completed – we have yet to get job outpu
descriptions written further down the line, we have yet to get al
our people managing more effectively and have yet to link reward
to performance to tighten the job descriptions.

There is no question that output orientation has acted as a cata
lyst for change. The changes which were desperately needed.

It *has* been costly, both in money terms and in terms of the top
team's time but, on the whole, worthwhile.

The Reddin organization made some mistakes, for example, they
tried to talk us out of addressing strategy, saying that we shoulc
only do this when we had completed the organization process
That would have been a tragic mistake, for we would have beer
unprepared for the merger with CBA. But even in our strategy
planning, we applied Reddin techniques and linked them with tech
niques developed by Science Research Institute (SRI) – in all, 81
people were involved in strategy taskforces, which led up to the
merger decision. We used some of those unusual combinations of
people to talk about the things we should talk about – and very
positive results emerged.

### How does the organization effectiveness programme apply to the merger?

There is no question in my mind that had we not had Reddin, we
would not have been as well prepared as we were for the merger
– indeed, I don't believe we could have made the decision in the
time.

Once we had made the decision, the Board was told that the Reddin method would be a powerful tool to enable us to get on with the job of making the merger work. As so it proved:

- We have used the Reddin techniques of candour, of consultation to take the decisions in the Integration Committee and the twenty Merger Committees originally set up to plan the merger of our two businesses.
- We have used the large team decision technique to determine the top team organization of the new bank – a number of meetings were held between Wales and CBA executives, to decide the details.
- We were due to revise the organization structure before the merger was even mooted. We knew there were faults – the general manager domestic business had far too much to do. He was virtually managing Australia. The general manager finance and planning was also too busy – not only managing the bank's accounting and treasury functions, but planning for the future. So we have to split those portfolios. Along came the merger, and it was logical to split the domestic job by creating the Southern Region; and it was logical to split finance and planning into finance and merger and planning.
- We've even carried the process into the merger department structure itself. If we had merged three years ago, I'd have had a staff of 50. Instead we have put the job out into the line, under a merger co-ordinator for each general manager – they decide, not someone behind the scenes. And we can run our department on six. We use a Merger Steering Committee to link the process together.

**For the future**

The merger has slowed down the adoption of the full OD programme: we have had to go back to relook at structures, we have had to slow down our planning timetable and we have had to put aside some things. But we are making decisions in a logical framework and with a set of concepts which are going to be more widely understood as the CBA executive and management go through managerial effectiveness seminars.

We've had a hiccup in the process – if you like – but in six months we will be a much stronger organization:

- we'll have a common language (and understanding of OD and the related jargon);
- we'll have logical ways of doing things;
- we'll have people who think more in output terms than in terms of bureaucracy;
- we'll have welded the two groups together, with a common purpose.

We at the Wales will benefit from CBA's current experience. They will remind us, as their top team have already, of some of the things we planned to do with Reddin but have not got round to doing. They'll make us relook at the textbook, so that we'll get a recommitment to the principles.

From all this you may think I'm a starry-eyed enthusiast – but this is only partly true, as the following makes clear:

1  I've always maintained that there are some weaknesses in the Reddin approach.
2  I've always said that the method is just the oil in the engine - the car had to be driven by the top people with their teams in the direction they choose. In a few years we may be using another oil.
3  Organization development is still heavily dependent on the quality of management. No system is better than the people using it.

But having said all that, I'm convinced that our version of OD is a good practical and effective way of making and meeting change.

As I hope I have shown, OD has played a great part in the changes which have taken place in the Wales; it has facilitated the merger process and we fully expect it to go on strengthening the Westpac Banking Corporation into the future.

# 11 The Chief Executive Officer who changed his organization

**BEFORE THE CHANGE**

'I think they dismissed us as a joke when we started.'

'The company wasn't going anywhere and I couldn't figure out why. I put the company in for analysis and it came out that it was being run by an autocrat who was killing his own company, had surrounded himself with bureaucrats and was destined to fail.'

**AFTER THE CHANGE**

'I felt the company needed change and, with output orientation, I now had a formula. I now had a common management language that we could use.'

'I went to my "unfreeze" with seven individuals and came back with a committed team and the message has flowed on.'

'I then came back to my company and removed my desk.'

'This new deal will make me financially independent for the first time in my life.'

'Atlas has recently broken into the Chinese market and has been officially recognized as a supplier to the Chinese government.'

'The area of greatest potential growth for the company is its recently released modular office air conditioning system. The system is said to be a world first and cost an estimated two million dollars to develop.'

'Without taking that two-day seminar when I did and then imple-

menting the ideas of outputs, it is extremely likely we could have
gone bottom up.


## WHAT DID HAPPEN WHEN A CEO REMOVED HIS DESK, DESIGNED AND CONDUCTED HIS OWN UNFREEZE MEETING AND RAN A SERIES OF TEAM MEETINGS

This manager-owner of an Australian airconditioning firm with
about eighty employees got rid of his desk and had a team
weekend 'unfreezing' meeting. Both things are slightly
unnerving, but he had the nerve. Profits doubled the next year,
and then doubled the year after. He has now secured his family
fortune. He took a risk and it succeeded. He wrote this letter to
the person conducting a seminar related to creating an output
oriented organization.

This account is as related by the chief executive officer (CEO)
himself with some minor terminology changes.


## A LETTER FROM A MANAGER

'Dear . . .
'You are on my mind as my desk is just being moved to my accounts
manager's office, and I am trying to adjust to my new executive
surroundings.
  'Actually, the cheapest part of the output orientation seminar I
attended was the seminar fee, for since then I have spent $5,000
refurbishing my office to my new non-conforming climate. I have
had a three-day, live-away "unfreezing" meeting with my seven top
executives and they have had a one-day "unfreeze" meeting with
their groups.
  'You mentioned when I phoned you on my decision to rid myself
of my desk that you don't always get feedback on results and that's
a pity for the changes that have taken place here in the last month
are nothing short of miraculous! I went to my "unfreeze" with
seven individuals and came back with a committed team and the
message has flowed on.
  'Tomorrow I have a one-day final review of all the effectiveness
areas and measurement methods and the 12-month plan for each
executive and then we start the new year – a new, revitalized,
reorganized and committed company: Your own seminar showed
that we were headed for trouble because of inbuilt and growing

stagnation which was stifling our real purpose and marketing objectives.

'There is a time and tide in the affairs of all men and I'm grateful I was ready for the message I got from you and your beautifully planned and deeply thought-provoking seminar which can give such quick and concise indicators and where I have proven that the disciple's message has just as much effect as the master's.

'Thank you and I am sorry I am not in the business of selling output orientation, for it is a message I could really move along.

'Sincerely,
Colin Ward
Atlas Air Australia Pty Ltd.'


## A SUBSEQUENT TALK TO MANAGERS

(*As a result of writing the above letter, Colin Ward has asked to talk to a group of senior managers on an output orientation seminar on his own experiences.*)

I will just feed you some facts and you can see if they are useful or not. I am very grateful to be invited. Our company isn't a big company and I'll give you some background on that.

Our particular group started some 15 years ago in the true fashion of husband-and-wife team, and $300, and we were in the airconditioning field. When you haven't got any money, you have to put in a lot of time, and we pursued that course. We grew to a point where we had about $5.5 million turnover.

We went into credit squeeze and lost $400,000 – nearly lost our house and nearly lost everything that we had, through the tradition of payment within our system, where builders obtain stage payments, and if they go broke, they take you with them. But we survived out of all that, coming down from 120 to 50 people and from $5.5 million turnover to $3 million and we restarted.

We then sold 15 per cent of our shares to an Italian group that we represented here and in South-east Asia, New Guinea and New Zealand, and we were formally looked upon as part of their international group, so that our company was now back to $6 million turnover. We rose to 80 people, but were certainly a very different profit-oriented company from what we were earlier, and broader based with different products, but while we were all that, I was very conscious of the fact that we were not making any real growth. I was conscious of the fact that I had pushed and pulled and I was very proud of my company. I thought I was reasonably intelligent; I travelled overseas twice a year; I am observant; I read and if someone asked me about my company, I would have said 'Well, we'd got a great company'. Yet we were not really making real growth, we were just keeping pace with inflation, and this worried me.

I knew there was something wrong with my company. We sort of restructured and did a few things. Finally, I looked in the mail and there was this Institute of Management booklet. I have always been too busy to go to seminars and, you know, who wants a lot of these seminars which have sort of trite people that stand up in front of you, who say the same sort of language and the same sort of talk? You finish and there has been no impact.

So I enrolled for the output orientation seminar that you are doing now and sat over yonder. I didn't really know what was in front of me other than output orientation, but I had an open mind I had need for change – for some reason or other, despite all our hard work and relative success, I was not happy about the way our company was going.

Then we started to do what you are starting to do – we began to get a common language, an output orientation language. By this time you had either made up your mind that you sort of understand it and you like what it's saying or you don't. You are rejecting it or you are open to it.

Our seminar workteam got along quite well. Sitting at the same table was a member of the top team of a 30,000-person bank, the CEO of Digital and the CEO of Olivetti. We had a good work session, mainly from across-the-board-type companies. When we had finished, we had a little time, so I said: 'Look, why don't you guys help me. My company is the smallest of the group. Wouldn't you like to feed my company in as case-study number seven which we have the opportunity to do?' And we did.

It came out to be a company with a completely conforming climate, which was quite different from what I believed my company to be. As an individual and as a person dedicated to the company, I would have told it quite differently.

So then I had the opportunity with this workgroup, and they were very kind to me, to look at the executives. I had one 'deserter' and four 'bureaucrats' in a group of eight senior executives, including myself. A lot of meetings that I thought were participative were not, as it turned out. I ended up to be an 'autocrat' and I guess really after a fashion, when I got over my initial reaction, I was. I guess a lot of guys who start a business off have to be autocrats and highly task-oriented to succeed. The four 'bureau-crats' and the 'deserter' were worrying also.

When I started to think about my company climate, I realized that it was in fact choking and was going to wither and die with a current inflation rate of 12 per cent. So, armed with all the seminar messages and books that you've got, I went back home to my group. I called them in and said, 'Look, I have just finished a seminar. OK you can say I am enthused about it and I like the output orientation message. There is a real message for us. Now I realize that I have been calling you in and talking with you, but the decisions were really pre-made and I have been handing tablets down from the mountain and saying what's great, while you have been sitting there anticipating the decision' – which was true, but I didn't believe it. I was one of those fair, wise, tolerant, thoughtful people that you keep hearing about.

Then I said: 'If you are interested and want to be a senior executive of this group, I would like a commitment and, in turn, I will make a commitment to you. To do that, I want you to give up a weekend of your time. That's your commitment for starters. Not in the company time, in your time – still the autocrat in me!' You have got to give something to get something, so I asked them for their own time. I said that we would go away and discuss the company in a way that it had never been discussed before. I felt the company needed change, and with output orientation, I now had a formula. I now had a common management language that we could use. If after the meeting they did not want to be part of this, or if they felt the company would not benefit from it – at least we would have spent three days discussing it. I actually did give them the Friday, let's be fair about it.

We arrived for the weekend meeting, eight people with a fairly tight schedule. There was a lot to go through and we started with an analysis of some of the case studies this seminar provided. Then we came to study ourselves. This was the first time, I guess, that they had ever been asked to comment in open honesty and candour on their own company's planned change objectives, level of resistance, the existing level of output orientation and how to make it higher, and styles of individuals. Previously, I was always planning the structure and doing all these other things myself, if they were done at all.

Then they had the opportunity of analysing me as a CEO. They gave frank comments on my style, my effectiveness areas and my effectiveness. They were really given the opportunity of analysing me along set terms which were impersonal. I think the main stress here is on the top person, as they must be ready to accept honest criticism and the fact that they can be wrong. Then, of course, we analysed the seven senior executives of the company, which was themselves. We had a room that we had hired that we could stick paper all the way round.

We wrote up our analyses, which brought a lot of revelations. As they started to look at themselves, they realized by this formula that in fact they had an inappropriate style – some of them.

Then they analysed the company and found, much to their shocked horror, that it was a conforming climate – eight out of eight agreed that it was conforming. Conforming may be an effective climate with some firms, but it clearly would not fit our line of business and our size of firm. That was the reason we were not getting anywhere, we were working hard and not being as profitable as we should. We had role behavioural clashes; but looked upon them as personality clashes. We had sales against production; this against this, but we always looked upon them as personality because we didn't really understand behavioural science. This was a great revelation.

We then asked everyone to write their effectiveness areas – the first step in output orientation; and bearing in mind that when a person joined our company, we gave them exactly what this seminar talks about – a job effectiveness description, but for us it turned out to be an input job description. We looked at all the advertisements that we had placed for staff over the past 12 months. They were all inputs. They were not output- and objective-projected advertisements; they were input advertisements. Which is why we were not getting top staff, I guess. This was a revelation to all of us in the room. Then when they started to write their effectiveness areas some of them were in fact total inputs, as they put them up in what they believed to be, and I believed to be, their areas of effectiveness. So we sat down and rewrote them.

First, we wrote the effectiveness areas of the CEO. We all agreed on what my job was and what my area of effectiveness was. Everyone doesn't have to come in at 8 a.m. because I did and they didn't have to stay until 7 p.m. because I did. And I did not have to keep proving to them that I could be first in and last out for the rest of my life. We did not have to keep proving to one another – we had to be effective. That was a great release of tension for all.

They then raised all of the areas that caused them consideration and problems, even to the point of whether they could select the colour of their own car. Some things were simple, but for them important. Some were big things. So if you would like to call it a grievance-and-an-open-honesty session, we went through that, to clear many of the blockages. We then agreed each person's effec tiveness areas, looking for overlaps and underlaps. This took all day and a lot of serious thought. They would be working next day, so they were supposed to stop at 5 but they were so keen they went on until 6.30 p.m.

It was a hard day, a hard three days, because they were tense days with people hearing things they did not want to hear, some of them, including me. We got through that, and we all walked out with new effectiveness areas, new objectives and a new planned company climate that we committed ourselves to. We were to be a dedicated climate company, suited to our size of company and the industry that we were in. We all mutually agreed on that – one vote, one person. Now I don't carry any more weight in those output orientation meetings than they do, because now I'm just another cog in the top management group.

We then agreed to have monthly team meetings. Most management improvement schemes fail because they don't have effective team follow up meetings. No feedback and review. They have floating little groups and after a while they get soft at the edges and die. We agreed to hold these link-back meetings away from the company; we hire a motel room from 8 a.m. until 5 p.m. Each person would be able to discuss their effectiveness areas and they would be judged on a budget, which they agreed to, set previously under this new scheme. I had set it with them, sitting on the other side of the table, so they were a committed group.

We then left our meeting-place, having achieved a tremendous thing. Tensions had been eased, and role behavioural clashes had disappeared, because people realized why they were having them. My relationship with my top staff had improved considerably. Because I was the leader, I was dominant and I did want them to move when I made the decision. The timing was my timing and the company revolved around me. And yet on the other side of me, I was trying to be related and nice, as well as all the things that autocrats try to do to keep people together, the seminar calls them hypocrites, but I couldn't quite face up to that. But the thing is we did leave as a very hard core and better-formed group.

I then came back to my company and removed my desk. Now when this seminar made the invitation to us as undoubtedly it will to you, or has, to take away our desks, suggesting we sit on them and be photographed for the local newspaper, being carried out of our office on them – I thought, well, you know this sounds good. I wouldn't mind a bit of public relations.

Then I thought, well, I won't go into the publicity, but I will do what output orientation suggests because if I am serious about change, I have to be committed to it. Why is my company confor-

ming? Why are we over-systemized? When we added up the piece
of paper, we had 120 pieces of paper. Well, engineers are confor
ming – they do rely on little walls and fences and systems, and we
had too many of them. We had some of the policies written ir
times of survival some years ago which people still trotted out wher
it suited them. They flicked through the book and quoted, 'You
said this then, that you could do this'. So we decided to rip a**
these things up and keep the ones that were valid and effective anc
get rid of those that were now ineffective and out of date.

But to return to the desk. I looked at it for a long while. I wa:
a guy who had worked from a long apprenticeship right througl
and had gone through public companies. Part of the status symbo
was to have a beautiful desk in a nice office, and 'attractive
secretary and a few phones and sort of feel as though one was ar
executive. It was a magnificent-looking desk, black leather on top
looking like it was worth several thousand dollars. It had a drawei
in the bottom where I had my secret files on salaries and perform
ances and a few other things. I looked at it and said, 'Well, where
should this desk be?' The group said it should be with the mos
effective 'bureaucrat' in this company. 'Who was that?' Answer
our Finance Manager. Great! So out of my office it went, rounc
the corner into the Finance Manager's, who happens to be :
woman. She sat behind it on the big swinging chair and she said
'This is beautiful. I can have my in-tray there and I can have m}
files here. Thank you.'

I walked back to my empty office and I thought, 'Bloody outpu
orientation has done this to me, what am I going to do?' So I callec
in a friend of mine, who is an interior decorator and explainec
what I wanted to do. I wanted to get out of the office. I didn't wan
an in-tray I wanted change and the change had to be permanent a
far as I was concerned – I wanted to commit myself. So she bough
for me some 'U'-shaped little modules of Italian brown velvet; :
little lounge suite that you push together, very nice. Also a grea
big coffee table, very deep and very long and the height where you
can write if you want to. Then I got this little work station on the
side of a smaller table that fits in the corner where the phone sit
– and that's all there is.

Next I called in my private secretary and said: 'Margaret, you're
great. But do you know what, I haven't been using you as a private
secretary, have I?' She said: 'No'. 'I have been using you as :
typist, haven't I?' She said: 'Yes.' 'So would you like to take all o
my private files and put them in your office?' 'Yes, I would.' Sc
out came all the secret stuff and went into her drawer. Out wen
the library, and I said that when I wanted a book, I'd press a buttor

and she could bring the book in for me. She said: 'Love to.' All of a sudden I had a private secretary.

In came all the new furniture, which cost me 7,000 bucks; but change you've got to pay for, and you know you get what you pay for. There I was, seated in this new office lined with wood, and glass down at the end so I could see myself. A little bit of an 'autocrat'. No desk, no in-tray. I sat and thought, 'Where do I put my pencil? Where do I put my pen? Where do I put all the things I have accumulated – calculators and things?' I didn't have a place to put things, and that's when the output orientation change started to take place. I either had to get a place to put them in or I had to delegate, so I delegated.

Now I go and sit with my executives in their office and we use my office as a general boardroom. If any of the senior executives have someone of importance they want to impress with Italian furniture and glass, they can use my office. It is now not the domain of the CEO. When I am there, I use it – but now I am out of the office. Now I am working for my output profile. Last year I was able to visit Israel, Stockholm, Italy, Singapore and Malaysia.

No one worried about me because I was out doing my bit. I didn't have to account to anyone that I wasn't in the office, and they didn't have to worry that I was watching them over my shoulder. They knew that we would all have to stand up and be counted at the monthly link-back meeting.

At the monthly meetings we have a complete re-appraisal of the budget achievements which is fairly normal. We also have a complete reappraisal of the adherence to the agreed and committed output profile and if it should be changed. It can only be changed with a group meeting – not just by me. Admittedly, I've got the flexibility at a One-to-One Meeting, but now I am committed, I want this thing to work and I want them all to carry on the message of output orientation.

I went to a board meeting in Stockholm and I introduced the ideas of output orientation to the International Group – a young Italian company now based in Luxembourg financially, but with Italian bases and new factories in America, Spain, Austria and Ireland. They are in a state where, frankly, they are bogged down. They need help. Talking with the founder and the CEO, I truly felt like a disciple. I said, 'This is what you need'. Then I went into my brief-case and out came materials on output orientation that I had with me. He said, 'What's that?' I said, 'This is what's made me so different. This is what has given my company a new revitalization. This is why I can be here not worrying about whether this or that has been dealt with because I trust my staff. They know I trust them – they've got known effectiveness areas and objectives and I've got known areas of effectiveness with objectives, this is what you need.'

In Stockholm they had their first 'unfreezing' meeting, so the message – the still pure message – is now flowing into an international group. The CEO has got his sixteen top executives around the world on output orientation.

Next weekend we go on our strategy meeting. They are all studying their pre-work and we go away for Friday, Saturday and Sunday. For the first time in our little company, we will be discussing a five-year strategy plan. I've always shunned five-year strategy plans because anyone can, sort of, extend figures – you don't have to be real clever. But if you start to do a serious one, it is indeed a mammoth task, as you know. All the inputs and ramifications of what is going to happen to you in five years just on 12 per cent inflation. And doubling your turnover, new premises and types of staff and utilization of all your facilities and resources. However, that's one of the things we will be discussing at our next meeting, and we will be bringing our new job effectiveness descriptions and checking them because they could have changed. We will be going over the whole thing again – setting ourselves up for our next year. That's what's happening next weekend.

So what can I say? I don't often do commercials and I'm not being paid for this one, but I do feel so enthused about it and it has liberated our company so much. That is why I wrote the letter. It's nice to get the feedback that output orientation is creating change; that some people do not just walk out of that door and say, 'Gee! output orientation is good', and then go off to the next seminar. It must help to meet someone who says, 'I have put the pure written word to the test and it's surviving'. We're not living in some unreal world, and the people I work with don't have to do what I tell them to do. If they don't like it, six or seven votes against one beats me. That's the end of the story, so really I owe output orientation a great deal. I owe the Institute of Management a great deal because, without them, I wouldn't have come on this seminar with its very true message. It's a wonderful message of integrity. Starting from here 12 months ago, my company has doubled its profit. If someone makes a statement that they have doubled their profit, I always look at them rather sceptically, but we are talking in-house here and that is exactly what we have done.

I am now managing by consultation. I only see some of my senior executives once a month at the one-day team meeting because I am a task-oriented person and I am involved with my output. Now when they want to see me, they just buzz through and sit in the lounge next to me, not over the other side of the former desk. I sit next to them; I look in to their eyes and we communicate because we are right next to one another – and it's all right with your secretary, too!

Gentlemen, I won't bore you, but I do thank you for the chance of giving you the message. It is obviously a different message from that of a very large company, where their unfreezing might involve hundreds of people. I only had eight and because of our size, I have been able to move fast and it has made a tremendous difference. I shall be very interested when next the group recast their votes on what company climate we have. Has it moved from conforming to dedicated, or hasn't it? Am I still an 'autocrat' or am I now a 'benevolent autocrat'? I will learn this from their votes. Now this is going to be very interesting. Do we have four 'bureaucrats' and one 'deserter'? Or do we have two 'bureaucrats' plus 'benevolent autocrat' people which we need in our type of company? And that will all be shown up indelibly at the meeting this weekend.

## The session moves to question and answer

*Question:* Who were the seven other people?
*Answer:* They are my top team. I might add too that since we introduced output orientation, they have taken the message. They have set up output orientation groups with their next line of management. So I gave the message to my top team and they have now set up output orientation with their group. We are now down to supervisor level, that's where we are. They hold their monthly meetings away from the company too, and they have found the same freshness, candour and honesty coming out on feedback and relationship with their people – so in our company in 12 months we have achieved not just the top team, we have now gone through our whole management layer.
*Q:* What are your Effectiveness Areas?
*A:* Well, basically, the number one is to give the shareholders profit return on investment. This is my number one. To make the company profitable based on an agreed shareholders return, bear in mind I have an overseas shareholder now as a partner. My output is to look for new products because, at this particular stage, we are broadening our profit centres; and to investigate the world for new products that dovetail into the way I want future strategy on profit centres; to maintain international corporate image from a profitability point of view. As you know, when you are dealing with the Chinese, when you are dealing with the Israelis, you have

to deal very personally with them. The rules that apply don't apply to many of their trading partners overseas and so I do spend, as I say, six months of the year travelling at this particular time of my life. When all this is set up, I'll be in a position to delegate quite a lot of those trips to other people. Of course, if I keep doing this, it will have detrimental effects upon my marriage, which I don't want to happen, but it is an agreed thing which my wife is involved with. She knows why I am going and we have the Board meetings at home now to keep her involved. She is aware of the reason I am going to Israel, why I am going to Singapore and why I am going to New Zealand and Italy, and why I should attend Board Meetings. I want better deals, and I want to try to unravel all of the problems that happen with telexes between us and Italy, because again we are all different people and that takes a lot of personal dealing at top level. It is something at this stage, that I have to do – it is part of my job. If I want to be CEO of my company and it wants to import goods from overseas, I have to be there. It is as simple as that, policies, and so forth, for the company. I didn't bring anything in writing with me, I just prefer to talk with you ad lib, but I can assure you that everything we do now is double-checked in writing when we've said it and then we get a bound little copy of all our agreed profiles, so that we can look at it if we want to refresh our memories of the company structure, which they comment on and help form.

*Q:* I've been wondering is there any problem with approaching union level with this output orientation scheme?

*A:* That's when I become an 'autocrat' again. Actually, we are a non-union shop. We are union by membership, non-union by the fact that we have profit-sharing within the company. I think this is one of the things that output orientation brings out as a link-back reward system. All of my senior executives are on profit-sharing basis on the achievement of the areas of effectiveness and objectives, the company has a holiday unit where we give them free holidays, and a few other things that small companies can do that are tax-free incentives, so we try to keep our people happy, which output orientation is helping us to do. We have far better relationships with our people who are, I think, more loyal to us than to some union boss, which is the way we have got to be because the union is going to kill us. I don't know if there is any union official here, but that's my honest opinion, so we are non-union in effectiveness.

*Q:* How about measurement of support things such as Finance/Personnel?

*A:* Well, the finance world is a difficult one. The only way we can

judge our financial department is that, number one, we get our
monthly profit and loss on time, we get our balance-sheets on time.
We have set dates for our Board Meetings and that division has
got to conform to that effectiveness feedback time, that the statute
returns are put in on time. We want to be in there by September,
to have a deadline date of being to the bank with our printed
audited reports by the 30th September. It's fairly hard going for
any company. We have monthly link-back meetings on outstanding
debtors and the whole trend of business, which is at a Board
Meeting, plus the fact that we play it through out profit and loss
accounts to each individual top-team manager, which never
happened before, so they now give a divided share of administration
costs and they have to have that for the monthly output orientation
link back meetings. The Accounts Department has to perform and
then I have got the Accounts Manager tied in to an overall
percentage of her co-workers, her peers, that she has to support.
When they achieve budget objectives, she gets an overriding bonus
on each of their achievements, which is the only way we can do it
because, as you say, it is very hard to set a profit centre for them.
There are some, but it is very hard to measure it, so we are giving
her an overriding commission. This gives her a chance to go around
and say, 'Look, I have given you these things, we have got to do
this. How are things going?' She is interested, and so is the whole
department that is centralized, as most finance departments are.
We find now that each manager is going along and saying, 'Gee,
my administration costs have gone up'. They are worried and they
are involved, whereas before they didn't care. Now they are fighting
for percentages because they want to sit at the link-back meeting
and say: 'I have been profitable and I am going to get my bonus
and I am going to be effective in my outside selective area of
outputs.'

*Q:* Are your franchises part of all this as well?

*A:* No. They are straight-out distributors, but when you say are
they part of it, previously my national manager for computer airconditioning would go out and he would just do a traditional job. Now
he's gone out and said: 'Listen, if you want to be the distributor,
this is a very important state to me, you represent a large per cent
of my budget. Do you realize what a wonderful thing you have got
going for you? Now look, where is your plan? I want an output
plan with objectives from you.' He is now carrying the message
over to the distributors by asking them questions, and putting it to
them: 'I want a complete plan, a marketing plan within one month.
If you want to reassure this, we have got to work together as trading
partners and I want to help you. I don't get any feedback from

you. I have got to come down and visit you and you are just a typical distributor. I want to tell you it's not good enough. I am now looking at terms of outputs. Let's have a look at this, let's look at your objectives.' Now, of course, he has changed his attitude, he is beginning to change the attitude of our distributors without them knowing what they are doing, just by putting the questions and taking a more positive involved attitude, which is why my profits increased by 100 per cent.

*Q:* While I've often seen high profit return from changing behaviour like this, did most of that 100 per cent increase in profit come from this change within your control, as a result of these things you've told us about, or was half of it outside?

*A:* More effectiveness, I think, was the answer, in one area for instance, the airconditioning manager who up to that point was carrying my message all of a sudden said, 'Do you know what, our costing is wrong.' 'Is it?' 'Yes, I've been doing it in one way because you did it that way, and I thought I wouldn't offend you, but we are losing money. I can make you more money.' 'Can you, show me, you bring it back.' This guy is like a flower, you pour water on him and it starts opening and opening. He's changed the whole costing philosophy. He's changed the call priority rate to people, he's changed the method of designing brackets and systems, so that we design off the site and go on the site with brackets, and so forth. He has assisted me with research and development – we've got four new products this year. I won't give myself a plug, but we've got a wonderful airconditioning system, a do-it-yourself home airconditioning, and its really something, but I was free to search that out, and this guy wants to help me, and I was able to do a job where my talents have been suited. Instead of worrying about everyone, carrying the weight of the whole company on my shoulders and going home having a nervous breakdown, stiff necks, palpitating heart, and all the things we have under stress, now I don't have all those very much and these guys are wearing it with me. They are sharing the burden and it's been a combination of just being more effective and profit conscious whereas before they were just workers.

## EPILOGUE

The success continued for this output-oriented company. Here is an article that appeared in Australia's leading financial newspaper a few years after the talk was given.

**ATLAS RECONDITIONS THE ATTITUDE TO SUCCESS**
*By Richard Heft*

The managing director of Atlas Air, Mr Colin Ward, wants other managers to hear the story of his company because 'there's a lot of doom and gloom out there and we need some success stories'.

Atlas Air, which manufactures air conditioners for computer installations and, more recently, for office buildings, is about to merge with a larger company in an estimated $5–15 million deal.

As well as giving Atlas a much-needed injection of funds for its ongoing development programs, Mr Ward said the deal would make him 'financially independent for the first time in my life'.

But for the fiercely patriotic entrepreneur, the merger has the added benefit of giving funds to advance the technology Atlas has pioneered.

The company was set up in 1964 as a husband-and-wife operation with 'enough capital to last three months'.

It installed air conditioning units and on the suggestion of IBM, began to specialize in computer mainframe cooling – a business which later burgeoned. Later the company began designing and manufacturing its own units. It was up against major international competition which included Leibert (a $200 million company) and Siemens (the giant German multi-national).

'I think they dismissed us as a joke when we started,' Mr Ward said.

According to Mr Ward, a large measure of the success of Atlas can be attributed to a business technique known as the output orientation system pioneered by Professor W.J. Reddin which he adopted in 1978. He attended an output orientation seminar when Atlas was languishing.

'The company wasn't going anywhere and I couldn't figure out why. I put the company in for analysis and it came out that it was being run by an autocrat who was killing his own company, had surrounded himself with bureaucrats and was destined to fail.

'Previously nothing moved in this company unless I knew about it. That is how most small companies start out and that's why most managers can't expand with their own companies.'

The crucial part of the success of the system was sticking to it, according to Mr Ward.

'We have hung in there and made it a part of our culture,' Mr Ward said. 'Other companies use it as a veneer and that's why things like management by objectives usually fail.'

Atlas has 12 division heads all of whom are now individually accountable and must meet goals on a monthly basis. As well, the company has a system of profit sharing for each of its managers.

According to Mr Ward, one of the most important secrets of the system is the free flow of information.

'They [Atlas managers] are better informed than most board members', he said.

Its South-east Asian branch is based in Singapore, and Atlas has recently broken into the Chinese market and has been officially recognized as a supplier to the Chinese Government.

Turnover now is about $27 million and Mr Ward said the company was on schedule to achieve this year's target of $35 million, about 25 per cent of which will come from exports.

But the area of greatest potential growth for the company is its recently released modular office air conditioning system.

The system is said to be a world first and cost an estimated $2 million to develop.

Further plans for development with its new partner include the development of the first commercially viable gas cooling system and the setting-up of a factory in India to facilitate entry into the booming computer market there.

(*Financial Review*,
8 December 1986, p. 30)

# 12 Change in Falconbridge Nickel Mines

'But it's behind the scenes that the most radical changes are continuing to take place.'

'Before the programme, there were twelve levels in the organization. After the programme, there are only six levels. Six levels have been removed and far greater effectiveness has resulted.'

'People are being a lot more candid and a lot more team-oriented and as a result more effective in their managing.'

'Teamwork means that you and I contribute to the decision-making process affecting the group with which we work.'

## USING THE 3-D ORGANIZATION EFFECTIVENESS PROGRAMME IN A 5,000 EMPLOYEE NICKEL MINE

*This is an account of the use of the 3-D Organization Effectiveness Programme in a 5,000-employee nickel mine. It was written by internal staff for internal use and was distributed to all employees through the employee magazine, 'Falcon'. This gives a good account of a comprehensive programme to achieve organizational effectiveness through emphasis on output orientation. Many types of meetings are described and their effects.*

*The chapter also contains extracts of a recent interview with Jack Boyd, Organization Effectiveness Programme Co-ordinator, about the success of the programme to date, which was reproduced in 'Falcon'.*

In the past two years almost 500 Falconbridge employees have gone 'back to school', not to learn new academic or technical skills, but to learn how to make better use of the skills they already have and how best to work as members of a team.

All this is part of our overall Organization Effectiveness Programme using the week long 3-D Managerial Effectiveness Seminars (3-D MES).

If one word had to describe the change at Falconbridge in the past two years, 'streamlining' would probably be an excellent choice. Streamlining describes in many ways the obvious change that employees can see, namely fewer levels of supervision.

But it is behind the scenes that the most radical changes are continuing to take place at our nickel mine such as increasing numbers of departments looking to teamwork as the best way of making decisions which affect them, and getting the job done.

Teamwork means that you and I contribute to the decision-making process affecting the group with which we work; we give our views and make our feelings known about what we see as the best solution to a problem. In other words, everyone on the team has the opportunity to contribute towards a solution and we strive for consensus among the team.

There are four active phases to what is now called the Organization Effectiveness Programme: 3-D MES, Team Meetings, Inter-team Meetings and Employee Surveys. The term 'manager' as used applies to any person acting as supervisor of other people.

## Management reorganization

The company's drive for better managerial effectiveness started right at the top about three years ago with a change in the management organization when John J. Mather came to Falconbridge from Indusmin, a Falconbridge Group company, as President of the Nickel Division. His mandate dealt in part with reorganization and he introduced the managerial effectiveness programme. Using the team approach, they set about to improve management performance and devise new reporting structures where appropriate. As an example of the type of organization structure changes that have been made, a 'before and after' comparison of the maintenance and services group is presented below.

## Change in number of levels in maintenance and services group before and after the organization effectiveness programme

*Before the Organization Effectiveness Programme:*

1   General Manager – Operations
2   Assistant General Manager
3   Manager Production
4   Assistant Manager Production

5  Area General Superintendent
6  Assistant Area General Superintendent
7  Maintenance Superintendent
8  Assistant Maintenance Superintendent
9  Area Master Mechanic
10  Master Mechanic
11  Foreman
12  Tradesman

*Two years after the start of the Organization Effectiveness Programme:*

1  General Manager
2  Manager – Maintenance and Services
3  Maintenance Superintendent
4  Master Mechanic
5  Foreman
6  Tradesman

Before the Organization Effectiveness programme, there were twelve levels; after the Organization Effectiveness Programme there were only six levels. Six levels have been removed and far greater effectiveness resulted.

### 3-D managerial effectiveness seminar

The Managerial Effectiveness Seminar (3-D MES) focuses on improving the managerial effectiveness of the individual supervisor and the theme of the six-day seminar is clarification of a manager's present standards of effectiveness and objectives.

In addition, the 3-D MES also deals with identifying the styles of others and sharply increases a person's awareness of the manager's own supervisory style and of how to use the most appropriate style to obtain optimum effectiveness in differing situations.

The 3-D MESs are conducted off company premises with employees in teams of four to eight. Team members on these seminars usually have no current reporting relationships to each other and spend about 80 per cent of their seminar time learning how to work more effectively together. The 3-D MES emphasizes effectiveness as the central issue in management and can be used to introduce output orientation methods in an organization. One full day is spent reaching agreement on the specific responsibilities or effectiveness areas team members have in their own jobs and the objectives they have over the next few years. At the conclusion of a 3-D MES the individual is usually more highly conscious of how participation by each member of a team is able to contribute to making the best possible decision in any given situation.

## The team meeting

Following the 3-D MES, particular on-the-job teams, such as a department head and reporting subordinates, meet to decide how best they may improve the way they work together. This three-day session of the Team Meeting is an emphasis on team measurement areas and managerial behaviour of each individual on the team.

It starts with reviewing the past managerial behaviours of team members, makes suggestions for behaviour changes and the major responsibilities (effectiveness areas) are developed specifying what each other team member could do for them that would enable them to improve their managerial effectiveness.

The Team Meeting leads directly to a clearer definition of that particular team's role in the organization and each member's role on that team. Team objectives can be better prepared through this approach. This may result in some team reorganization which the team has the opportunity to design.

## Interteam meeting

Another step in the programme is the elimination of non-productive blockages between different teams in the total organization. These may be staff/line organization problems or issues between particular departments,

Blockages usually become more visible and people more amenable to changes to remove blockages because of Team Meetings and the 3-D MES Seminar. The central question both teams address in these one-day meetings is: 'What can I do to increase your effectiveness without decreasing my own?' In these Interteam Meetings between key members of two teams a plan of action is worked out and agreed upon by members on both teams as to how blockages will be removed. Commitments are made, and follow up agreed upon to ensure changes are carried through.

## Employee surveys

An important part of the overall Organization Effectiveness Programme is development of plans to meet employees' needs.

Identifying needs and concerns of employees is done through surveys sent to all employees.

In June last year and again in June of this year, all employees were asked to complete a survey, called the Organizational Health Survey, developed and processed by an independent company. Results of these surveys are tabulated and provided to management. Overall company results as well as breakdowns by departments, by collective bargaining groups and other groupings are produced to indicate how employees view the company. The survey results are compared to other companies who have completed the same survey, and to other years the survey has been done by us, to see if action undertaken to address issues is being effective in getting desired results.

There are three components to the surveys: a Job Satisfaction Survey which asked how satisfied employees were with their jobs at Falconbridge; an Organizational Health Survey, which through a series of questions deals with areas such as communication, creativity, conflict management, leadership, productivity, participation, human resources management and organization structure issues; and a Management by Objectives Survey, which is used to assess to what degree we are using elements of the management by objectives process in the management of our operations.

Response from employees has been good, and further administration of these surveys is planned in successive years, so that developments can be monitored.

Feedback sessions are held with employees about these surveys and results have been made available to executives of the three unions. A personal letter is sent to all employees providing a brief analysis of the overall results of the survey for the whole division. Departmental meetings are also held to discuss the results of the surveys in each department and employees are given an opportunity to participate in plans for improving those areas where weaknesses were indicated.

## INTERVIEW WITH JACK BOYD

*The following are excerpts from an interview with Jack Boyd, Co-ordinator of the Organization Effectiveness Programme, conducted by Falcon of the in-house journal.*

*JB*: The Organization Effectiveness Programme is a name given to a programme being used by management to assist in organization development. Its emphasis is in areas of developing individual and team approaches to problem-solving in key areas that affect a team and its relations with other teams in a large complex organization.

*Falcon*: How long has the programme been in operation?

*JB*: About two years. Following the late John Mather's appointment as President of the Nickel Division, a group of senior people attended the first 3-D Managerial Effectiveness Seminar. Mr Mather had successfully used this type of programme for organization development in Indusmin prior to coming here. From this came a commitment to develop a similar Organization Effectiveness Programme by our management team.

*Falcon*: How many employees have been through the programme?

*JB*: The programme is not yet completed as there are various stages to it. So far, all salaried employees have been through the 3-D MES stage which is the first part of this programme. It concentrates on individual supervisory styles and how to use appropriate styles to achieve optimum results. The second stage is the Team Meeting, which is now being done with concentration on department team performance improvement.

*Falcon*: You said there are other parts to this programme. If so, what's next?

*JB*: Yes, there are other parts to the programme and some have started already. For instance, the employee surveys in June of this year and last, and various Interteam Meetings between specific teams to sort out long-standing problems. I'd like to talk a bit about the employee surveys because they were and will continue to be a very important part of this programme. The survey feedback was tabulated by an independent company and they were able to tell our management team how employees viewed the company under various categories, department by department.

*Falcon*: That sounds like an annual 'physical'.

*JB*: Well, it is in a way because it effectively takes the 'pulse' of our organization. There are 80 questions in these surveys which cover eight important areas: communication, creativity, leadership, productivity, conflict management, participation, human resource management and organization management. It was important that we learn how employees feel about the company in these vital areas, so that we can improve any of the negative factors which are there.

*Falcon*: What's one of the key points of this approach to individuals working in teams?

*JB*: One of the key points is learning to use teamwork; to use all of the resources any given group of people has within it; and to use all the attributes the members of a team can bring to solving a problem. Through the 3-D MES and Team Meetings, individuals can learn how best to contribute and use the resources of others.

*Falcon*: I've heard a lot of comment from people who have gone through the 3-D MES course about the strain and pressure of long days and late nights.

*JB*: Yes, well there are reasons for the long hours. The first task at the 3-D MES is that participants have to reach consensus on the answers to 80 questions with a team of six or seven people who do not know each other that well. Being so new to the whole 'consensus' thing, they often struggle for two to three hours on the first eight questions or so. But what happens with fatigue is that it tends to eventually break down resistance to things; people are apt to be very polite and kind and not very candid when they're all well rested but this eventually breaks down with long hours. And let's face it, one of the keys to this whole business is learning to tell it like it is and yet not be unduly harsh in the way you present something. If you have something on your mind you have to say it because if you hold back on something you'll never be able to make a commitment to the decision in the end. At the end of these seminars we usually find that all members on a team are so committed that no one minds putting in the long hours.

*Falcon*: So you're not only looking for consensus to decision, you're looking for commitment as well?

*JB*: Most definitely for commitment.The two reasons for working as a team and there are only two, one is that the team may come up with a better solution than one person alone could have developed and the other is to get commitment from everybody on that team to the solution in the end on the lines of 'that's our plan and we're going to make it work!'

*Falcon*: Do you see this programme as having a positive impact?

*JB*: Yes, I certainly think so. People are being a lot more candid and a lot more team oriented and as a result more effective in their managing.

# 13 Change in a power commission

'One fundamental change in our philosophy as a result of this programme is that we are now committed to rewarding excellence and treating incompetence appropriately.'

'The Team Meeting is the most important step in the programme.'

'The enormous number and rapidity of changes being encountered provided a major reason for the programme.'

'We deliberately attempted to sample many of the development programmes available . . . for one reason or another these did not suit our needs.'

*R. E. Tweedale, General Manager of a Power Commission, describes his organization's experience of 3-D Managerial Effectiveness.*

In the last few years our supervisory and managerial staff have participated in an extensive management development programme. The majority had one-week 'country house' seminars using case method covering finance and human relations. Over seventy of our supervisory and managerial force participated in one week T-Groups. In addition many of our senior management had an intensive five-week programme of case study.

We deliberately attempted to sample many of the development programmes available. In addition to pure case and T-Groups, we sampled the Blake Managerial Grid, the American Management Association's seminars and many others. For one reason or another these did not suit our needs fully, although each could be useful in an optimum programme of organization effectiveness.

## A comprehensive 3-D theory

We became acquainted with Professor W. J. Reddin and his work on organization effectiveness. Professor Reddin, whose background includes Harvard and the Massachusetts Institute of Technology, developed his programme by stressing three elements: task, relationships and effectiveness. It was the third element of effectiveness that engaged our attention as we thought this was often overlooked. His associated programme was quite flexible and could be tailored to meet the needs of our organization. The 3-D managerial style model, in particular, was flexible enough for ease of identification within our organization. In fact flexibility was what attracted us to his management style model and his organization effectiveness programme. The model suggests that there is no single ideal management type. It proposes that managers should not be judged by how they act but whether their actions are appropriate and effective. The hallmark of a good manager, then, is diagnostic skill in sizing up a situation and effectiveness in handling it. This was so close to our commonsense view of management that we thought his programme was worth a trial.

Apart from job knowledge, intelligence and task orientation, a manager should have flexibility. Organization life demands that a manager continually adapts to changing situations. The managers who are most useful, it seems to me, are those who can size up a situation and then follow through in the most appropriate way. Sometimes this may seem hard, sometimes soft, but always effective.

Professor Reddin was given freedom to move within the organization and managers were free to consult with him as they wished. We had considered employing an inside person for this type of work, but found that the external person brings a detachment which might otherwise be hard to find. Professor Reddin has made it clear, and we have accepted, that his client is the organization and not any particular individual, team, or division.

## OUR ORGANIZATION PROBLEMS

Naturally our organization has had some problems. In the main, these were caused by very rapid growth and consequent unseasoned staff. The key problem was that as an organization, we had not fully adjusted to the fact that we had suddenly grown. The problems that arose from this were:

- Too many managers involved in some decisions and not enough managers involved in others.
- Some dysfunctional interdivisional communication problems.
- A need for clear objective setting and output orientation.
- A need for more decision-making at lower levels.
- Some resistance to change in the organization.
- Insufficient emphasis on job performance.

These problems are common to many rapidly growing organizations. We wanted to do something about them.

How could we change all this? It is very easy to change an organization by inducing fear. This is done simply by firing a few key people – or demoting them. We are opposed to this idea unless absolutely necessary. We believe that organization life often enforces managers and workers into inefficiency, so that they as individuals are seen as incompetent when it may not be their fault. Very often, they may not have all the resources with which to work or they may simply be in the wrong job.

Our management staff is basically engineer-oriented. This is common and appropriate in an electrical utility. However, some engineers are not basically relationship oriented. They should not all, therefore, be expected to pick up a managerial hat just because there is a vacancy.


## THE PROGRAMME

Our change programme as it finally evolved had several types of meetings, plus the 3-D Managerial Effectiveness Seminar (3-D MES), which came first. They collectively performed the functions of unfreezing the organization, changing it and then stabilizing it at the new level.

The meetings and the 3-D MES overlap each other in time and the dates below give the starting time for each successive meeting.


### 3-D managerial effectiveness seminar (May, year 1)

The first stage was the 3-D MES. All our top managers participated. Here we learned the 3-D style theory and its application to organized life. We became acquainted with sound teamwork principles, with our own style and were provided with a direction for style change. As planned, the main impact of this laboratory was a general 'unfreezing' of the organization and of individual managers.

There is little doubt that this stage alone had a profound impact on the organization. As the general manager, I attended all but one of the eight seminars for a few hours and discussed with the managers the direction we thought the organization should go. In addition, I solicited their comments by giving each team the task of identifying organization weak spots. All of the comments of the 28 teams were distributed to the top managers in the organization. I cannot say I agreed with all the comments made, but I must say that, in aggregate, they exerted a shock on the organization.

At this point, we decided that the 3-D programme had something to offer us, and I called a planning meeting to chart the direction and timing of the programme. At that meeting we decided to use our largest division, the Distribution Division, as a pilot group for team training and the subsequent 3-D stages. We wanted a pilot programme to make sure we knew what we were getting into. As it happened, many of the changes in the pilot division spread naturally to the other divisions.

**Team Meeting (February, year 3)**

The Team Meeting is the most important step in the programme. It takes advantage of the unfreezing effect of the 3-D MES. In effect, it gives a management team a perfect opportunity to decide just how they intend to work together in the future. We decided to go as far as to ask each team to reorganize itself. Many teams did make some long overdue changes. I know of none of these seminars that did not have a marked influence in making each team more effective. The programme we evolved was tested on a senior management team and then conducted on demand in other parts of the organization. Many teams have reconstructed their internal organization after these meetings and the methods used to make decisions have changed. 'We-team' decisions rather than autocratic 'one-alone' decisions are now commonplace, although not used everywhere.

The 3-D MES and the Team Meetings had a profound impact on our management force. Withdrawal of involvement and commitment is nothing new in organizations, but changing this condition is. Many of our less involved managers when confronted with their behaviour in the 3-D MES decided to modify it. The Team Meetings gave them this chance.

**Managerial objectives conference (April, year 3)**

Through the medium of the four-hour supervisor-subordinate one-to-one meeting we have introduced output orientation into most parts of the commission. This was introduced with remarkable ease and appears to solve many of our problems of both direction and motivation of the managerial and supervisory force. Historically we have been geared to control of input rather than measurement of output. Obviously this will take years to change completely, but major structural changes are underway.

An interesting phenomenon has occurred which I call 'development by proxy'. In our pilot division many changes in procedures, and for that matter management philosophy, were introduced. These changes, seen as successful, were picked up by many of the other divisions. This is proof, I think, that once a direction is clearly established, the whole organization can quickly adopt it or adapt to it.

**Corporate strategy meeting (September, year 3)**

Another stage of the programme was the Corporate Strategy Meeting. The three-person top team of myself, my deputy and chief engineer, and the comptroller met for three days to discuss the organization and its future. In particular, we looked at the internal design of our organization as well as its comprehensive role. We know we were ready for such a change and the three days gave us a chance to get into the new design in some detail. We made many changes which may not seem profound but were significant in their effect on the organization. These included:

- Redesigning the composition of the Executive Committee.
- Decreasing the number of managers reporting to the general manager.
- Introducing a senior engineer into an economic analysis function.
- Collecting several staff departments together in a newly created unit.
- Creating two senior positions for functions not previously distinguished separately.

There were many more, of course, but the point is that the strategy meeting was not simply an intellectual exercise.

## Work unit idea conference (February, year 4)

One problem in a geographically decentralized operation such as ours is the difficulty in getting changes introduced in the field. This was facilitated in three ways. One was by bringing into head office the various groups to discuss proposals for improvement. Another was by going to the field. For me, this stage was a most exciting and personally satisfying part of the programme. We sat down with the field units, one by one, to discuss their objectives. These small meetings were usually attended by five levels. They helped to tie the head office and field effectively together and tapped many new ideas. There was constant expounding by managers and others of the real need for change to take place, so that proper responsibility could be given and taken.

## Interteam meeting (September, year 4)

The impact of the effectiveness programme was by this time having a profound effect on the commission. One outcome was that the various parts of the commission were finding new relationships with other parts. We saw this as a necessary phase rather than an unnecessary evil. One major misalignment problem occurred between the HQ staff elements and the line. This and other similar problems were moved to resolution through the Interteam Meeting. Here staff and line sat down to hammer – I think that is the word - out their appropriate relationships. What has resulted is a functional and major redistribution of responsibilities for the good of the commission. We see staff as architects and catalysts rather than control or vertical feedback mechanisms.

## Large group meeting (October, year 4)

Up to this point the programme has concentrated on the manager alone, the vertical relationship and teams. We next decided to work in similar fashion with a division as the basic unit for change. The Distribution Division, our largest, decided to have a Large Group Meeting with six levels at one meeting. This was attended by 80 personnel – about a 10 per cent representation of all regions and all trades including linemen and meter readers. It was carefully designed for maximum participation. The objective of this meeting was to give the division manager an opportunity to explain his management philosophy and give all present an opportunity to question him in detail on past, present or future events.

The enormous number and rapidity of changes being encountered provided a major reason for the programme.

The conference went extremely well and another is planned. An ideal future topic with enormous payoff will be one concerning the methods of introducing change. If the division, as a whole, could agree on change introduction procedures the productivity potential would be tremendous.


## CHANGES

Training or development is not a profitable proposition unless something happens. I personally am not influenced too much by what people simply say about training courses. In fact, I do not know of a training programme which is not rated highly by participants, even though it may have been relatively useless in terms of introducing changes. The pay-off in training is not more training activity, nor is it what people say in answer to researchers. The pay-off has to be visible change.

As I have indicated, in the past few years our organization has made several major changes. In the past two years we have:

- Reorganized key parts of the management structure.
- Reoriented managers 'to manage'.
- Established a programme of output orientation throughout the company.
- Pushed decision levels downward, so that particular decisions are made at appropriate levels.
- Modified procedures, so that performance or output data is operated as well as input or control data.
- Changed the attitude to change itself, so that acceptance of change is becoming the norm.
- Established teamwork methods in parts of the organization that could use it and established other methods where teamwork was not needed.
- Introduced the norm of performance measurement though the reward structure is not yet decided on.

One fundamental change in our philosophy as a result of this programme is that we are now committed to rewarding excellence and treating incompetence appropriately. This is easier said than done, but I think we have been able to get the word out and can now take some concrete steps. Other specific changes dealing with human resource utilization included:

- Line crew foremen fully replaced head office engineers on a committee to select line tools.
- The meter readers established their own work norms and disciplinary manual.
- I announced that (for the first time) a lineman could work his way up to become general manager.

## MASSACHUSETTS INSTITUTE OF TECHNOLOGY RESEARCH

From the start we decided to conduct research as the programme proceeded. Several technical articles have appeared and will appear in professional journals. This research has provided good feedback to the units generating the data, but I think our main reason for encouraging research was to facilitate the advance of social science. Ohms Law was developed some time ago. As yet, as far as I know, social science has a long way to go before such a simple and concrete formula can be established.

An independent study conducted by Massachusetts Institute of Technology (MIT) produced such answers as:

|  | *Yes* (%) | *No* (%) | *Don't know* (%) |
|---|---|---|---|
| 'Should "unfreezing" (3-D MES) be accomplished in stranger groups?' | 92.5 | 7.5 | 0.0 |
| 'Was there need for this type of programme in the company?' | 87.3 | 12.7 | 0.0 |
| 'Did the programme assist you sufficiently with behaviour change?' | 88.9 | 11.1 | 0.0 |
| 'Should there be more team training?' | 85.0 | 15.0 | 0.0 |

## NOT ALL PROBLEMS SOLVED

While I believe the programme has been a success, we still have problems:

- There has been a little difficulty on the part of some in adjusting to new philosophies.
- Some departments whose roles have changed are going through what amounts to an identity crisis.
- The rule-books take much longer to change than we imagine and this slows down the change process.

## IF YOU WANT TO START

Based on our experience, I would make these suggestions to other top executives who are thinking of getting involved in an organization effectiveness programme:

- Before you do anything, decide what your idea of a good corporate policy is, in other words – where do you want to go?
- Understand the implications of the various management style models that are current – in particular, 3-D, McGregor and Grid.
- Discover the nature of the various change programmes now available. Get some data on nuts and bolts success.
- Find an external change agent who you think is competent, has experience, and has or could earn the trust of the top executives.
- Work with the change agent to develop an organization programme to suit your needs.

And do not:

- Think that your organization will change without your changing as well.
- Rely on a mechanical approach that suggests all companies have the same problems.
- Think that the programme will be over in 12 months.

## IS THIS A PROGRAMME?

On reading this, you may get the impression that this organization effectiveness plan was highly programmed – it was anything but that. The programme as it evolved met the needs of the organization as it evolved. It may be that this programme has general application. I cannot judge that, but it fitted our needs well.

Development is too important to have it ritualized. As far as it has been feasible, which was practically always, organization subparts could move to the next step as soon as they liked or wait as long as they liked. As far as I can tell, this has improved the reception of the programme tremendously and heightened its ultimate impact.

# 14 Change in a computer firm

'One criticism my subordinates made of me was that if I do not want to listen, I just cut off. They gave me examples, and I had to admit they were right.'

'Accountants thought that, just because they were accountants, they were automatically good profit centre managers. They thought the job was all figure-keeping. The "unfreezing" exercise finally showed them that there was little relation between the two things. Now they are good profit centre managers because they know how to apply their knowledge.'

'There was a danger that, because we had grown so fast, some areas of responsibility may have slipped between the cracks, or overlapped each other.'

*This chapter, written independently as an article by David Clutter-buck for the magazine 'International Management', shows the effects of the 3-D Management Effectiveness Seminar (3-D MES) and Team Meetings on improving organization and managerial effectiveness through an increased emphasis on output orientation and teamwork.*

When Graham Aldridge, comptroller of a national subsidiary of International Computers Ltd, in the UK, disagreed with a colleague he didn't mince his words. 'I guess I had quite an abrasive style of management', he admits. He either banged the table and said, 'No way', or told them rudely they were talking rubbish.

Aldridge changed his behaviour considerably since he attended a 3-D MES earlier this year. Over the past 12 months every manager, from directors to supervisors, had attended the same seminars, intended to 'unfreeze' their managerial styles. Managers from other companies who attended the same seminar as Aldridge pointed out to him that his manner put other people on the defensive and hindered real teamwork.

'I used to think I was making people think more deeply about things,' says Aldridge. 'Now I try to achieve the same result by asking leading questions.'

The company started the programme because it was worried about the side effects of its fast growth. the national subsidiary had grown from 750 people to 1,200 in three and a half years. Turnover doubled to about $35 million in the same period. Explains managing director John Starkey: 'There was a danger that, because we had grown so fast, some areas of responsibility may have slipped between the cracks, or overlapped each other'.

The computer company claims that Reddin's technique, which he calls 3-D, has helped to improve co-operation between departments. Managers have also been made to look critically at their effectiveness both as a team and as individuals. As a result, decision-making has become faster, with greater participation by managers lower down the line.

Reddin bases his ideas on the theory that every manager's job contains a mixture of getting along with people and getting things done. He calls the two aspects relationships orientation and task orientation and uses them to define management styles.

Unlike many other management theorists, Reddin does not necessarily aim at changing the manager's style. Instead he wants managers to recognize their own style and to use the knowledge to react more flexibly.

The styles are used as the discussion point to help managers to face up to their own behaviour and to criticize candidly that of others. In the 'unfreezing' seminars they practise with people outside their normal working group. When every manager from a team has attended a seminar, the team meets to repeat the critical analysis part of the process. These meetings are called Team Meetings.

In the seminars, the participants learn to identify variations on the different management styles through films and management games. They split into teams, who observe each other's behaviour, and make each other aware of the management styles they are using and how effectively. In addition, participants have to define and list what Reddin calls their 'Effectiveness Areas' – those essential outputs of the job that would damage the company by their absence. The aim of this exercise is to help them concentrate on the most important objectives when they return to their jobs.

The seminar made Starkey look at his own job in a new light, even though he disagreed with the assessment his team colleagues made of his management style. The team diagnosed him as an integrated manager, but Starkey thought he paid too little attention to the personnel aspects of his job.

For some people, the candour can be too much. In an extreme case, an apparent high-flyer, who appeared to have a great deal of confidence and ability, collapsed like a balloon when faced by a sharp analysis from team-mates. Because of bad behaviour in the seminar team-mates asked this participant to leave the room on several occasions. This individual left the company soon afterwards.

At the end of each internal seminar, Starkey spent three hours asking participants for their recommendations of ways to make the company more effective. Kenneth Simper, of the company's training function, says: 'They named company policies they considered to be inappropriate and even criticized members of the top team whose management style they thought should be improved. In four seminars of 40 managers each, some 150 points were raised.'

Starkey promised to answer all the recommendations in two weeks, but the sheer volume made it impossible. 'As a result, some managers at lower levels became very cynical about it all', says Simper.

Explains Anthony Whetton, head of the newly established large systems division: 'People assume that because they air organization or management problems there it is a magic wand to solve them in no time. When their expectations are not realized, they may not understand the amount of work that is needed to put things right.'

Some problems were tackled very quickly, however. Managers in the first two seminars pointed out overlaps in responsibility between functional departments. For example, the personnel department would send out memoranda on a new car policy without consulting the finance department, which was also concerned. Starkey set up a committee to co-ordinate this kind of policy-making. The committee had produced a number of manuals, indicating who should be consulted in each area before a policy decision is announced.

Meanwhile the top team held its Team Meeting. The ten top managers analysed one another's styles, and says Simper, 'There were strong things said to every member'. They also looked at how effective they were as a team.

One thing that quickly came to light was a conflict of objectives between the department selling computer hardware and the department selling computer time on a bureau basis. Both were making independent and conflicting bids to the same customers, where there was an alternative of supplying computer time or a small computer. Says the consultant, 'Sometimes the personal needs of the sales staff who have targets to meet, were put before those of the company'. The matter was resolved by putting both departments under the control of the same director and hiving off large computer systems to a separate department.

Another area where interdepartmental co-operation improved was the technical training department. Says Simper: 'We have not defined its function in terms of what was needed for the business. The technical training department teaches customers' personnel how to use our machines. We used to see that as an end in itself. Now we realize that it is only a means to the end of developing the customer as a growing market for our products. Managers responsible for training now see themselves as helping sales.'

The top team also found it could save time by closer co-operation on missives from head office in the UK. Says personnel, education and training manager Colin Peters: 'In the past someone at head office would send the same document asking for information to four different members of the top team. All four would answer it independently. Now, one says to the other three – "I am doing it. Send your input to me".'

'The quality of our decision-making has improved and meetings are shorter between a third and a half', says Starkey. 'We now define our objectives for a meeting before we start, and see they are met.'

Team Meetings further down the line had similar results, exposing weaknesses both in people and departments. Says field engineering manager Norman Goulding: 'One criticism my subordinates made of me was that if I do not want to listen, I just cut off. They gave me examples, and I had to admit they were right.'

People are also much clearer about what they are expected to do, claims Peters: 'Accountants thought that, just because they were accountants, they were automatically good profit centre managers. They thought the job was all figure-keeping.' The unfreezing exercise finally showed them that there was little relation between the two things. 'Now they are good profit centre managers because they know how to apply their knowledge', Simper concludes.

Not everyone understood what the Team Meetings were trying to do, however. Says Simper: 'Some managers wanted to run their Team Meetings too early, before all their subordinates had attended 'unfreezing' seminars. They wanted to solve their problems then and there to boost this year's profits for their departments. We pointed out that the pay-off period is much longer.'

In another instance a group of middle managers in one part of the company decided they were already so effective and candid a team they did not need to conduct Team Meetings at all. 'But three months later pressure from their subordinates made them change their minds', says Simper.

The success of these team meetings encouraged top management to delegate more. A particular opportunity arose when ICL internally took over the computer subsidiaries of Singer Co. Starkey and his top-team colleagues worked out an overall superstructure for the merged organization, and defined new effectiveness areas. Then the next thirty people in the hierarchy were given a free hand to sort out the rest of the organization and responsibilities over the next five months.

'The top team began by asking themselves how much participation they could get into the exercise', says Simper. 'They organized the managers into working teams, each of which reported up We could not have done this 18 months ago, because people would not have been able to operate effectively in taskforces. Branch managers would have been over ruled by regional managers, for example.'

# 15 Change in John Player & Sons

'The company was not looking for immediate, quantifiable results. Organization development is a roughly self-descriptive term, a device for "developing" or "changing" an organization.'

'This is the kind of organization which tends to breed complacency and certainly spawns bureaucracy.'

'You can never tell which bit of the work has done the trick.'

'Over the last few years, there is no doubt that the company has changed enormously. It is less stuffy. Managers can unbend with their subordinates. Subordinates can have a go at their managers.'

Terry Dodsworth explains why this tobacco company spent £200,000 and 3,500 senior manager days on organization development. This case study appeared in the *Financial Times*. The term organization development (OD) is used in this article. It has close similarities to what this book refers to as 'output orientation'.

Prior to the company's decision to embark on the output orientation programme, they had been implementing management by objectives (MBO) for five years and had three full-time staff engaged in MBO implementation. The seventy top managers, including the full top team, had participated in the one-week Blake Grid Phase I Seminar. The key opportunities for improvement that were identified included higher candour which was thought to be likely to lead to higher productivity, higher commitment to the company unit and organization outputs and a major lowering of resistance.

By March next year John Player, the Nottingham tobacco company, will have spent £200,000 on the management technique known as organization development (OD). It will have used up the £200,000 in approximately three years. Three hundred managers, almost all the Player management from chairman down to junior ranks, will have gone through the hoops on which the company has already lavished a total of 3,500 (senior) working days.

Player's will never know exactly what it has achieved with the programme. It will never know whether it could have saved the £200,000 or whether some of the changes that have come over the company in the past three years would have happened anyway. There is simply no way of accurately quantifying the results of an OD exercise.

Why, then, is John Player, one of the biggest companies in the Imperial Tobacco group, investing so much expensive management time in OD?

The answer John Player gives is quite simple. The company was not looking for immediate, quantifiable results. Organization development is a roughly self-descriptive term, a device for 'developing' or 'changing' an organization.

The object is to make managers behave in a more open and participative manner to set them talking and arguing and solving their problems together. In laymen's language, it is a technique designed to inject some entrepreneurial drive into a stodgily bureaucratic company. It aims to do this by breaking down the barriers which grow like barnacles on a well established company structure.


**Programme Objectives**

The programme objectives agreed by the top team were:

- Improved objective setting.
- Increased commitment to managers' objectives.
- Increased commitment to team objectives.
- Increased acceptance of, and readiness to, change.
- Increased identification of the need for appropriate change.
- Increased implementation of changes needed.
- Improved interfunctional co-operation.
- Increased use of participation in decision-making when this improves the decisions or obtains necessary commitment.
- Increased job satisfaction.
- Increased candour.
- Increased trust.

There were two basic reasons for adopting OD. The Player's Board was changing rapidly with the influx of new directors including the then chairman, Geoffrey Iden. 'I think', he says, 'that there was a growing pressure at that time to query the benevolent autocracy type of management. There was a greater desire for participation in the company.'

John Player is a big, traditionally wealthy company. It employs about 8,500 people and has a long history of success behind it.

This is the kind of organization which tends to breed complacency and certainly spawns bureaucracy. Player wanted to develop a style of management which would be much more responsive to rapid change.

Iden, a newcomer to the Board, was chiefly responsible for the move to OD. 'We almost hit upon it by accident', he says. 'But it seemed to be the answer to some of the problems that faced us.' He chose a system developed by the ebullient, Canada-based Professor Bill Reddin. Reddin is an indefatigable inventor of management jargon who uses a technique which he calls his '3-D system of managerial effectiveness'. To go through one of his courses, as most of the Player's management have, involves a visit to the 3-D Managerial Effectiveness Seminar (MES), the Team Meeting, the Interteam Meeting, and so on.

Behind this phraseology lies a fairly clear-cut idea. Reddin believes that organizations function best when their separate parts understand and are working towards a common goal.

Thus the 3-D MES is designed to show managers how they appear to others, and how team working can be the most effective way of tackling problems. The Team Meeting is for a group of managers within a department to get together and thrash out their points of difference. The Interteam meeting, on the other hand, is supposed to bring different departments together for similar clarifying discussions.

The meetings are not simple across-the-table encounters in the conventional sense. They are led, as unobtrusively as possible, by Reddin or Player's own three-member OD department under Barrie Haley. The groups of managers never spend less than a day, and may spend up to a week, on the meetings, which are always held in hotels well away from the company. The problems are generally ones they have faced at work or those they can see looming.

Sometimes they are also encouraged to comment on each other's behaviour, the technique that has led to much criticism of the activities of the behavioural scientists in industry. 'The aim', says Haley, 'is to avoid being destructively critical, to make people see the differences between how they see themselves and how others see them'.

By the end of the year the major programme of OD meetings will probably be finished at Player. The managers will have learned the basic techniques. From then on, it is a matter of the OD department keeping managers talking about their problems and eventually, Haley hopes, insinuating the techniques until they become an accepted part of corporate life.

Over the last few years, say Player's senior managers, there is no doubt that the company has changed enormously. It is less stuffy. Managers can unbend with their subordinates. Subordinates can have a go at their managers. 'I like to think that my staff say what they think of me', says Nevil Poole, Production Operations Manager.

But however much the company changes, and however successful it is, it will never be easy to pin down the part OD has played. For example, Player has closed down its Nottingham pipe tobacco making plant and redeployed a large number of workers with no major hitch. It has also launched a successful attack on its direct labour costs. Player's No. 6 has established itself as Britain's biggest-selling brand. Who can tell whether all this would have happened without OD?

Again, it is difficult to believe that Geoffrey Iden would not have taken the company in much the same direction as it has gone anyway. He is the archetypal modern manager, the man who started as office boy, worked his way through the company, and now at 59 sits on the Imps main Board. He is a naturally relaxed, open, consultative type of manager.

Iden recognizes that he will never be able to pin down OD's contribution. 'It's like the famous quip on advertising', he says. 'You can never tell which bit of the work has done the trick.'

What he has done is accept one of the basic truths about large modern corporations in a dominant market position. They are inevitably bureaucratic, and they need a lot of pushing before they will change. If OD has made the blood pump through Player's management arteries again he will be happy.


**Some Key Programme Elements**

In summary, some of the key programme elements were:

- A full 3-D programme using those meetings as needed was initiated.
- Three hundred managers were involved and all participated in the 3-D MES except the seventy who had participated in Blake, all of whom instead participated in the two-day '3-D conversion course'.

- An internal full-time staff of two were appointed for three-year terms. Half-way through their term, one other was appointed.
- An independent research programme was established with the London Business School.
- All of the top team participated in three separate Team Meetings about one year apart.
- All of their subordinate teams participated in Team Meetings and many other team meetings were conducted during the course of the programme.
- A large group meeting was conducted with the general question to be addressed as 'How do we improve productivity, add profits and lower costs?'

## AN INDEPENDENT RESEARCH STUDY

Not part of the above article but worth mentioning was the organization's interest in formal research on their change programme.

The organization contracted with a team of five psychologists from the London Business School to monitor the changes and report directly back to the top team. The client supplied a budget for the research project which by today's standards would approximate to £50,000. Table 15.1 shows positive results on all five scales measuring aspects of climate.

Table 15.1  Summary of climate differences between time one, time two and time three in the organization as a whole

|  | June (year 1) | December (year 1) | October (year 2) | N |
|---|---|---|---|---|
| Readiness to change | 21.0 | 22.6 | 23.4 | 465 |
| Satisfaction with colleagues | 26.1 | 26.5 | 27.2 | 466 |
| Satisfaction with subordinates | 31.2 | 32.0 | 33.2 | 455 |
| Leaders' psychological distance | 3.6 | 3.3 | 2.8 | 458 |
| Interpersonal aggression | 3.1 | 2.8 | 2.3 | 454 |

The scales used in Table 15.1 are those that showed a significant change. There are five, the first one being readiness to change. The study was conducted three times. One was the base time period, the second study was about six months later and the third study was about nine months after that. All these scales showed a significant change. The sample sizes are indicated in the last column and are all over 450. What these results show fairly clearly is that the 3-D

MES may be used as an organization change device for some softer variables than simply profit and managerial effectiveness. Here the 3-D MES was used to deal with the softer variables first, such as climate, as a method of unfreezing the organization before broader changes take place which will lead to improved effectiveness.

# 16 Change in Siemens, West Germany

This is an article written by Dr Dieter Hempel, head of the Industrial Psychology Unit of Siemens AG, in Munich. It describes the extent of their use of the 3-D Managerial Effectiveness Seminar (3-D MES) and the criteria by which they chose it and decided to 'buy' the seminar rather than attempt to 'make' it themselves. After this article was written, Siemens decided to greatly expand the use of the seminar above the 1,000 or so managers that had already participated. They saw its usefulness in their international operations and its provision of a common language concerning effectiveness across the Siemens system. They purchased the rights to use the 3-D MES for any Siemen's managers in the world.

This is an account of our experience with the 3-D MES. We are now approaching a figure of 1,000 managers who have participated in this one-week seminar, designed by Professor W. J. Reddin. Clearly, we have found it helpful.

## SOME BASIC ASSUMPTIONS

This chapter is based on the assumption that the success of any large industrial organization depends to a large extent on how its human resources are utilized and that there are two basic approaches in mobilizing these human resources. One is to try to influence people as individuals. The other approach is to use systems as a means of steering the behaviour of people.

Budgeting would be an example of the systems approach. Introducing seminars on managerial effectiveness for upper management provides an example of the people-oriented approach.

Within Siemens AG we believe that generally speaking both aspects are equally important. Of course, it depends on a given situation whether one puts more emphasis on the one or the other.

This is one of the reasons why we feel managers should strengthen their abilities to diagnose the rapidly changing situations correctly, and to improve their ability to act flexibly according to the different demands of various situations.

So while reading this account of the implementation of a seminar on managerial effectiveness for upper management of Siemens AG, one should keep in mind that it is just one measure within a very complex set of efforts to mobilize human resources.

## Some Key Figures

Siemens is one of the world's leading companies in the electrical and electronics industry; in terms of sales in this sector it ranks among the five largest in the world. The broad spectrum of products, focusing on power engineering and communications, extends from the electric motor to the power plant, from the telephone to the large computer, and from electronic components to X-ray departments. The intensive research and development work draws primarily on the innovative potential of electronics. Products and systems based on electronic technology account for almost 50 per cent of our sales. Through a world-wide sales and manufacturing organization established in well over 100 countries, we make more than half of our sales outside the Federal Republic of Germany.

Siemens employs well over 300,000 people throughout the world; of this number, roughly one-third work abroad. The workforce includes scientists, engineers and technicians, as well as commercial staff, professional workers, skilled and semi-skilled labour, trainees and temporary student labour.

Its size and variety of projects enable the company to offer its employees job opportunities suited to different talents and capabilities. Size and variety of job demands also create considerable challenges to management and call for a personnel policy and organizational structure which allow for extensive delegation and a good match of responsibility and authority.

## Off-the-Job Training Programme for Managers

In order to help managers to cope with problems deriving from these challenges, Siemens has established various measures for management development which include both on- and off-the-job training. The off-the-job programme starts with a set of three seminars which build up one on each other.

Starting with first-line managers (not foremen for whom there is a separate programme), each seminar draws participants from different rank levels. Roughly speaking, the aims of these seminars are:

- to acquaint participants with company goals;
- to make responsibilities, aims and problems of both groups and central divisions transparent;
- to develop an understanding for each other's problems through personal contact among participants and top-level managers.

Following these seminars, which all managers should attend during their career development, there is a set of problem-oriented seminars which are more or less optional and which draw their participants mainly from upper- and top-level management. Contents of these seminars are general management, political issues, problem-solving techniques and languages. This is where the 3-D Managerial Effectiveness Seminar (3-D MES) fits in.

## THE PROCESS OF SELECTING THE RIGHT SEMINAR

It is difficult to answer the question as to how the process got started. There were many discussions in seminars, during projects of organization change, both formal and informal, which finally led to an overall consensus that we would need some kind of training in leadership behaviour for upper management. So the next question was: what should this seminar look like, and how can we get the commitment of the Managing Board?

A first step in solving these problems was to make the topic of 'Leadership style and effectiveness' part of a workshop or information forum for upper management. This information forum was set up to discuss problems the company would have to cope with in the future. The method used was mainly group discussions and poster sessions.

One outcome of these discussions was that, as seen by upper managers themselves, there was a need for more training in leadership. As a further step the Central Personnel Department was commissioned to conduct some research into what the needs for training were in more detail.

From the results of this research we developed the basic criteria for the design of the seminar, some of these criteria were as follows:

- The seminar should go hand in hand with the principle of delegating and matching responsibility and authority.

- It should help the individual managers to analyse their situation by themselves.
- It should not sell some kind of ideology, but rather help towards more clarity in setting objectives and measuring results.
- It should help towards better co-operation within teams and between teams.
- It should help to develop human resources.
- It should match with international standards.

It would have been quite a challenge for the specialists in the Central Personnel Department to develop such a seminar themselves. But for reasons which need not be explained to the practitioner, they decided to answer the question 'Make or buy?' in favour of 'Buy'.

After some market research, we came to the conclusion that we should take a closer look at the 3-D MES. We sent a group of managers from different functions – e.g. production, research and development, sales, administration and personnel – to an open 3-D MES in England. These managers reported to the respective committee of the Managing Board, and it was decided to have two in-company seminars and ask the participants for further evaluation.

Accordingly we asked W. J. Reddin and Associates to conduct these two seminars with their staff in English at our management institute in Germany. Evaluation of the seminar by the participants at the end is part of the seminar design, and it turned out to be very positive. In addition to each seminar, we had a follow-up meeting six months later. At that point, the evaluation of the seminar showed an even more positive attitude towards it and there was quite an amount of evidence that the participants had started working with some of the seminar concepts in their own area of responsibility.

This finally led to the decision of the Managing Board to continue with these seminars, to have our own staff trained as trainers and to co-operate on the translation of the materials into German.

## RESULTS AND FURTHER DEVELOPMENTS

It took us, as a company, about two and a half years to decide on the implementation of these seminars. It took us five years to approach some 1,000 upper managers as participants. We introduced the follow-up meetings as a part of the seminars because the participants wanted to share their experiences in transferring what they had learned at the seminar into practice.

The process of implementation is still going on. At this moment, one can say that the seminar has been broadly accepted as a means of individual development. There is quite an amount of transfer as far as the personal area of responsibility of the individual participant is concerned. There are difficulties in communicating some good ideas where participants meet partners who have not been to the seminar, and thus there is still some hesitation as to how some of the seminar concepts are in harmony with company regulations and the cultural environment. But the decision to continue has been taken, and to make participation mandatory for managers who are to be promoted to certain functions and levels of hierarchy. Finally, we hope that more and more participants will send their own subordinates to the seminar and then start working to design the organization of their own unit in a more effective way.

Maybe we could have been more effective ourselves in managing this implementation process. But there is one thing we have learned: it takes time and needs a continuous effort to spread new ideas in a large organization.

# 17 Change in Arthur Young & Company

'Business people are conditioned to respond to power.'

'No one wants to do anything important on the basis of direct-ness, trust and candour.'

'I learned a lot about myself in team-building, and that made the course worthwhile.'

'I gained confidence. I have done a better job as a result of that change. I've done better work – done things I never thought I'd be able to do – and the confidence has kept building.'

This is an account of how the 3-D Managerial Effectiveness Seminar (3-D MES) was used to help senior audit partners in one of the largest accounting firms in the world to become far better managers and far better team members. This is extracted from a much longer article, entitled 'Casting light on what makes us tick' by Henry Marksbury, a member of Arthur Young & Company. The introduction to the article read as follows:

What happens when experienced, successful managers are brought together in small groups and told that for the next six days they must function as teams? A partner in Arthur Young & Company (AYC) who 'passed' the Reddin 3-D Managerial Effec-tiveness Seminar, which has been conducted in the USA and other countries by senior AYC staff for more than 10 years, analyses the personal agonies, frustrations and satisfactions of team building dynamics.

Team-building can make a manager more effective by exploring, in a group setting, the age-old question of 'what makes people tick?' This can be enhanced by doing the exploring not in abstract discussion, but in living, objective-oriented situations.

That is what management personnel of Arthur Young & Company (AYC) an international accounting firm, have discovered over the past several years by taking the five day Reddin 3-D Managerial Effectiveness Seminar (3-D MES), which is called informally in the company 'team-building'.

In the 18 months since I took the course I have interviewed 32, and talked at some length with another 42, of the AYC people who had then taken the Reddin design seminar. Most of the 74 from whom I gathered comments and observations had had a year or more of trying to make team-building work in the real world of business and of life in general.

Sixty-eight of the 74 found the seminar to be of considerable use in business and personal life. Five others indicated it was valuable education, but found that it did not work for them in the business world. For example, one person said: 'Business people are conditioned to respond to power. No one wants to do anything important on the basis of directness, trust, and candour. Trust is a nice thing to talk about, but if trust is basic to this seminar, there is simply no such thing outside the classroom. Who is ever really candid? I learned a lot about myself in team building, and that made the course worthwhile. But that was the limit of it.' Another dismissed the 3-D MES as 'an attractive gimmick of no real value. It's a lovely dream, but it has no relevance to my work or to my life.' I asked this person if the course was, in any sense, time well spent. The answer was 'No'. This was the only wholly negative appraisal among the 74 persons I talked to.

## THE MANAGERIAL EFFECTIVENESS SEMINAR: ITS GOAL AND OPERATING PRINCIPLES

'The seminar doesn't offer the answer to the process of management or of relating to people in motivational ways', says Ted Sable, director of Arthur Young's Management Development Programme and the prime-mover and one of the first teachers of its Managerial Effectiveness Seminar. The structure of the seminar and its documentary 'matrix' – a textbook, manuals and charts – were created by William J. Reddin, an authority of managerial training, and author of *Managerial Effectiveness* (1970), translated into eight languages.

'The purpose of the course', says Sable, 'is to give people an opportunity to see into the dynamics of group situations, to give and to get feedback about the way people differ in their views. But what matters is that through the course individuals develop sharper perceptions. They develop keener understanding that individual styles and reactions in situations can be modified to get results.

'Almost everyone – especially successful people – gets rigid through the years. Success is narrowing. The 3-D MES stimulates flexibility. The paperwork the group has to do in the course makes its members try to move ahead. But they can only move by working together. The paperwork gets at least some of them concentrating on a group purpose. How do they decide what to do? It's up to them. Sometimes this brings about friction, sometimes co-operation. It's a microcosm of the situations most of us are involved in every day.'

## Views of a Team-building Management Unit

Here are some comments from the entire management team of an Athur Young practice office. All seven management members of this office had taken the 3-D MES. They made these points nine months or more after taking the course:

- Taking the course opened up communication.
- That's right. It's like saying, we're going to level. We're going to speak to the point, say what we really have in mind.
- I like the freedom, we have to be ruthlessly candid. There's an awful reluctance – or used to be – to tell people their idea or their memorandum or whatever isn't really first rate.
- Teamwork is a great thing. When you discover that, you are on your way. We've demonstrated that the team can come up with better answers.
- We did not think of ourselves as a team. Now we do.
- We're not there yet. We've made progress. The lines of communication are open. It takes a lot of effort, but we understand the concept and we're trying to apply it.
- I think it helps if the top people in the office take the course, as they have here. It's tough to make it work if the people in charge don't know what you're getting at.
- You become more flexible. Less wedded to your view. More open to other viewpoints.
- That is something that came through to me in the course. It was scary how sure I was that my view was right – at the beginning of the course. You can have a view, but you need to be ready to temper it or change it or just hold it in abeyance while you hear the other people out. I suppose everyone knows that. But the 3-D MES shows you, showed me, how 'stuck' on my views I was.

- Another important thing you learn is that style of management is critical in many situations.
- The course talks about managerial style and also about situational management. Complicated sounding, isn't it? I think the earlier you reach people in their careers, the better, if you want to improve them in those areas.
- I don't agree, I'm older than most, and I think those concepts - style, flexibility and situational management – made me much more aware of what's involved, what's possible. Change is often the answer to management problems – trying to change your approach or trying to change the situation. There's a limit to what can be done in a six-day course, but I think quite a lot was offered.
- I'll second that. A hell of a lot was offered. Going to that seminar was like going through hell week. Like walking out of the desert after a plane crash. We made it and, as a result, we know some things.
- That makes plenty of sense to me. There's so much I can gain from my associates in the office and in the firm – that's what the course got through to me. And we're working to make that more possible than it would otherwise be, doing it through team building. We're not there; maybe we never will be. But we co-operate a lot more. We share a lot more.

## THE 3-D MES AND THE 'REAL WORLD'

What do 'team-building graduates' who find themselves in a small minority among the management group in their offices have to say? They are, on balance, highly affirmative about the seminar and its personal rewards, but they lack the pervasive sense that 'it's really working' that I encountered in the practice office where every management member had taken the course.

Here is a sampling of the range of comments from most of my 54 contacts who are in the minority:

- You don't need to be right all the time to be you. That's what comes through to me. I've become much more relaxed and productive by keeping that in mind.
- I gained confidence. I have done a better job as a result of that change. I've done better work – done things I never thought I'd be able to do – and the confidence has kept building.
- The MES helped me with personal growth. But you can't use it across-the-board in dealing with people who haven't taken

the course. The everyday world isn't tuned into it. It's a fine
personal guide. You can keep using the momentum the seminar
gives you. It's hard to put into words, but I think it's like being
an evangelist among non-believers. You set an example, but
you don't preach too much. Openness and candour are strong
medicine to those who haven't lived that way and don't see any
reason why they should. I lie low with the message.

- Several in my office have been through the seminar. We tried
to use it on our top partners who haven't been to the course.
We even had a dinner conference about it. We laid the candour
on. We got the feedback that they didn't want any more of
that stuff. Nevertheless, I think the course was the greatest
management development experience of my life. Whenever I
meet someone in the firm who's been through it, it's all we talk
about. We're all believers. It works enough of the time. It helps
me.

- The group saw me as I saw myself. There was no great personal
revelation. But I learned a lot about the others. They were
certainly not the people I thought they were at first. I have
gone out of my way to get to know the people who report to
me. They all have more to offer than I would have known
about if I had just let our communications channels develop in
routine fashion.

- It's a difficult grind, sure. But I think I am making a lot of
progress in situations where nobody but me has been to the
Reddin MES. You keep letting others know that you want their
best. You never stop trying to fit the workload to the people
better and to relate the dynamics of your personal management
style to the people more effectively. Those who have participated in the seminar keep trying to improve the environment
to fulfil their credo, their team goal: Give us – you and me –
your best.

- It's pointless. Team-building won't work with people who don't
know what it's about. I find it interesting, the insights keep
coming. I'm far more aware than I would have been if I hadn't
taken the course. But candour and openness? You have to be
kidding. I'd be dead by next Tuesday. People almost never tell
you what they think about anything that matters. I spend the
day trying to protect my flank and keep from making some
damaging mistake. Is there any other way – really?

- The 3-D MES reveals the bullies and dictators for what they
are. A bully or an egotist is just not a leader. The team ought
to be free to follow a true leader free to reject any obstruc-
tionist. And during the course the team has that freedom. But

in the real world? Of course not. It's the difference between a fairy tale and real life. You learn to be satisfied with a small percentage of what the seminar has shown could be possible. You make gains, but short ones.

- People are jealous and some are scared, and so many inhibitions stand in the way of the 3-D approach. In the classroom, after the break-in period, people let go of all their defences. They find they have nothing left to lose – that's not it. They just get taken over by the process. I try to make it happen, but only very gently, in the practice office. Several people remarked on the change in me. I never used to try to take a creative part in our planning sessions. I talk more. I try to draw others out. It works.

## A SUMMARY OF THE 3-D MANAGERIAL EFECTIVENESS SEMINAR

The seminar is presented two or three times a year to a total of approximately 45 persons. Arthur Young management personnel have taken it, as well as 22 clients. Those 161 Arthur Young people form 9 per cent of the 1,792 management personnel of the firm (578 partners, 358 principals and 856 managers). Far short of anything approaching a tidal wave has happened within the firm, but it is a beginning – perhaps considerably more. One meets 'team-builders' in almost every office in the course of travel for assignments.

Today, a year and a half after going through the 3-D MES, I think of my team-mates with so much more than fondness that the only word to express my feeling is the unaccountable word 'love'. They struggled with me, and against me, to come up with 'the answers'. We were from different backgrounds; a lady tax manager and five males, an office managing partner of very senior tenure, a young tax principal just past 30, a fortyish management consultant, an audit manager in the early thirties and myself, a writer then aged 45.

We had terrible trouble moving the dialogue ahead. But the trouble was the making of us, it seems to me. The trouble brought us together, and as a result of it, we learned what was beneath the veneer. It is a wonderful morale-building experience to talk purposefully with people who speak straight, free of the constraint that says 'be terrific', and free of the restraint that says 'be cool'.

They saw me in ways markedly different than my life until then had 'taught' me to see myself. They saw me as an executive, a 'take-charge' person, and would have, they said, welcomed far more discourse from me than I had seen fit to give, though they indicated I had said far more than I thought I had. Which indicates that I, a reclusive writer (in self-image) who had resolved I would go there only to take notes, had been caught up in the process.

## The seminar itself

We arrived on Sunday evening. Now it is Thursday. After three-and-a-half days of slogging through paperwork exercises and tests and of contending with the close-up egos of several 'team-mates', the team members appraise each other's performance.

The rules hold every commentator, or critic, to observations about behaviour during the course. Motives are not imputed. Conjecture about 'how you got that way' is not permitted, nor is conjecture about 'what you ought to do about yourself'.

One by one, the team members go before their team-mates. The person being commented on sits and listens. If he or she wants to know more on some point – something that nettles, perhaps, or otherwise arouses curiosity – two comments are permitted: 'Tell me more' and 'For instance'.

In observing my behaviour the group has missed nothing. My repeated glances at my watch, for example. My frequent trips to the coffee urn, including the several times that I lingered to stare out of the window before returning to my chair at the worktable. My habit of staring when I have reservations or otherwise dislike what someone has suggested. A better gesture, surely, would be to say what's on my mind, including my reasons for disliking the speaker's tack.

Each member of the team, in turn, hears the group's reflections. The views differ on some specifics, but taken together, they present a fairly uniform and plausible picture in every case. If the commentators don't agree on every point, it is still clear that they are in general agreement and are touching on some behavioural changes that can increase ability to contribute to and influence a team or group.

## The non-contributor

These are some typical comments that team-builders make to the non-contributor:

- If you don't want to be here, why don't you leave?

- This team needs your ideas. Why won't you give them to us?
- Give us a chance. I think we can show you not only that the ideas of all of us are better than the ideas of an individual, but that you will contribute more if you enter into the conversation. Tell us what you think about question number seven . . .
- If you're not going to talk to the purpose but only about your accomplishments, you're wasting our time. Why not climb aboard? You'll like the ride after you decide to pay your way.

All of these comments were heard during the 3-D MES by me or by someone I later interviewed. And the truth for all but a few has been that the ride was well worth it; 68 of 74 (92 per cent) said it was valuable as applied to their work and personally, while five (7 per cent) said it had educational value; and only one of 74 said it was worthless.

## The start of the ride

At 5 p.m. on a Sunday evening, the participant enters a room with fifteen or twenty others, hears a general introduction by a 'facilitator' (who in our company, and I gather virtually all others, is a well-trained staff or even line person from the company itself, trained by the Reddin organization) and 30 minutes later is free to have dinner. But you must join the team - four or five other persons – in a 'team-room' at 8 p.m. There is work to be done.

That work consists of exercises. Generally the pattern of those exercises is that each participant takes a test, and then the team members compare answers, thoughts and ideas, arriving somehow at a team answer. The 'somehow' of this team answer is the key to the dynamics of the Managerial Effectiveness Seminar, for the team is left on its own to decide how it operates. Whether one person's answer becomes the team answer depends on his or her impact on the group. Whether the team answer is a synthesis of individual answers or comments, whether a vote is taken – the team decides. Such decisions must be made for some 50–80 answers in each exercise, twice a day. The day's work runs, for some teams, well into the night.

Once the team answers are arrived at, the team submits them for grading, and its performance is compared with the results – the right and wrong answers – submitted by other teams. In the great majority of cases, the team gets better grades than most or all of its members.

These tests and exercises are the foundation, the measuring

devices, for the team's work – in the beginning. And in the beginning, the 'laboratory environment' of the materials has a surrealistic effect on the mind: a journey into the realm of '3-D Theory', 'task orientation vs relationships orientation', 'situational management' and 'style management'.

The task questions – a basic part of the first day of the team-building course – carry the flavour of the special vocabulary of their creator. People taking the course read the text (*Managerial Effectiveness*) and certain related materials and arrive steeped in new ways to talk about managing people and situations. During the course they work on their own to come up with answers to questions. They then meet to arrive at a team answer.

Most exercises – each lasting about two hours – consist of some 80 questions. The team must, therefore, discuss and resolve one item every minute or so. Not much time, when allowance is made for occasional quips, jokes and mutters of exasperation, to say nothing of the time sometimes consumed by impassioned advocacy for a point of view.

How to move ahead? Take a vote? Appoint a dictator? It's up to the team. The answer is undoubtedly 'in the team'. But whose answer? Mine? Yours? The majority's?

The team members thus travel into the other-worldly realm of the 3-D jargon and the seemingly non-helpful facilitator. Some teams, according to my research, have a comparatively smooth journey; the team members work well together. This does not necessarily mean that they score high, though some do; it means that they arrive at answers without extreme stress and strain.

But that was not my experience, nor was it the experience of approximately half the people I talked to. For this half – the 'strugglers' – the early part of the course is a time for wondering why you ever agreed to put yourself through an experience that is off-putting at best and absurd ('a waste of time') at worst.


**The team knows**
Individual grades and performance are not revealed in the general meeting-room. What individuals contribute remains a secret, except to them and their team members.

But in a deep and volatile sense, there is pressure upon the individual: they know and the other team members know, through the compilation and comparison of the scores in the team-room, when they had the right answer and did not 'hang in' during the group discussion and thus let the group persuade itself of the 'rightness' of the wrong answer decided upon. Further, the group comes to know each member well, fathoms the workings of his or her mind, and judges whether the individual is contributing.

Thus the answer is indeed in the team. And soon, by Tuesday night, after 30 or more hard-slugging hours, the common denominator ceases to be the material; that matrix has given birth to something between the team members, a personal rapport (or antipathy) involving the team's performance. The common denominator becomes what the team knows and wants; what the team sees as the potential contribution from each member and what the team determines to be the obstacles – quirks of behaviour, straying from the point, any disaffection or any squashing of someone else – in the way of that contribution.

For me, the first indication that something was happening was an awareness that my team-mates were changing. I don't remember when I first perceived it; I know it happened sometime before the appraisal session on Thursday. I realized they were not the same people I had met on Sunday evening. There was much more to them. But the change was not only in my 'eyesight'. They were showing sides of themselves that were not visible on Sunday evening.

Some who had been distant became talkative (and some of that talk consisted of heated outbursts). Some who had been affable but superficial became deadly serious; easy courtesy or idle remarks gave way to crisp injunctions as to what should be done.

People who had appeared to promise little leadership became leaders. New strengths appeared in some – contributions of persuasive reasoning, creative suggestions for moving the work ahead.

Along about Wednesday (for me) a sort of indifference set in – a callousness to go with the heightened sensitivity to others. This was another element in what I call the 'common denominator', something akin, perhaps, to an actor or a tennis player getting over an attack of nerves as the action gets under way. The others are like me, after all.

They've made mistakes, become peevish and said exactly what they thought under pressure. And they've stayed with it, through thick and thin. I like them. There is a lot more to them than I originally thought there was.

The habitual mask and gestures of self-concealment, playing it safe, 'mindlessly' playing it the way that has worked many times before – they all fall away. The others see and are seen. They see me and I see them.

# EPILOGUE

Nearly two years after taking the Reddin 3-D MES, I returned to the Arthur Young Educational Centre in Reston, Virginia, to speak to a group of the firm's management development instructors. The invitation from Ted Sable, director of management development, was to 'come tell us what you've learned about team-building'.

It is often said that speaking to a group tells the speaker more than those who are listening. And that was my experience. In reviewing the nearly two years since I took the 3-D MES – a better way to say it is since team building happened to me – I made these notes:

1  My fellow workers have valuable things to tell me. I must make every possible effort to hear these valuable things.
2  Patience is fundamental. I have become more patient – but not across the board; only where I have the knowledge or the intuition that a person's talent merits patience.
3  Listening is a crucial part of patience. Let people talk, but not to the point of going off the rails (missing deadlines or other important objectives).
4  Take the time, make the effort, to understand problem situations as well as opportunities. I can't do this alone. I must deal 'one to one', to share, to build, to solve problems and to optimize opportunities.
5  People look at things differently. No way around that. Accept it. Live with it. Discover again and again that though it can be frustrating and time-consuming, the fact that people inevitably disagree and are sometimes in conflict can be the seedbed of maximum contribution.
6  Team-building can only exist in an atmosphere of well-managed confrontation. Provide 16-ounce gloves or the combatants will use bare knuckles. (Seriously: adhere to the principle of discussion about behaviour or about work objectives, not about personal motives.)
7  No miracles. It has taken thousands upon thousands of years to make human beings what they are.
8  Progress is not only possible, but inevitable. The 3-D MES experience – the inner teacher, the recollection of what was reflected back to me – endures. Other people have much to tell me (us), if I (we) will let them.

# 18   Short case studies

This chapter contains a number of abbreviated case studies which will give you further insight into how the ideas in this book can be used. The case studies are as follows:

- The Use of the 3-D Managerial Effectiveness Seminar for General Motors' foremen.
- Improving managerial effectiveness in Ethiopia.
- Introducing output orientation in a government power utility.
- Increased profit in a UK division of an international packaging group.
- Changes in an international petrochemical plant contractor.

## THE USE OF THE 3-D MANAGERIAL EFFECTIVENESS SEMINAR FOR GENERAL MOTORS' FOREMEN

Flint, Michigan is the home of the General Motors Institute (GMI). Essentially, this is the GM University. The GMI started using the 3-D MES in 1972 and is still using it at the time of writing.

Clearly, General Motors did not need to become more output-oriented, but equally there was little question that lower levels of supervision and management could benefit from the 3-D MES to increase flexibility. While participants on the Managerial Effectiveness Seminar went as high as plant manager level, the bulk of the hundreds of participants were general foremen. These general foremen were fairly senior by most world standards and supervised five to fifteen foremen who, in turn, supervised a total of approximately 300 workers. These general foremen were experiencing some difficulty in coping with changes introduced by rapidly changing technology and also the changing expectations and values of new employees who, in some cases, they simply had to hire because of government regulations concerning minorities. Naturally the general foremen tended to use methods which had worked for them in the past, and methods they had seen their superiors use. Unfortunately, this did not work so well in the current circumstances in which they found themselves. There was a clear need for increased behavioural flexibility in order to deal with a far greater variety of situations than they had previously encountered.

While the programme did not use anything from 3-D other than the MES, the GMI still did create programme objectives; These were:

- Increase skill of general foremen to recognize that situations vary and require varying approaches to increase effectiveness.
- Identify the key output requirements of their jobs and gain knowledge and skill in managing managers
- Increase skill of general foremen to use a variety of approaches to introduce or to adapt to change

The 3-D MES was used in a creative way. The GMI decided to use three one-week training modules. The first week was the 3-D MES. The second week concerned the major changes in the company situation and how these should be best dealt with by the general foremen. The third week consisted of training in objectives setting and planning.

The company research programme was based on comparing general foremen, who did not participate with those who did. The results showed clearly that flexibility in behavioural response to changed conditions did occur.

## IMPROVING MANAGERIAL EFFECTIVENESS IN ETHIOPIA

Ethiopian Airlines is the dominant management training institution in Ethiopia. It conducts public management seminars on a wide variety of topics, has a comprehensive seminar catalogue and frequently brings overseas visitors to conduct seminars related to management. Two of their executives visited the UK to participate in an introductory output orientation seminar. Based on that experience, they decided to introduce the 3-D Managerial Effectiveness Seminar (3-D MES) into Ethiopia on a public seminar basis. Naturally the senior management of Ethiopian Airlines attended, as did the most senior levels of the military, the Air Force and various government departments. Some Ethiopian trainers are being developed to conduct the seminars. These seminars, the first long series of senior management seminars ever conducted in Ethiopia, are being well received. To some this may be surprising as Ethiopia is a Marxist country, and some confuse managerial effectiveness with profit orientation and assume it would not fit a

Marxist approach. The 3-D MES is concerned with increasing added value. If it was profit-oriented solely, it would not be used by government departments. The seminar is not in any way against profit, but the emphasis it gives to the concept of added value makes it applicable in a variety of organizations and political systems. Several full-length 3-D MESs are now being conducted in Ethiopia every year.

With the various problems which Ethiopia has had, and continues to have, some might ask why anyone would be concerned about the managerial effectiveness improvement, rather than about the health of the country's children. Improvement has to move on several fronts. Those involved in the 3-D MES are quite convinced that, while it may be a longer-term effect, improving the effectiveness of senior government officials and senior managers in Ethiopia must lead to some of the problems that have occurred recently having a much lower likelihood of occurring in the future or being dealt with more effectively.

## INTRODUCING OUTPUT ORIENTATION IN A GOVERNMENT POWER UTILITY

The introduction of output orientation in one power utility has already been described; here is another case study concerning a different power utility. The utility was government owned and had approximately 1,000 employees. It operated quite independently, except for being tied into a national power-grid system. Before the introduction of output orientation and the use of 3-D Managerial Effectiveness generally, there had been no major organization or top personnel changes in ten years; there had been no prior internal management development of any kind; and there had been a growth, over ten years, of 350 employees. The planned change objectives chosen were:

- reorganization;
- job rotation;
- improved managerial effectiveness;
- improved teamwork;
- improved organizational flexibility;
- improved managerial flexibility.

The commission decided to use the 3-D MES and planned to put the top managers on it. After experiencing the programme over a two-year period, sixty more were included. So, 21 per cent of the total workforce attended the 3-D MES. Rather obviously, they thought positively of the programme and were taking 'unfreezing' seriously. The Team Meetings were widely used and cascaded through the organization, starting with the top team and then levels two and three, and so on. Several Large Group Meetings were held on various topics, including reorganization, how to implement the organization and how to provide better service generally.

Many changes occurred which seem to relate to the overall programme. These included:

- Within twelve months of the top-team Team Meeting most departments had changed their reporting relationships, owing to the creation of five new functional divisions.
- Twenty-eight of the top thirty managers had moved to different positions.
- Four years after the programme, the commission took over a public power commission of similar size.

Not one manager was fired.


## INCREASED PROFIT IN A UK DIVISION OF AN INTERNATIONAL PACKAGING GROUP

This 10,000-employee division foresaw a period of radical change ahead. Historically it had held over two-thirds of its market, but several overseas companies had entered the market with new technology and additional capacity. The division had been very production-oriented and company policy was to decentralize and turn the twelve plants into profit centres grouped into two 'businesses'. The division had not been successful at introducing the new technology itself.

The new divisional chairman, who had used 3-D ideas successfully in an overseas subsidiary, decided to apply them in the UK. The objectives of the programme were:

- role clarification, to work out the implications of the new decentralized structure, particularly the reduced powers of staff and technical departments;
- renew management by objectives and increase marketing orientation;
- plan and set profit-related performance objectives and gain commitment to objectives;
- review and appraise individual managers' performance;

- improve teamwork and interfunctional relationships;
- more effective meetings;
- greater mutual confidence and cohesion;
- improved problem-solving climate;
- better decisions;
- greater openness and candour.

Two hundred and fifty directors and managers participated in the 3-D Managerial Effectiveness Seminar; and over thirty team meetings, starting with the directors, were held. Meetings to resolve interfunctional problems were held and the programme carried down to the supervisory level in some areas.

The programme objectives were widely achieved, many managers became more confident and competent and made significant changes to their style and to their outputs. The new technology was successfully introduced and there was a spontaneous and unlooked for increase in the attention paid by managers to the continuous development of their subordinates.

The 3-D programme, in addition to meeting its objectives, created the flexibility and the focus on outputs that substantially helped the division to reduce capacity, control overheads and raise efficiencies. As a result, the division returned to profit significantly in advance of other divisions in the company, despite a drastic shrinkage in the total market. Morale and efficiencies sharply increased and 'the division is far better able to meet the demands of the business'.

## CHANGES IN AN INTERNATIONAL PETROCHEMICAL PLANT CONTRACTOR

This UK process plant contractor of 1,000 employees operating worldwide with contracts valued at up to £500 million had a long history of low profits and big contract losses. Corporate planning was poor, directors and managers were not aware what was expected of them, roles were ill-defined and relationships between directors and their departments were poor, resulting in too many decisions being fed up the line.

The Managing Director wanted to open up communications and replace the previous autocratic and paternalist style with a more open team style of management. He wanted to establish clear performance objectives, to which management was highly committed. He also wanted to increase the skills of managers required to obtain effective co-operation and to manage subordinates in a highly variable and demanding contracting environment.

One hundred and twenty directors and managers attended the 3-D Managerial Effectiveness Seminar and fifteen Team Meetings were held over a period of three years.

There was general agreement that a number of changes and benefits were achieved:

- A corporate plan with quantified objectives was established and subsequently reviewed and updated. It provided the basis for developing the company and its business.
- The whole operation became more objective, based on the clarification of unit and individual roles in output terms by team agreement of effectiveness areas. Managers knew what was expected of them and took necessary initiatives. Decision levels were moved downwards.
- Team working and communications were greatly improved and interdepartment conflict reduced.
- Effectiveness Areas were linked as a basis for managerial appraisal and formed the basis of a new appraisal and manpower planning and development system.
- A more open style of management came into operation.
- There was a complete re-examination of the way everything was done. Many changes, major and minor, in organization structure and procedures were smoothly introduced, some of which would have been impossible without 3-D. A highly flexible approach was adopted in organizing taskforces for major contracts.
- Morale and motivation were sharply increased.
- Many directors and managers were considerably developed.
- The budgetary and cost-control systems were based on results (Effectiveness Areas) rather than on activities.
- The creation of two new divisions was achieved quickly and easily to form the nuclei of new businesses.

The managing director stated: 'The introduction of 3-D provided a framework within which existing talent was able to come together and operate in a much more effective and cohesive manner. In a very fast-moving business environment, it created the essential flexibility needed to meet the business demands without losing the cohesion of the management team. As a result, greatly increased profits have been earned, leading after four years to a level in real terms never previously achieved in the company's long history.'

# Glossary

'If you want to converse with me define your terms.'
(Disraeli)

**achievement climate**: Climate which reflects high task orientation and high relationships orientation in a situation where such are appropriate, thereby creating an output orientation and thus more effectiveness. Perceived as having a high level of achievement of objectives: mutual encouragement for high performance; high co-ordination of people in work; and much use of teamwork in decision-making.

**acquiescent climate**: Climate which reflects low task orientation and high relationships orientation in a situation where such are inappropriate, thereby creating an input orientation and thus less effectiveness. Perceived as an organization which is pleasant, kind, warm; has low initiation; somewhat passive with unclear directions given; unconcerned with outputs and standards; and good at smoothing over conflict.

**AE** *see* **apparent effectiveness**

**ambivalent climate**: Climate which reflects high task orientation and high relationships orientation in a situation where such are inappropriate, thereby creating an input orientation and thus less effectiveness. Perceived as accepting grey acceptable situations; having some encouragement of ideas and high performance but low support and not much response, even where good performance is delivered, and much yielding and giving in to pressure and too much use of inappropriate participation.

**apparent effectiveness (AE)**: Extent to which manager gives the appearance of being effective.

**authoritarian climate**: Climate which reflects a high task orientation and low relationships orientation in a situation where such are inappropriate, thereby creating an input orientation and thus less effectiveness. Perceived as critical, threatening, suppressing conflict; downward communications only; much acting without consultation; many managers feared and disliked; emphasis on day-to-day productivity rather than a longer-term, low performance level maintained primarily by threats.

**autocrat**: Manager using high task orientation and low relationships orientation in a situation where such is inappropriate and thus less effective; perceived as having no confidence in others; as unpleasant; and interested only in the immediate task. Indicators are: critical; threatening; demands obedience; suppresses conflict; downward communication only; acts without consultation; and sometimes feared, disliked.

**basic climates** *see* **system climate, people climate, production climate and team climate**

**benevolent autocrat**: Manager using high task orientation and low relationships orientation in a situation where such is appropriate and more effective. Indicators are: decisive; shows initiative; industrious; energetic; finisher; committed; evaluative of quantity, time and costs; and obtains results. Perceived as knowing what is wanted; and how to get it without creating resentment.

**bureaucrat**: Manager using low task orientation and low relationships orientation in a situation where such are appropriate and thus more effective. Indicators are: follows orders; rules and procedures; reliable, dependable; maintains the system as a going concern; watches detail; efficient; and rational, logical, self-controlled, fair, just, equitable. Perceived as being primarily interested in rules and procedures for their own sake; wanting to control the situation by their use; and as conscientious.

**change targets**: Those parts of an organization where change is to be introduced. This may include such things as the top team, middle managers and a particular unit.

**climate** *see* **basic climates, input climates and output climates**

**compromiser**: Manager using high task orientation and high relationships orientation in a situation that requires a high orientation to only one or neither and thus less effective. Indicators are: yielding; sometimes weak; avoids decisions; produces vague acceptable decisions; ambiguous; and distrusted, not understood. Perceived as poor decision-maker; as one who allows various pressures in the situation to influence too much; as avoiding or minimizing immediate pressures and problems rather than maximizing long-term production.

**conforming climate**: Climate which reflects low task orientation and low relationships orientation in a situation where such are appropriate, thus creating an output orientation and more effectiveness. Perceived as being highly concerned with orders, rules and procedures; reliable, dependable; good systems; details watched; rational, logical and fair; prefers written communications; typical response to disagreements and conflict being to refer to rules and procedures.

**corporate strategy meeting**: Three-day meeting attended by only top team or executive committee to reconsider organization policies and structure, focusing more on the organization and its environment rather than the organization from within and relationships between individual roles in that organization.

**dedicated climate**: Climate reflecting high task orientation and low relationships orientation in a situation where such are appropriate, thus creating output orientation and more effectiveness. Perceived as having high levels of initiative; energy in industry; being committed to finishing well; highly evaluative of quantity, quality and time; results-orientated; ideas that arise tend to be implemented; and with efficiency and productivity valued.

**deserter**: Manager using low task orientation and low relationships orientation in a situation where such are inappropriate, thus less effective. Indicators are: works to rules; minimum output; gives up, avoids involvement and responsibility; gives few useful opinions or suggestions; and makes things difficult, resists change, uncooperative. Perceived as being uninvolved and passive or negative.

**developer**: Manager using low task orientation and high relationships orientation in a situation where such are appropriate, thus more effective. Indicators are: maintains open communication channels; develops talent of others; coaches, understands others; supports; works well with others, co-operates; and trusted by others, trusts, listens. Perceived as having implicit trust in people, and being primarily concerned with developing them as individuals.

**EAs** *see* **effectiveness areas**

**effectiveness areas (EAs)**: General output requirements of a management position.

**executive**: Manager using high task orientation and high relationships orientation in a situation where such are appropriate, thus more effective. Indicators are: uses teamwork in decision-making; uses participation appropriately; induces commitment to objectives; and encourages higher performance and co-ordinates others in work. Perceived as a good motivating force and manager who sets high standards; treats everyone somewhat differently; and prefers team management.

**flexible organization**: Organization having suitable and rapid range of appropriate responses to a changing environment. Its characteristics include emphasis on effectiveness; acceptance of change; free power flow; flexible resources allocation; marketing orientation; technological orientation; free information flow; project team; and focus on outputs.

**frozen**: An organization or an individual in a state of no change.

**humanistic climate**: Climate which reflects low task orientation and high relationships orientation in a situation where such are appropriate, thereby creating an output orientation, thus more effectiveness. Perceived as having high level of shared understanding and co-operation; much trust and openness; high involvement in planning and productivity; and talents reasonably well developed and open communication channels.

**input climates** *see* **stagnant climate, acquiescent climate, authoritarian climate and ambivalent climate**

**interteam meeting**: Meeting between two teams to solve outstanding problems between two units. Typically this might be production and marketing or design and engineering or engineering and production, or even headquarters and field.

**JED** *see* **job effectiveness description**

**job effectiveness description (JED)**: Written statement specifying effectiveness areas, measurement areas and authority areas of particular management position.

**large group meeting**: One- to three-day meeting attended by 30–300 people, who may or may not be managers, designed to group problem solve a particular topic. Highly participative, not in any way the top person making a statement about the future.

**MAs** *see* **measurement areas**

**manager**: Person occupying a position in formal organization, responsible for the work of at least one other person and having formal authority over that person.

**managerial effectiveness (ME)**
Extent to which manager achieves output requirements of that position.

**managerial effectiveness seminar (3-D MES)**: Six-day residential seminar for each manager from top person down, participating in teams composed of other managers without line relationships to one another.

**ME** *see* **managerial effectiveness**

**measurement Area (MA)**: How an effectiveness area is measured.

**missionary**: Manager using high relationships orientation and low task orientation in a situation where such is inappropriate, thus less effective. Indicators are: avoids conflict; pleasant, warm and kind; seeks acceptance of self; dependent; makes things easier; avoids initiation; and passive, gives no direction, unconcerned with outputs and standards. Perceived as being primarily interested in harmony.

**objectives**: Effectiveness areas which are as specific, time-bounded and as measurable as possible or specific output requirements of a management position.

**one-to-one meeting**: Half- to one-day meeting between team top member and each team member in turn, to strengthen relationship by clarifying respective roles in terms of effectiveness areas and to build better open, coaching relationship, not in any way the traditional appraisal type meeting.

**OOO** *see* **output-oriented organization**

**organization climate**: Factors influencing behaviour in organization which are common to essentially unrelated positions in that organization.

**organization development**: Development of organization as a whole to become more effective, rather than simply the individuals in it.

**organization output statement**: Statement of organization's basic purpose, sometimes referred to as 'driving force', 'company strategy' and 'company goal'.

**output climates** *see* **conforming climate, humanistic climate, dedicated climate and achievement climate**

**output-oriented organization (OOO)**: Organization of any type designed, operated and trained so focus of all subunits and individuals is towards the achievement of that organization's purpose.

**outputs planning meeting**: Three-day in-company meeting attended by top team of organization or unit, usually concerned with eight planning steps; change targets, change objectives, change target climate, managerial style, outputs, 3-D MES, meetings and staffing.

**PE** *see* **personal effectiveness**

**people climate**: Climate recognizing the individual, where people tend to talk to each other more than in other climates.

**personal effectiveness (PE)**: Extent to which managers achieve their private objectives.

**planned change**: Planned method of introducing change in organization, as opposed to evolutionary change or no change at all.

**production climate**: Climate which tends to give dominance to work process, where time perspective is immediate to short term and preferred choice is 'do it now'.

**relationships orientation (RO)**: Has major emphasis on people, listening, trusting and encouraging.

**RO** *see* **relationships orientation**

**skills managerial**: The three skills required for managerial effectiveness: situational management, situational sensitivity and style flexibility.

**stagnant climate**: Climate which reflects low task orientation and low relationships orientation in a situation where such are inappropriate, thereby creating an input orientation and thus less effectiveness. The climate is perceived as highly insular; uncreative; having low involvement; resistant to change; low concern with efforts except to cover them up; working to rules; and with too many people making it difficult for others.

**style awareness**: Degree to which managers can appraise own style correctly.

**system climate**: Climate characterized by managing prudently and therefore also by being very concerned about correction of deviations.

**task orientation (TO)**: Has emphasis on productivity, getting the job done, initiating, organizing and directing.

**team climate**: Climate characterized by high interaction among individuals and units and giving high value to communication in group settings, thus the use of formal and informal meetings.

**team meeting**: Three-day meeting with objective to build team around common outputs and improve both team and team member effectiveness; usually held off work-site, attended by full team of top person and all team members.

**TO** *see* **task orientation**

**unfreeze**: Conditioning of managers and organizations to more readily accept change.

# Index